All rights reserved. No part of this publication may be reproduced, stored in a retrieval system, or transmitted in any form or by any means, electronic, mechanic, photocopying, recording or otherwise, without permission of the copyright holder.

© Stephen Wainwright 2023

Printed in England by Flexipress Printing Ltd., Ormskirk, Lancashire.
Tel. 01695 576339 | www.flexipress.co.uk

About This Book

The author pictured with the Mayor of St Helens Cllr Sue Murphy and mayoral escort Mike Murphy (Pic: Tony Foster)

Thank you to everyone who purchased the second volume of *"The Hidden History of St Helens"* and told me that they enjoyed reading it. I promised that £1 from the sale of each of the first 1,000 copies of the book would go to the Alzheimer's Society, via the charitable work of Soroptimist St Helens. I'm pleased to say that sales were sufficient to allow for

The cheque presentation to Diane Charnock of St Helens Soroptimists (Pic: Anne Jones)

a cheque for £1,000 to be handed over on July 10th 2023.

This third book is "more of the same" of the previous two volumes with more fascinating stories that I have uncovered from their hiding places deep within the local newspaper archives. Cruelty figures quite a lot in this edition with a history of the work of the NSPCC in St Helens from 1895 to 1931; the story of the violent St Helens vet and the husbands brought to court accused of persistent cruelty to their wives.

The St. Helens Reporter

WITH WHICH ARE INCORPORATED

The St. HELENS STANDARD & The St. HELENS CHRONICLE, Established 1865.

4.---NEW SERIES. | FRIDAY, NOVEMBER 7, 1902. | 10 PAGES.

JOSEPH HEWITT.

Lighter moments are provided in the opening and closing chapters which are devoted to the court appearances of some odd characters. There are also comic aspects to the chapter on lynch law in St Helens and you may also find yourself smiling at the compilation of stories from the St Helens Newspaper's beat group column called Teen Topics.

Slavery survivors also tell their disturbing accounts of life in bondage; there is a history of the St Helens Circus in North Road and there are glimpses of what St Helens was like in the early 19th century when it was little more than a village.

Much of the content of this book has been sourced from newspapers stored on microfilm at Eccleston Library and I would again like to thank their ever-helpful and cheerful staff and those at St Helens Archive Service in the Gamble Building for their kind co-operation. **SRW**

Contents

The St Helens Characters That Enlivened Court Hearings	1
The Freed Slaves In St Helens and Other Slavery Stories	27
The Adoption of Lynch Law In St Helens	41
The Story Of The St Helens Circus	57
Conmen and Imposters In St Helens	75
John Shaw Menzies – The Violent St Helens Vet	93
The St Helens Newspaper's Beat Group Column	103
"Dear Sir" – A Collection Of Curious Correspondence Part 2	137
Four Curious Cases Of Bigamy	155
The Hanging of a St Helens Painter / The Death of a Waterloo Hero	171
The Women Who Accused Their Husbands Of Persistent Cruelty	179
When St Helens Was Only A Village	199
The Champions Of Child Cruelty Cases In St Helens	219
Unusual Things Said In Court	251

The St Helens Characters That Enlivened Court Hearings

"For some time there was confusion in the court. Officers went to restrain the woman, who, snatching up the child continued to shout: "You dirty, rotten cads, that is what you are.""

Most folk when they appeared as defendants in St Helens' courts would show respect to the Bench and attempt to create a good impression of themselves. That did not mean they had to be completely submissive. On January 2nd 1869 after indulging too much in New Year celebrations, Catherine Cosgrove made an appearance in St Helens Police Court charged with being drunk.

When the Clerk asked the woman whether she was guilty or not guilty, Catherine replied: "I am, love". The Clerk then said to the magistrate: "Then, she pleads guilty". To those remarks Catherine responded: "Oh, yes, darling. I had a sup too much. Oh, your honour, darling, I will never come before you again." The sole magistrate was William Pilkington who saw the funny side and sent the elderly woman on her way.

But there were always those who preferred downright hostility and abuse of the Bench. There were also the comics, the constant talkers, the confusers and weepers. Everyone likes a joke but there is a time and a place for everything. And although magistrates liked defendants to demonstrate contrition, uncontrollable bawling was taking things a bit too far!

Witnesses were also brought into the courtroom that caused confusion, including interpreters that proved completely incapable of speaking the foreign language that they were supposed to translate. And so this chapter is dedicated to examples of those who enlivened court proceedings with their behaviour – even if it did not necessarily do them any good!

THE PAIR OF WEEPING TRAMPS

During the 19th century the term "tramp" was endowed on anyone who, for whatever reason, had a nomadic lifestyle. For some it was only a temporary occupation whilst searching for work and being "on tramp". But the police and courts treated all who roamed the streets with great suspicion.

In January 1871 Superintendent James Ludlam – who was in charge of St Helens police – told magistrates that tramps gave them considerable trouble. However, the bobbies certainly reciprocated, as the police routinely arrested tramps for begging or sleeping where they shouldn't – and then the courts almost always despatched them to prison.

For example, on December 14th 1868 a vagrant called James Beesley was imprisoned for 28 days with hard labour by the St Helens Bench for simply sleeping in a yard in Church Street. And in June 1871 a cheeky tramp named James Boyce was charged in the St Helens Petty Sessions with vagrancy after sending some pigs packing. The Liverpool Daily Post wrote:

> He had driven the pigs out of [a] farmer's stye, and lain down in their place. The presiding magistrate commended his taste, and ordered him to have a clean bed in Kirkdale [gaol] for fourteen days.

St Helens police arrested almost as many female tramps as males – but the women were treated no less sympathetically in court. In March 1869 Supt. Ludlam charged Eliza Coleman with begging in Victoria Passage *(located between Bridge Street and Naylor Street)* in St Helens. Ludlam told the Bench that there

Victoria Passage in the town centre

were a great many tramps about and he had received complaints about their behaviour. The woman was sentenced to ten days in prison with hard labour.

Tramping the country in all weathers hardened the vagrant and so for them to break down in court was rare. A male and a female tramp journeying together was also not common. But on February 1st 1873 the St Helens Newspaper described a case that bore both of those unusual aspects:

> William Thomas Yarwood and Mary Thomas, tramps, were brought up in custody, charged with creating a disturbance that morning in Raven-street. P.C. Harrison deposed that he heard them making a noise for a considerable time, and he was at last obliged to lock them up. They had been drinking. At this moment the male began to cry like a child, and the female, seeing him in such distress, did the same. His Worship asked the fellow what he had to say, and observing that his weeping prevented him from making a statement that could be understood, advised him to bear up like a man and tell his story.
>
> Yarwood rubbed his face a good deal to smooth out the wrinkles of emotion, and then managed to tell his Worship that a good Samaritan from the Brewery had given him some drink last evening, and as he was not accustomed to intoxicating liquors, and had an empty stomach besides, he was quite overcome. The woman said she was going home to Wales at once, and would not be again found in St. Helens while she remained in the flesh. Supt. Ludlam in reply to the bench, said the prisoners were a pair of tramps. Yarwood made an appeal for discharge, which his Worship declined to grant, and then he blubbered more than ever, the woman joining sympathetically. They were ordered to

find one surety each, or go to prison for fourteen days; and being utter strangers, they went to prison.

> ## The Wife Stabbing Case.
> ### COMMITTAL OF THE ACCUSED.
> Josiah Beech was brought up on remand, at petty sessions on Saturday, charged with stabbing his wife Elizabeth, on the previous Wednesday evening. It will be remembered that when the woman was brought forward to give evidence on Thursday morning, she endeavoured to have the fellow let off, and would only tell a few facts, and then under a good deal of pressure. During the interval from thence until Saturday her mind changed somewhat, and Mr. Marsh was retained to conduct the prosecution. Mr. Beasley was for the defence.
> Mr. Marsh said he could not exactly call the woman the prisoner's wife, but they had been living together as man and wife for some years. Three months ago they separated, although some serious differences: but Beech

The St Helens Newspaper August 12th 1871

Josiah Beech was another blubberer in court – although the charge levelled against him was more serious than what the two tramps faced. The 26-year-old fishmonger appeared in St Helens Petty Sessions on August 5th 1871 charged with stabbing his wife.

Some time earlier Eliza Beech had told her husband to leave their marital home in Tontine Street in St Helens. However, the man kept returning to plead with Eliza to be allowed back. But she stuck to her guns and on the last occasion that he turned up, a row led to him stabbing her in the thigh. Now in the dock facing a serious charge of wounding with a knife, the St Helens Newspaper wrote that Josiah Beech had "intermittent fits of vigorous crying".

When his very weak wife entered the courtroom to give evidence, the fishmonger had "roared loudly, buried his face in his handkerchief, and rocked to and fro in an apparently frantic manner". In fact both parties did a lot of sobbing "in concert", as the newspaper put it.

Josiah denied that he'd used a knife during the row but Dr Thomas Griffiths from Hardshaw Street gave evidence that a sharp blade had unquestionably caused the one-inch wound. The defendant was remanded to another hearing, with the Newspaper writing:

> He acted like a baby as the police led him away, and he covered with reproaches the woman he had injured, as often as he could afford to stop sobbing for a moment.

Like many battered women that were so heavily dependent upon their husbands, Eliza Beech was a very reluctant prosecutor and in October when tried in the Quarter Sessions at Kirkdale, Josiah was acquitted of the charge of wounding her.

ARE YOU A FRENCH COMMUNIST DEVIL?

On October 11th 1872 Charles Montague appeared in St Helens Police Court charged with endeavouring to obtain two pence by false pretences. The defendant said he preferred to be known as Captain Montague and described himself as a former officer in the French army and of the Paris Commune.

However, the captain – albeit an interesting character in his own right – is not the focus of this story. Instead tailor William Rimmer of Tontine Street takes that honour. This is what the 46-year-old told the magistrates about his first meeting with Captain Montague:

> I came into my house and found the captain talking to my missus. He shook hands with me, and I shook hands with him, although I did not know him. I asked his business, and he said he was one of the French Communists. "Are you one of them devils," I said. "Well, I have been looking for a long time to find two or three,

and now that you are here I'll settle you. Give me down my rifle, missis, till I shoot him.

He said he had been a captain in the French army, and he bared his wounds to show them to me. He also said that he was once a master tailor at Paris, and now wanted work. I told him he was at a poor game here, and that he had better get back to France, and then I gave him twopence. He said he had been to Pilkington's, and a tall gentleman with a big beard, had given him 1s.

ST. HELENS PETTY SESSIONS.

FRIDAY — (Before Major Pilkington.)

A COMMUNIST TURNED VAGRANT — TEMPORA MUTANTUR.

Charles Montague, described by himself as Captain Montague, was brought up on remand, charged with endeavouring to obtain money under false pretences. He looked a middle-aged man, strongly built, and with some evidences of a respectability which misfortune had almost obliterated. When he arrived in the town, he represented himself to be an ex-officer of the French army, and of the Paris Commune; and amongst those on whom he waited to pay his devoirs, and probably ask for assistance, was Major Pilkington himself. Having the ill luck to take a few glasses of Irish whiskey, before he was familiar with the levelling tendencies of that beverage, the sturdy Communist became so demonstrative and disagreeably conspicuous that a policeman illus-

The St Helens Newspaper October 19th 1872

Well, William Pilkington – the aforementioned big bearded man – just happened to be on the Bench trying the case! He admitted seeing the Frenchman at his glassworks but denied that he had given him any cash. After listening to the captain's rambling defence statement, Pilkington declared Charles Montague to be a "mendicant and vagrant" and sent him to prison for a fortnight.

THE SLEEPING DEFENDANT

The police often brought offenders into court just hours after they had been arrested and in John Fleming's case it was clearly far too soon! The young man appeared in the St Helens Petty Sessions on April 26th 1869 to face a charge of being drunk and indecent in College Street. The St Helens Newspaper described how Fleming had quickly fallen asleep after being placed in the dock:

> He had been brought into court about an hour before his case was called, having been arrested immediately after the offence was committed, and from his general appearance it was plain that he would find insuperable difficulty in disproving a charge of drunkenness. Having been deposited in the dock, and sandwiched between a couple of fair creatures who had not found the requisite funds to meet certain fines imposed upon them, he thought he might make good use of whatever interval of quiet was before him; and disregarding alike the interesting revelations of litigants, and the paternal speeches from the bench which accompanied and ornamented many decisions, he industriously set himself to sleep composedly. The proximity of the damsels kept him from falling, and he dreamt away until his turn came. When his name was called he did not vouchsafe the slightest movement in response, and a repetition of the patronymic [his surname] only elicited a prolonged and much-to-be-envied snore in response.
>
> Thereupon a constable shook him gently by the shoulder, and whispered into his ear that he was required to get up, but he slumbered on. Then another officer seized him by the collar, and shook him, and went through every gradation of force up to dragging him from the seat, vainly. In fact it seemed either as if we were going to have a modern Rip Van Winkle, or that he was sleeping from malice prepense

[deliberately] to worry the court, and general merriment was becoming very audible. The officers were lothe [sic] to give up the task in despair, and they hit upon the expedient of compelling this living prototype of the "fat boy" in Pickwick, to walk a few steps. It is to be expected he is no somnambulist [sleepwalker], for when he felt himself going through the necessary exercise of putting each leg to the front alternately, he delighted his body guard by opening his eyes. It was thought all was now satisfactory, and the awakened sleeper was placed before the bench, and formally charged with the offence entered against him.

Mr. Cross [Court Clerk] asked him whether he was guilty or not guilty in the most suave tone possible, to which the prisoner replied by a look of affection at his querist, but refrained from uttering a word. The question being repeated, with a like effect, Mr. Cross inquired, in a fraternal and sympathising way, if the prisoner heard the words uttered. He then found voice, and in a tone of the most happy case, answered that he heard distinctly but understood not a word. It now seemed hopeless to proceed, and a remand was granted until Wednesday. Fleming was led away, and he doubtless resumed his repose when deposited in his cell.

THE MOTHER WHO CALLED THE MAGISTRATES DIRTY SCAMPS

The term "scamp" used to have a much more insulting meaning in the past than today. When Richard Naylor was charged with sleeping in a brickfield in Peasley Cross in October 1872, William Pilkington was again sitting on the Bench and made this extraordinary statement:

> You are the most unmitigated scamp and blackguard in Sutton. You always associate with poachers, and you rarely

work for more than a week at a time. You have a good home and bed, but you prefer to meet with the lowest scamps and blackguards.

Then in June 1931, Joseph Gaskell, landlord of the Springfield Hotel in Thatto Heath, was ordered to pay £25 damages in Liverpool County Court after being accused of slander and assault. The 34-year-old licensee owed more than £9 in income tax and had told a taxman that he was a "worthless rascal, bloody scamp and thief".

And six years later the mother of a 16-year-old defendant called magistrates scamps. By 1937 the justice system was far fairer than in the 1870s when prison was seen as the solution for most minor crimes – even when committed by children. The probation service under its motto "advise, assist and befriend" was by now well entrenched in the court system – although not everybody who was in trouble wanted to be advised, assisted and befriended!

The St Helens boy and his two parents were extreme examples of individuals who fought against a system that in its own way was doing its very best to assist them. The St Helens Reporter described what occurred on October 22nd 1937 under the headline *"Mother Offers Baby To Bench – Strange Outburst In Court – Father Wishes He Had A Bomb"*:

> The Chairman was just finishing his final remarks to the sixteen-years-old defendant who stood before him in the Juvenile Court on Tuesday morning. "...That is the sort of return you have made to those who have been trying to help you," he said. "You are going away to an approved school for as long as they find it necessary to keep you." The words had hardly left the Chairman's mouth before there occurred an unprecedented scene. A woman, mother of the defendant, who had been sitting behind her boy, by where he stood facing the Bench, stood up suddenly. With a swift

movement, clutching an infant child in her arms, she advanced to the foot of the Magisterial desk.

At first it almost appeared as if her intention were to hurl the child at the members of the Bench. Instead the woman slammed her burden heavily upon the Magistrates' table, saying loudly: "You can help to keep that. I will go out and work, you dirty scamps." For some time there was confusion in the Court. Officers went to restrain the woman, who, snatching up the child again, continued to shout: "You dirty, rotten cads, that is what you are." "Take charge of that woman," the chairman (Mr. W. G. Gentry) instructed the police. Weeping now, the woman was led away. Her husband, who had also been in Court, addressed the Magistrates. "Don't mind her," he said. "Can I appeal against this? It is hard on her. It will drive her and me away."

Then he, too, appeared to lose control of himself. As he walked away from the Bench, he burst into tears, and was understood to say: "I wish I had a Mills bomb. I would throw it at you." The boy defendant joined in the confusion. Rushing to his father he cried: "Never mind, Dad." Then – and he too was now in tears – he turned to Mr. F. E. James, Probation Officer, who had given evidence a few minutes before. Clutching Mr. James, the lad shouted: "I will get you when I come back." Order was restored as court officials escorted the lad, his father and mother from the room, but the woman's raised voice could be heard outside for some time afterwards. The woman apparently waited outside the Court, for, as the Magistrates were leaving later, she again accosted them and walked behind them from the Mining School, where the Juvenile Court is held, to the Town Hall, constantly shouting opprobrious [abusive] epithets.

The scene was the conclusion to a case over which the Magistrates had spent much time. The boy before them made no answer to and gave nothing in explanation of an accusation of committing a breach of recognisance, one of the conditions of which was that he should attend at the office of the probation officer. Mr. F. E. James and Mr. Cyril Beasley both testified to the fact that during his term of probation, he had given them considerable trouble, and had on many occasions not attended at the office at stipulated times. It transpired that the lad had left home, apparently to attend at the probation office on these occasions, and had later returned, telling his parents that he had seen either Mr. James or Mr. Beasley, whereas in fact he had not done so.

Records that were produced showed that the lad had been before the court at intervals since 1934, and on one occasion he committed a further offence within a few days of being placed on probation. The lad gave no explanation of his conduct to the Magistrates, and when they had heard the evidence, and decided that he was guilty of the offence, it was stated that on two previous occasions the lad had appeared before Magistrates for breaches of recognisance and been fined. When spoken to on one occasion about not attending at the probation office, he was alleged to have replied: "You will never get me to attend." When they had considered the case in private, the Bench recalled the defendant and the Chairman addressed him.

"You are the type of young fellow who nearly breaks the hearts of Magistrates, Probation Officers, social reformers and all others who go out of their way to try to do a good turn for someone who needs it. Of the scores of boys and girls who come to this Court I can recall none for whom more consideration has been shown, to whom greater sympathy has been extended, and for whom greater excuses have been made in every shape and form, in a genuine and sincere effort to help you. What have you done? In effect you have stuck your fingers to your nose. In effect, it has been equal to flinging a bucket of dirty water over us. You have come to the end of your tether. You are going away to an approved school for as long as they find it necessary to keep you." It was at this point that the scene described above occurred.

By the 1930s anonymity was being given to young defendants in court, making it impossible to research further details that might explain the family's foolish behaviour. Their motivation can only be guessed at – but the mother and father probably felt they were doing their very best for their kids in very poor circumstances and resented others interfering.

The boy was likely to have been earning a wage that was boosting the family's low income but now they'd have to contribute to the cost of their son's stay at an Approved School. A final point about the only individual identified in the St Helens Reporter piece. That was the Chairman of the Bench, William George Gentry, who as well as serving as magistrate – was also editor of the Reporter!

In another case in the Juvenile Court in October 1946 in which Gentry was the Chairman, he became so exasperated by a mother's remarks that he thumped his table and told the woman she was "impudent". Her boy had been one of four lads that had pleaded guilty to stealing goods and damaging property and had been placed on probation for two years.

Interruptions and outbursts at Juvenile Court

Father's threat to appeal; Mother's protest

Interruptions, outbursts, criticism of the Magistrates' decisions, and an occasion when the Chairman (Mr. W. G. Gentry) struck his desk and told the mother of a defendant: "Madam, you are impudent!" were unusual features of Tuesday's sitting of the Borough Juvenile Court.

The Court sat for two and a half guilty on the charges of house...

MOTHER OBJECTS

St Helens Reporter October 18th 1946

It was the lad's first offence and so in the magistrates' eyes they were being generous and giving him a chance. But the unnamed mother did not seem to agree and argued that the punishment was too strict. Gentry probably did not help matters by comparing her precious son to a dog! This is the dialogue that took place:

Mother: Do you think it is fair to put him on probation?
Gentry: Absolutely, it is the fairest thing we could possibly do. A boy has the same privilege as a dog. The dog is entitled to its first bite. If a boy does wrong, we give him a chance to be good.
Mother: Yes, but it is not often you do that!
Gentry: As you are not in court when we do that, excuse me if I say that to you that you know nothing at all about it.
Mother: I know that much.
Gentry: Madam, you are impudent. You are talking about something of which you know nothing. We have treated these boys with transparent fairness. We have given them a chance.

The woman also took some time before she agreed to be bound over as a surety for her son's behaviour, eventually agreeing but saying: "But I do not think it is fair, all the same."

THE FRANTIC EXCITEMENT OF BARBARA SCARRY

The reporters covering 19th century court cases in St Helens were clearly not given a written list of the defendants appearing in the dock. The journalists appear to have recorded the names of the accused as they were verbally stated in court, as their spellings varied considerably.

Barbara Scarry was quite an excitable character and is listed in the 1871 census as a 40-year-old living in Liverpool Street in Greenbank. But in describing her outbursts in St Helens Petty Sessions, the newspapers referred to her variously as Barbara Scally or Scully. But however her name was spelt, the woman certainly enlivened court proceedings with her antics!

On July 11th 1874 the St Helens Newspaper described how Barbara's latest appearance in the Petty Sessions had "exhibited all the frantic excitement which characterises her public appearances". Then she had been charged with breaking the windows of Cornelius Gleeson of nearby Sandfield Crescent. During the hearing Mrs Scarry appealed to Supt. James Ludlam, the head of the town's police force, for help, saying:

"Stand up for me, Mr. Ludlam, or they will hang me this day." Although capital punishment was then in existence, it was not, of course, merited for breaking windows! The Newspaper then described more of the woman's activities in the courtroom:

> She went on to conduct herself in such a wild manner that she was quieted with some difficulty. When the complainant [Cornelius Gleeson] was sworn she broke out again, calling him an "old bite," and other names equally complementary. Mr. Swift [prosecuting counsel] made an effort to state the case, and then he came in for the battery of her tongue, which poured such a verbal fire upon him that he was completely silenced. When she was exhausted for a moment complainant stated that while he was shaving himself – and he was careful to say he performed the operation with a razor – Mrs. Scully threw several large stones through the window, and he had to beat a retreat lest one of them should strike the razor just at the moment it was scraping the surface hair from his throat. "How could you see me throw the stones when you were shaving yourself?" she asked; and she seemed inclined to pull the witness box to pieces when complainant declined an attempt to solve the poser.

> His Worship threatened to remove her from the court, and she calmed down for a moment, only to rise to boiling point again when complainant's wife came forward to corroborate. The chairman, in despair, declared she must be mad, and fit

for a lunatic asylum, an assurance which so wrought upon her tenderest feelings that she straightaway fell upon her knees, clasped her hands, and would have prayed, but for a material-minded policeman, who raised her up. The chairman begged of her to be quiet for a little time, and she promised she would, but immediately afterwards declared that she had not taken any "toxicating" drink for a long time, and the complainant wanted to cause disturbance between her and her "married husband." A nice thing for a mother of thirteen children! His Worship said it was best to send her to prison, and ordered her to be confined for fourteen days.

The sentence was a shock to her for a moment, but she recovered, and gave perfect freedom to her tongue, bestowing left-handed compliments on all around. As the police escorted her from the court she asserted, in her loudest tones, that she had built the old Town Hall in fines, but that not a single halfpenny of her money should be contributed towards the new one. With this declaration she vanished, but her voice was heard for some time afterwards from the stairs and passage as she edified her escort by her ravings.

Mrs Scarry was not very good at arithmetic – at least she was incapable of accurately counting the number of children that she'd had! The 1871 census lists three kids in her Liverpool Street home aged between 1 and 7. In court in 1874, as we have seen above, she claimed to have had 13 children. And five years later when making her 34th court appearance, Mrs Scarry told the St Helens Bench she'd had 26!

Her age had also jumped from forty in the census to sixty in 1879. But it was down to forty-six in the 1881 census and two years later when she died, Barbara Scarry's death certificate states fifty-four. So take your pick!

THE ITALIAN INTERPRETER –
THAT COULD NOT SPEAK ITALIAN!

The three main Italian ice cream families of the 20th century in St Helens were the Fredericks, the Randolphs and the Vincents. All three families anglicised their surnames *(and Christian names)* having come to the town originally with surnames of Frederici, Randolfi and Vernazza. However, when in court they usually used their real Italian surnames. By 1920 their empires were on a small scale and as those in charge of the businesses were still first generation, their understanding of English was very limited.

On July 23rd 1920 a woman called Geoveffa Vernazza appeared in St Helens Police Court charged with trading after eight o'clock at night. She was married to Giuseppe Vernazza and the couple worked for and lived with Roberto Vernazza *(aka Robert Vincent)* in his premises in Boundary Road.

The wartime restrictions on trading hours were still in place and a constable had seen Mrs Vernazza selling ice cream from her barrow in Elm Road in Thatto Heath at 8:25pm. However, the court proceedings got off to a comical start.

A young woman accompanied Mrs Vernazza into the dock and told the Bench she had come to interpret for the defendant. Asked by the Clerk to the Magistrates whether she could speak Italian, the woman said she could not. "Then how are you going to tell her?", replied the Clerk.

"I don't know that there is much to tell", came the reply to some laughter in the courtroom. "Why have you come here?", enquired the confused Clerk. "I've come to see what the fine was and what they [the Bench] had to say."

The "interpreter" was not named in newspaper reports but she appears to have been Roberto Vernazza's St Helens-born wife, Eliza. She told the court that her husband spoke Italian and the defendant Geoveffa Vernazza had explained to him what had occurred on that evening when trading hours were breached. Her husband had subsequently translated the conversation to Eliza in English, so that she could explain the details to the court. Then when she returned home she would tell her husband what the fine had been and he'd explain it in Italian to the other Mrs Vernazza that had broken the law.

So the woman was sort of interpreting but in a very roundabout way and English justice cannot, of course, operate like that. The case was adjourned for three days so that an Italian interpreter that could actually speak the language could be in court. The magistrates then heard that Mrs Vernazza had not realised what the time was on the evening in question when she was selling ice cream and she was fined ten shillings.

But there were not just Italian foreign nationals living and working in St Helens during the early 20th century. Like today east Europeans were attracted to the town by the prospect of higher wages than could be obtained in their homeland and many Polish and Russian workers found employment in coalmines and in the St Helens glassworks.

Often members of these small communities would live together and occasionally there would be friction between them. On October 17th 1902 the St Helens Newspaper described a court case that had arisen from such a row and how there had been trouble finding suitable interpreters:

> At the Police Court on Saturday before Councillors Leach and Green, John Grip and Peter Albert, two Austrian Poles, of Prospect-road, were charged with assaulting a Russian Pole. The case caused considerable amusement. Complainant gave his name as Tauden Filemanoff, but at the colliery where he works he is called "John Smith." The police also adopted this name, and Filemanoff evidently made no objection. The case was before the court the previous day, when it was adjourned, and the Clerk

suggested to a man who came forward as interpreter that he should bring some one with a better knowledge of the language. On Saturday, a young woman, with a baby, came forward, but the defendants professed they could not understand her. Police-constable Lewis said they both spoke [English] well enough when arrested. "John Smith" and his witnesses spoke to [about] the two men coming into his house 2, Clarence-street, Peasley Cross, [on] the previous Saturday night, and assaulting him. In order to cause a row, they invited him to gamble, but he went for the police, and came back to find Grip with a grip of his wife's throat, and beating her. Grip jumped through the window and then smashed all the glass. The magistrates bound the men over to keep the peace for six months.

"NOW WHAT DO YOU THINK OF THAT?"

It only cost around six shillings to obtain a summons against someone who had upset you – some neighbour, perhaps, that you had fallen out with. Then in court the complainant would describe what their foe had supposedly done, routinely missing out any acts of provocation or violence that they themselves had committed.

Occasionally the opposite strategy was adopted in court. Instead of cutting to the quick, a long-winded description of behaviour irrelevant to the charge was given by some chatterbox. On January 17th 1874 the St Helens Newspaper described the conduct of Ann McNally in the local Petty Sessions:

> Ellen Anders was charged with assaulting a very ancient dame named Ann McNally. Complainant, who spoke very energetically, began her story by telling all the incidents which had occurred two years ago, when defendant lodged with her. She was very voluble and circumstantial, and although some quarter of an hour was spent by her before

she reached the gravamen of her charge, the bench listened with the most wonderful patience. At last she asked in the most serious manner possible: "What do you think of that?" to which the Chairman felt constrained to return a hint that he would think a great deal more of the story of the assault complained of. Complainant then said that during an altercation, which took place a few days ago, defendant assaulted her, and unless the magistrates interfered she was just the sort of a woman who would kill her (complainant). The bench did not think there was any case to answer. The complainant: She threatened to make mincemeat of me – now what do you think of that? (Laughter.) Besides she often tears the shirt off her husband's back. (Great laughter.)

DIALECTIC CONTRASTS

As described above some people had no idea how to behave in a court of law. They became very excitable, talked non-stop about irrelevant events and infuriated the Bench. Another such case took place in St Helens County Court on March 15th 1870 when a woman called Jones sued a female called Hicks.

Few details of the actual case were revealed in the St Helens Newspaper's report, as they preferred to concentrate on the behaviour of the two loud-mouthed ladies. But it had something to do with a bedstead and a handbrush for which Mrs Jones sought damages. The Newspaper wrote:

> The plaintiff is a Welshwoman and the defendant an Irishwoman, and during the pros and cons of the case it was amusing to listen to the dialectic contrasts. While Mrs. Jones was telling her story, which she did with considerable volubility, despite her imperfect pronunciation of English, the defendant continued a persistent system of interruptions and

ejaculations. It was no use to endeavour to keep her in order, much less induce her to hold her tongue. Once she was permitted to open the ball in her own behalf, she poured out a torrent which his Honour managed to stem, after a very great deal of difficulty, and a few threats of coercion, and she was temporarily quieted. A young woman named Warren was examined on behalf of the plaintiff, and the scene between her and the defendant was fully as chaotic as that with the plaintiff.

As is customary in all cases where friendly females fall out, the adjectives were most uncomplimentary on both sides and as a second witness was being sought for, the defendant continued to jerk out her complaints. The registrar in vain requested her to be silent, and when, in sheer despair, he held out a threat of severity, the incorrigible woman flatly told him there was no use in his appealing to her, as she could not repress her feelings. An order was given for the payment of 17s. 6d.

THE DAFT THREAT THAT LED TO A MONTH IN PRISON

As stated justice in the past tended to be swift. At 11:15am on November 5th 1930 PC Taylor collared Thomas Nolan in Stanhope Street in St Helens. Twenty-five minutes later the pedlar from Church Street was before the magistrates charged with selling envelopes without a street trader's licence and was fined five shillings.

But that was not the fastest implementation of justice on record, as the sentence meted out to Alice Blake in St Helens Police Court eclipsed it by about twenty minutes. The woman from Crossfield Street *(near Parr Street)* did not appear to think the old adage "When you find yourself in a hole, stop digging" applied to her.

On June 27th 1905 she was charged with committing a savage assault on a Mrs Heyes, along with her husband Joseph and a woman called Ellen Underhill from Parr Street. The three prisoners in the dock vigorously denied the charges but the victim looked a sorry sight.

Mrs Heyes' head was bandaged up and her doctor said she was not yet completely out of danger. So the defendants were convicted and Joseph Blake and Ellen Underhill were sentenced to two months hard labour and Alice Blake received a month in gaol.

However, Mrs Blake was furious over her conviction and as she was being removed from the dock she turned to Mrs Heyes and said: "You will be in fear of your life when I do come out; you will, that." Hearing that threat the Clerk to the court ordered the woman to be returned to the dock where she was charged with threatening Mrs Heyes.

In response Alice Blake complained that she was completely innocent and had received a month in prison for nothing. Everyone in court had heard the threat being made but a process needed to be observed and a formal witness statement made. So PC James Winnard was chosen to give evidence of what had been remarked only seconds before and then Mrs Blake was asked what she'd got to say in her defence.

There was not a lot that she could say – she could not deny making the threat as even the magistrates had heard her say it! All she could do was repeat her claim of innocence of the original charge. Unsurprisingly, the magistrates found her guilty of threatening Mrs Blake and said she would be bound over to keep the peace for 12 months. She would have to find the sum of £5 herself, as well as two additional sureties of £2 10 shillings each.

If in default of paying the money a further 28 days would be added to her sentence. It was very unlikely that she would have been able to find the sureties and so almost certainly would have served an extra month in prison for making her silly threat in court.

THE FECKLESS FEIGH FAMILY

Denis Feigh was a somewhat comical character that was a regular in court and known as the "irrepressible Denis". His dozens of convictions were mainly for drunkenness and disturbing the peace for which he usually served jail time. Although such offences would normally result in fines, Denis rarely had the cash to pay them and so had to go to Kirkdale Prison instead.

> AN INCORRIGIBLE DRUNKARD.—At the St. Helens petty sessions, on Monday, Dennis Feigh, a brick-setter's labourer, was charged with drunkenness and disorderly conduct. It was his forty-fifth appearance, and the chairman thought it was high time to resort to strong measures with him, and accordingly fined him 40s. and costs. Dennis's exchequer being as usual *sans* bullion, he was committed to prison for a month.

Report from the Wigan Observer January 15th 1869

But Feigh's notoriety meant his three sons John, James and Patrick had no chance in life and the lads were often brought to court charged with begging or stealing. And his wife was no better. On June 3rd 1872 Denis Feigh made his 57th court appearance in the Petty Sessions and his wife Margaret was in the dock for the eighteenth time.

The St Helens Newspaper wrote: "Both are as well known in the court as the magistrates themselves, or the clerk, or the superintendent of police." However, it was unusual for the couple to be in court together facing the same charge. But every time one of the pair was before the Bench, there always seemed to be some colourful tale that was told. And the Newspaper related how on this occasion it was the Feighs' faces that were centre stage:

> On this occasion Denis had a most melancholy black eye – an eye that seemed to mourn for the misfortunes which its owner was continually meeting with. He leaned against the box like a man thoroughly at his ease in official society, and

too accustomed to the position to feel the slightest novelty. The wife took things less coolly. Her face was very considerably scratched, and the marks were as fresh as if they had been inflicted within half an hour, while her outer clothing, scanty in quantity – hung about her like ruffled plumage, or a number of jagged wings.

Denis, when the clerk addressed him, pleaded "Guilty, your reverence," without a moment's hesitation, but Mr. Spencely was less successful with the female. While she was in the police cell (she said) – and she kept patting the scratches with a handful of the ruffled plumage – a woman whom the officers had considerately left with her for the sake of company – attacked her, tore her face, removed some of her hair, spoiled her cap, and reduced her plumage to the ragged condition in which it appeared. She pointed out her assailant in court, and then stopped. The clerk took advantage of the breathing space to push on the evidence, and no defence being offered, the congenial pair were sent to prison for seven days.

CHARNOCK, THE HOLY PROPHET

The distinction between someone perceived as a character and an individual that is mentally ill can be a fine one. John Charnock passed the certifiable test in 1931 when a prison doctor declared him to be sane. But the behaviour in court of the self-proclaimed "Charnock the Holy Prophet" was at the very least bizarre.

The man from Billinge – but at the time of the hearing of no fixed abode – had been prosecuted for leaving his wife and 4-year-old child chargeable to the General Rate Fund. In other words, Charnock had walked out on his family three months before leaving them destitute – and the ratepayers had been forced to bale his wife out to the tune of 18 shillings 6d per week.

When he first appeared in court on December 30th 1930, Charnock had created quite a stir by ripping open his shirt to reveal a large crucifix tattooed on his chest. He then shouted to his wife: "You have got to confess before God's high priests before I maintain you."

In response Mrs Charnock turned to the Bench and with considerable understatement simply said: "He is religious". After that outburst, the man was remanded for a week in order to be medically examined.

"CHARNOCK, THE HOLY PROPHET"

GETS TWO MONTHS IN PRISON

LEFT WIFE DESTITUTE

John Edward Charnock, a native of Billinge, of no fixed abode, who startled the Borough Police Court by his extraordinary actions when he was charged with running away and leaving his wife and child chargeable to the General Rate Fund, again appeared before the Bench on Tuesday, after a week's remand for medical examination.

St Helens Reporter January 9th 1931

Upon returning to court Joseph Cooper, the St Helens relieving officer, told the magistrates:

> It has been a very sad case. He went away and did not care whether they starved or not.

At that point the magistrates asked Charnock if he had anything to say and he responded with "I wish you a Happy New Year". Det. Insp. Anders revealed that Charnock had been admitted to Rainhill Hospital in 1919 but last week while remanded to Walton Gaol after showing signs of religious mania in court had been examined by a doctor but not considered certifiable. He was sent to prison for two months.

THE HARD LIFE OF A MOTHER OF THIRTEEN

I can't really claim that the mother who delivered a touching speech in St Helens Juvenile Court on May 4th 1943 could be described in any shape or form as a character. But I am including her as the final example in this chapter to remind us how many of those that appeared in court were very poor and had a very tough life.

HARD LIFE STORY OF MOTHER OF THIRTEEN

This is the story of the hard life of a mother with thirteen children, one of whom was before the Juvenile Court Magistrates, on Tuesday, on a charge of breaking and entering a saddle room and stealing a horse collar, brush, and brass ornaments, of the value of £1 7s. 6d.

"HE is one of thirteen children... 19, and I have one 17, at home, and this boy aged 13.

"I have struggled and even mended boots as far as I can. I do all the cooking, washing, make and mend the clothes, cut old pants and make do and mend. They have had a good bringing-up. He had no need to do anything at all like that. I am ashamed for him that he should be part of my body."

Part of the St Helens Reporter's article from May 7th 1943

I cannot identify the women or say where she lived in St Helens as newspapers had by then been banned from identifying in any way child defendants.

But I can explain that she was before the magistrates to support her 13-year-old son who was faced with a charge of breaking and entering a saddle room and stealing a horse collar, brush, and brass ornament valued in total at £1 7s. 6d.

The dilemma for the magistrates was that this was the boy's second time in court. As magistrate William Gentry had alluded with his misbehaving dog analogy in a previous case, child offenders were by now being given a second chance. Their first offence would likely result in a warning and, perhaps, probation – but repeat convictions would not be treated so sympathetically.

This is what the distressed mother told the Bench in between sobs:

> He is one of thirteen children. I am too full for words. They are not like me. I think about this disgrace and shame, and I

am sorry they are my children. I grieve for the boy because he has good habits. I have only two boys working at home. I have had thirteen children, and a hard life and no pleasure, nor any recreation. All has seemed work and strife. The boy goes out with firewood. His father was hurt in the mine years ago, and he does not get a halfpenny from any source whatever, and I get £1 a week from one of the boys. The oldest at home is 19, and I have one 17 at home, and this boy aged 13. I have struggled and even mended boots as far as I can. I do all the cooking, washing, make and mend the clothes, cut old pants and make do and mend. They have had a good bringing-up. He had no need to do anything at all like that. I am ashamed for him that he should be part of my body.

The lad was put on probation for two years with a condition that he resided in a hostel at Newcastle for at least six months.

The Freed Slaves In St Helens (And Other Slavery Stories)

"The sight would have made an Englishman's blood run cold – slaves so flogged as to cover their bodies with blood."

INTRODUCTION

The town's links to the slave trade largely involved Combshop Brow – as Croppers Hill in Prescot Road was also known. That had been the main site in St Helens where ivory combs were manufactured and then sold at Liverpool. The Dagnall family who owned several comb works in the town had even signed a petition protesting against the abolition of slavery.

When the American civil war ended in 1865 a number of freed slaves sailed to Britain. At that time there were many black performers on the music hall circuit in this country. Some of these entertainers were home-grown and in the theatrical mix there were also white artists using burnt cork make-up to wear blackface.

Studying newspaper entertainment listings from this period is a disturbing experience for 21st century eyes. For example, in February 1872 Lamb and Chapman were part of the company that performed at the St Helens Theatre Royal in the premises known more recently as The Citadel. Next to their name in their listing in The Era newspaper was the single word "Ni***rs" *(without asterisks)* – which supposedly described the nature of their act.

A more informative review, after the pair had performed in Gloucester, said: "Messrs Lamb and Chapman have become immensely popular in their entertainments as delineators of grotesque Negro life. Their witticisms and comicalities have produced roars of laughter."

Above is a promotion for the troupe of former slaves that spent over a year in 1870 performing a minstrel show in Liverpool. As can be seen from the images within the advert, the troupe also played up to the comic stereotype of black life in the Deep South.

Other slavery survivors came to this country primarily to relate their shocking experiences, as well as to entertain. One of these was B. W. Brown, which is where I shall begin this chapter as when his troupe came to St Helens he received some appalling treatment from a local newspaper.

THE ATTACK ON A SLAVERY SURVIVOR

About 1881 a small Christian troupe of freed American slaves called the Coloured Singing Pilgrims came to Britain to undertake a tour of Methodist and Congregational chapels. The group was led by a man called Benjamin W. Brown and sponsored by the Methodist Episcopal Church of Baltimore.

Over the following three years the Pilgrims conducted dozens of events all over the country, with most having no admission charge.

Instead a retiring collection was held with half the proceeds going to the host church – or some other worthy local cause – and Brown's troupe took the rest. Fortunes were not made but that clearly was not the point with education in a Christian setting being the purpose of the tour.

What were described as slave and sacred songs were performed at each venue, usually over two evenings. However, the highlight of each performance was a lecture by Brown entitled *"Scenes In A Slaveland"*. His horrendous, first-hand account of a slave market and the savage treatment of slaves that had attempted to escape from their owners must have shocked members of his audience.

Benjamin W. Brown and family

Some insights into B. W. Brown's character are provided by local newspaper reports when reviewing his troupe's performances. For example, the Stroud Journal of February 18th 1882 described him as a handsome man of mixed-race:

> …with very little of the negro except the hair. He is highly intelligent, cultivated to a considerable extent, possesses much natural eloquence, and a modest and pleasing demeanour and fine presence.

In March 1883 and June 1884 the Coloured Singing Pilgrims appeared in St Helens and Earlestown, respectively, with the latter performance held at St John's School. But it was B. W. Brown's 1883 show at the United Methodist Free Chapel in Ormskirk Street in St Helens introduced by the Rev. James Sarvent that angered the Prescot Reporter. They published two lengthy articles on the event in the same edition of their paper. The first piece provided an informative account of what had been said on the night – but the second denounced Brown as a virtual fraud. In its first article the Reporter explained how Brown had been bonded in slavery for nineteen years and had made a failed attempt at escape that resulted in him being put up for sale:

He managed to get five miles away from the plantation, but he was captured and sent to the slave market by his master, who declared that he would not have a runaway "darkey" on his plantation. He would never forget the sight he witnessed in that slave market. In the pens were old men, young men, women, and children, some of whom were to be sold to supply their drunken masters with money; and others, who, like himself, had tried to make their escape, but had been hunted down by the bloodhounds, captured, and whipped, had been sent to the market to be disposed of in some way or other. He had seen and the sight would have made an Englishman's blood run cold – slaves so flogged as to cover their bodies with blood; then washed down with salt water and cayenne pepper, greased, and fed well for a time to get them fat for market. On the market day on which he was sold, there was a gathering of slave owners from various parts of the country. A big fine fellow, handcuffed, was placed on the block, and the auctioneer commenced the proceedings by inviting bids for a "strong hearty negro." He was knocked down to the highest bidder.

The next man placed on the block was a relative of his (the speaker's), and the auctioneer impressed upon the buyers the necessity of taking this "ni**er" as far as wind and tide could take him, as he had a wife and six children, and might attempt to run away to see them. He was knocked down for 1500 dollars. The next to be put on the block was a woman, with her baby in her arms. At the request of a slave owner to break the "lot," the mother and child were separated. The child seemed to understand the meaning of the words "break the lot," and clung closer and closer to its mother's breast. Great tears rolled down the mother's cheek, and the mother and child were sold to different masters. The child was then torn screaming from the mother's arms, and the mother bade it farewell and promised to meet it in heaven. She was then put on one side, and because she was crying, the slave owner struck her over the face with his whip, and told her to dry up her tears. He would not describe further the scenes he witnessed that day; suffice it to say that towards evening he was bought by a man named Wm. Bryan. The cries of the children rang through his ears for a week afterwards; the children seemed to be going in one direction and the mothers in the other.

THE COLOURED
SINGING PILGRIMS

(Ex-slaves from U.S.A.) will take part in the

MEETING AT THE MISSION ROOM, HIGH STREET.

On SATURDAY, MARCH 17th, at 7.30.

On **Sunday, March 18th, at the Town Hall,**

There will be a special

SERVICE OF GOSPEL SONG BY THE PILGRIMS,

When one of them will give an Address. The Pilgrims will also take part in the 8.15 p.m. Meeting at the Warwick Hall.

A Collection at the close of each meeting.

On **Monday and Tuesday, March 19th and 20th,**

THRILLING LECTURES

Will be delivered in the

CROMWELL ROAD, LECTURE HALL,

Describing the Slave Market, where human beings were bought and sold like cattle, including their quaint and original sacred songs.

Admission 1s., 6d., and 3d.

Tickets at Mr. Sutton's and at the British Workman. You are asked to take your tickets early; only 350 for each night will be sold. [1662

SLAVE LIFE.

INTERESTING LECTURE AT ST. HELENS, BY AN EX-SLAVE.

An entertainment at once unique and interesting was given in the United Methodist Free Chapel, Ormskirk-street, on Monday evening, in the presence of a fairly large audience. The Rev. J. Sarvent occupied the chair. The programme, which, judging from the applause with which the several items were received, was very much appreciated by the audience, consisted of a service of song, by the "Coloured Singing Pilgrims" (ex-slaves from U.S.A.), and a lecture by Mr. Brown, who for many years before the slave emancipation in 1863, suffered the degradation of thraldom; while Mrs. Brown, her husband, and a young lady sang a number of quaint negro melodies. Mr. Brown, who delivered his lecture in an effective and at times pathetic manner, said he had come amongst them that evening to narrate the simple story of his life. He would not tell them what he had read or heard, but simply what he had seen and felt. Having been in slavery some 19 years, he was one of these four-and-a-half million slaves who were set free by the Proclamation in 1863. His first recollection of slavery was when he was about eight years old. His mother was a slave, but his father was a free man, and rented an old cabin where he took the younger children to live. When he (Mr. Brown) was old enough to go to work, his master sent for him, and he would never forget the first night in slavery. There were rules and regulations in force which forbade them to speak of freedom or free countries, although it was whispered in the old cabin and in sacred places, that

Advert in Surrey Mirror March 17 1883 & Prescot Reporter August 18 1883

That heart-breaking account of the talk was published on page 7 of the Prescot Reporter's edition of August 18th 1883. But three pages further back, an 850-word-long editorial denounced Brown's account of his experiences, saying:

> It cannot be denied that we have monsters of cruelty in this country, who ill-treat, maim, and even murder their fellows, or their wives and little ones. Yet who would describe the crimes of such people as applying to English people generally....The planters of the late slave states of America are no more to be universally described as monsters of cruelty, who delighted in torturing their slaves, than the English people are open to the charges which we repudiate for them. Mr. Brown's story was badly told, and the way in which he related it must have begotten doubts in the minds of the most thoughtful of his hearers.

Presumably those were the words of the paper's editor, who probably did not attend the lecture. In contrast his journalist who was present wrote how Brown's presentation had been delivered in an "effective and at times pathetic manner". It was also explained how the ex-slave had stated in his introduction that he would not be telling them what he had read or heard – but simply describing what he himself had seen and felt. Nowhere in that account – or in the many other reports of his speeches in other towns that I have read

SLAVERY AS IT WAS.

Stories of slavery and slave owners told by emancipated negroes, or by New England abolitionists, must as a rule be accepted *cum grano salis*. The story told by a coloured gentleman, named BROWN, at St. Helens, on Monday evening, of his having " seen slaves so flogged as to cover their bodies with blood; then washed down with salt water and cayenne pepper, greased, and fed well for a time to get them fat for the market," is one which requires the proverbial grain of salt. It cannot be denied that we have monsters of cruelty in this country, who illtreat, maim, and even murder their fellows, or their wives and little ones. Yet who would describe the crimes of such people as applying to English people generally. We have had perpetrated in Ireland during the past two years many crimes of the greatest magnitude, and of the most bloody character, yet who, but those bereft of reason and conscience, would describe the Irish people as a race of assassins? The planters of the late slave states of America are

Prescot Reporter August 18th 1883

– was Brown described as condemning all plantation-owners for cruel practices. He was simply relating his own experiences.

As well as condemning Brown's claim of having seen slaves so flogged as to cover their bodies with blood, the editorial refused to believe that a young child would be separated from its mother at a slave auction. That – it was argued – would be the equivalent of throwing good money away:

> The infant would have fetched literally nothing, and the mother very considerably less than she would with her infant, as experience of human nature, both white and black, had taught the planters that to take an infant or child from its mother was not the way to make her either a good domestic servant, or an industrious field hand.

The newspaper blamed the novel Uncle Tom's Cabin by Harriet Beecher Stowe for inducing the people of Britain to accept any "Munchausen statements as to the horrors of slavery, or the cruelties inflicted by slave owners". However, the American non-profit organisation called the Equal Justice Initiative have written that separation of enslaved mother and child was common, adding:

> In the decades leading up to the Civil War, Southern slaveholders defended slavery against critics' characterization of the slave trade as barbaric and cruel by claiming that slavery was a benevolent system that benefitted enslaved Africans. Advocates of slavery maintained that slaves were sold locally, families were kept together, and slaves could pick their new owners. Even today, the myth of the benevolent slaveowner persists, and the impact of slavery on Black families still is not well understood.

So it appears the editor of the Prescot Reporter had been sucked into believing that such stories were grossly exaggerated. I also wonder if the lecturer in Ormskirk Street had been a white man, whether his story would have received more credibility?

UNCLE TOM'S CABIN

Illustration by Hammatt Billings for first edition of Uncle Tom's Cabin

Harriet Beecher Stowe's anti-slavery novel 'Uncle Tom's Cabin' made a powerful impression on many in St Helens. In previewing a silent film version that was due to be screened at the Parrvilion in Jackson Street in December 1916, the St Helens Newspaper said:

> During the second half of the week "Uncle Tom's Cabin" will be shown as the premier attraction. "Uncle Tom's Cabin" has stood the test of time. Since it was written, many years ago, by the famous American authoress, Mrs. Harriet Beecher-Stowe, thousands of writers have tried to imitate it, by basing their stories on the same theme, but no one has since succeeded in so faithfully depicting the lives and conditions of slaves in America before the emancipation. Never has there been drawn a character like dear, gentle

Uncle Tom. Most of us know the story. In our youth how we revelled in it, how we laughed over Topsy, cried over little Eva, and shuddered over Simon Legree.

GRAND CIRCUS AND THEATRE,
NORTH ROAD, ST. HELENS.

Proprietor and Manager......Mr. Wallace Revill.
Acting Manager..........Mr. E. St. Quintin Dent.

MONDAY, OCTOBER 14, 1889, and during the week,
Mr. Charles Hermann and Powerful Company,
in Mrs. Beecher Stowe's celebrated Drama,
U N C L E   T O M ' S   C A B I N,
Introducing a Troupe of Real Freed Slaves,
Trained Bloodhounds, &c.

Doors open at Seven o'clock, to commence at Half-past; Saturdays half-an-hour earlier.
Prices of Admission.—Chairs, 1s.; Side and Promenade, 6d.; Pit, 4d.
Half-price to all parts of the house (Pit excepted) at Nine o'clock.
Smoking strictly prohibited.   563

Advert in the Prescot Reporter October 12th 1889

'Uncle Tom's Cabin' has been represented on stage in St Helens on several occasions with freed slaves involved in its production. In October 1889 the Grand Circus played host to a musical version by a company that included freed slaves, jubilee singers, trained bloodhounds and the Louisiana Troubadour Quartet.

The history of the North Road venue is described later in this book in the chapter 'The Story Of The St Helens Circus'. But the wooden structure could accommodate up to 3,000 persons and on October 19th 1889 the Prescot Reporter in its review of the play wrote:

> The building on Monday evening the opening night was crowded to its utmost capacity, and the favourable

impression created on its inaugural production was a most favourable one....The slave troupe during each evening sang a number of melodies in excellent style.

Two years later in reviewing another production the St Helens Examiner said on October 31st 1891:

The favourite melodrama of "Uncle Tom's Cabin" has been presented by Mr. Charles Harrington's Company, at the St. Helens Theatre Royal during the week, and has attracted some good houses. A troupe of real negroes and freed slaves have added considerable realism to the piece, and their old plantation songs and sketches have evoked much applause.

SLAVERY ACCOUNTS IN LOCAL NEWSPAPERS

The Prescot Reporter *(like most other local papers)* also covered national and international news, as many folk could only afford one paper a week. In November 1868 the Reporter reprinted a remarkable article from the New York Tribune on robbery and murder by racist bandits in Texas and this is an edited extract:

The Post has a letter from Marshall, Texas, saying that murder, robbery, and outrage are rife in that region, the sufferers, being, in nearly every instance, freed men [black slaves]. The civil magistrates are described as inert and negligent, and it is said that the people actually boast that no man was ever hanged in their neighbourhood for murder. In North-Eastern Texas are two or three gangs of desperadoes, well armed and under discipline, commanded by two men, one named Baker and the other named Bickerstaff. Cullen Baker is the chief of the most powerful band of desperadoes in the land. He rules the country for miles with the double-barrelled shot-gun and revolver. He takes delight in styling himself the 'God damned ni**er killing Baker' [my asterisks]. He killed a negro about six weeks ago while quietly working in Mr. Crawford's field, emptying his double-barrelled shot-gun and two revolvers in his body; and then whipped the murdered man's wife and forced her to leave her home. A short time ago he hanged four negroes.

The freeing of American slaves did not end slavery worldwide and for many years the St Helens and Prescot newspapers carried disturbing accounts of the despicable trade.

The St Helens Newspaper published a particularly shocking report on March 22nd 1873 when they reprinted a list of slaves that had recently been offered for sale in Havana.

Not all those poor souls in bondage were sold at market but could be bought by reading what we would call the classified sections of newspapers. This is a short, albeit shocking, extract:

- Just arrived from a plantation, a Cuban negress; aged 14 years; there is no other negress so lusty and robust as she is; she can endure any plantation work, and can plough as well as any man.

- A female servant, thirty years of age, and her son, eight years old of very endearing manners, and can be taught to do anything. The mother can cook, wash and iron well, and has been twelve years in her present position.

- A Congo negress for field work, very humble, thirty-five years of age; can cook and wash; price, 650 dols.

- Must be sold – four young, handsome negresses, all good servants, can be had on trial; also a fine American black horse, will go in single or double harness.

LONDON MISSIONARY SOCIETY

St Helens had its own branch of the London Missionary Society and the Congregational churches in the town held meetings in which special sermons and lectures by missionaries were given. The legacy of slavery and its continuing practice in some countries was a regular topic and the Congregational Sunday Schools raised around £100 a year to help fund the society's work. In October 1903, Dr. Peter Forsyth, Principal of Hackney College in London, told those gathered in the Ormskirk Street Congregational Church:

> The policy of the Christian world towards the rest of the world for centuries was not "give" but "grasp." We had gone to the heathen with greed for a gospel, we had poisoned them with horrible liquor, given them gunpowder, the slave trade and horrible diseases. We have an awful debt to repay. Many of the people we had debased and destroyed were finer people than the scum that ruined them or the Christian traders that fattened on their slavery.

THE REMARKABLE MASHA KATHISH AT COWLEY

FATHER MURDERED IN SIGHT OF SON

SON OF SOUDAN CHIEF VISITS COWLEY GIRL'S SCHOOL

Members of the branch of the league of Nations Union at Cowley Girls' School, on Monday, had the unusual privilege of a visit from Hatashil Masha Kathish, the son of a chief of the Dinka Tribe (Soudan), who was liberated from the most brutal of slavery fifty years ago.

He told of the Dinka tribe's affectionate...

St Helens Reporter March 21st 1930 and Hatashil Masha Kathish

An African prince called Hatashil Masha Kathish had been a slave in Sudan until in 1880 British soldiers freed him and missionaries later brought him to England. During the 1920s and '30s Kathish toured the country on behalf of the Wilberforce Society's Anti-Slavery Campaign, with enslavement still a widespread practice in the world – particularly in Africa. An estimated six million people were believed to be still in bondage in 1930.

On March 21st of that year the St Helens Reporter described Masha Kathish's visit to the town:

> Members of the branch of the League of Nations Union at Cowley Girls' School, on Monday, had the unusual privilege of a visit from Hatashil Masha Kathish, the son of a chief of the Dinka Tribe (Soudan), who was liberated from the most brutal of slavery, fifty years ago. He told of the Dinka tribe's, affectionate, honourable nature, of their ability and wealth, and of the happiness of their tribal and home life. His father was chief of the Dinka, an office combining the duties of priest, lawyer, judge and general. Masha Kathish was by birth "Continuer" in the succession. But he never continued.
>
> His father was seized by slave-dealers, and killed before his son's eyes. Kathish was taken, and endured three years of almost unbelievable brutalities, until he, and thousands of other young men and women were liberated by General Gordon. Missionaries took Masha Kathish, on his release, and finally he was brought to England and educated at the Home Cliff Missionary College.
>
> The great regret of his life is that, up to the present, no open door has presented itself to return to his own people, or to any of the adjacent tribes, with whose language he is familiar, to be to them Christ's ambassador, proclaiming salvation. Those who heard Masha Kathish will never forget

his appealing sincerity, or imagine the world is free from the terrible crime of slavery, and many will be inspired to do all they can to hasten the day when man shall no longer be allowed to buy and sell his fellows and to treat them as lower than beasts.

The Adoption Of Lynch Law In St Helens

"His ears were boxed, his hair and ears pulled, his nose tweaked, and his clothes torn. He was thrown from one to another without ceremony, and to the delight of a crowd. He roared for mercy, but none was granted."

My first volume of 'The Hidden History' contains a chapter called 'The Burning of Effigies in St Helens'. That was a communal activity in which local people took great pleasure in demonstrating their displeasure at some person's behaviour. The effigy of the unfortunate one would often be carried high in a procession accompanied by the beating of kettles and pans.

Violence was rarely employed against the target of the crowd's ire. Not only was humiliation more fun – but sensible victims would batten down the hatches inside their homes until the storm passed. Their "crimes" were invariably minor – such as having an affair. But when the perceived offence was more serious, then "lynch law" could be invoked.

Modern-day dictionary definitions concerning lynching and lynch law involve a hanging or some other form of execution. However, during the nineteenth and early twentieth centuries, the terms were more commonly employed in British newspapers to describe less extreme acts of violence in which communities rallied against perceived offenders.

The acts might range from rough handling to a severe beating and serve as preliminary punishments before being handed over to the police – or "persuaded" to leave town. Those accused of offences against children were most at risk of lynch law acts, such as in my first example.

LYNCH LAW OF A CHILD MOLESTER AT PARR

Whereas today the police and courts warn members of the public not to take the law into their own hands, that was not necessarily the case in the past. When Robert Frith appeared in St Helens Police Court on June 29th 1914 the St Helens Examiner said the magistrates "complimented the men who gave him a thrashing".

The 40-year-old labourer from Black Horse Street in Parr had been charged with indecently assaulting two little girls. Under their headline *"Lynch Law At St. Helens"*, the newspaper explained how two children, aged six and seven, had been playing near some chemical waste heaps off Park Road. Frith was seen to be with them and Emma Dingsdale became wary of his behaviour. So she alerted John Kinley *(or Kinsey)* of Parr Mill Cottages and he and a man called Tunstall watched Frith for a while before giving him a severe beating. The paper added:

LYNCH LAW AT ST HELENS.

A WELL-DESERVED THRASHING.

Robert Smith, a stalwart labourer, of 1, Black Horse-road, exhibited evidences of very rough handling when placed in the dock at St. Helens Police Court yesterday charged with indecently assaulting little girls. Mr. W. Hutchen defended.

The Chief Constable said the offence was alleged to have taken place on Saturday afternoon near the chemical waste heaps by the side of the canal near Park-road. Two children, aged seven and six, were the complainants in the case.

A woman saw the man with them, and she called two men named Kinsey and Tunstall, who, after watching him for some time, set on to him and beat him severely, cutting and blackening his face extensively.

After dealing with him on the principles of lynch law, they handed him over to the police, to whom he stoutly denied that he had.

The Liverpool Daily Post of June 30th 1914 identified Frith incorrectly as Smith

After dealing with him on the principles of lynch law they handed him over to the police, to whom he stoutly denied that he had done anything wrong. He was sent to gaol for two months.

The Liverpool Daily Post's report used the same headline as the Examiner and said the beating had been a "well-deserved thrashing". And the St Helens Reporter under their headline *"A Beast Well Thrashed"*, wrote that it had been:

"Another case of indecent behaviour with respect to little girls" and added that Frith's face "bore the marks of the attentions of Messrs. Kinley and Tunstall, in the shape of two black eyes and a badly-bruised face". The Reporter also quoted Ald. Henry Martin, the Chairman of the Bench, as telling the two men:

> I congratulate you for what you did. You gave him a good thrashing, and it served him right. I am very glad you did it, and I congratulate you on having the pluck to do it.

Arthur Ellerington, the St Helens Chief Constable, added:

> I endorse that. No doubt a much more serious offence might have taken place had these two men not acted as they did. They acted splendidly, and deserve every thanks.

The magistrates that adjudicated on the case were far from being alone in considering such extra-judicial punishment to be acceptable. *"Coroner Advocates Lynch Law"* was the Belfast Newsletter's headline to an article from September 2nd 1907 that described the words of Samuel Brighouse.

The Coroner for SW Lancashire had been conducting an inquest in St Helens in which two cyclists had crashed in Corporation Street. One of the men involved had waited for a while before riding off and police efforts to locate him had proved unsuccessful. The Coroner described how he'd conducted a similar hit and run case in Ormskirk in which a cyclist had struck down and killed an old woman. Brighouse then said:

> Men like that ought to have the law administered without the aid of justices, when they met them on a lonely road.

I'm not aware of any gathering in St Helens that might be deemed as having been a kangaroo court. But in April 1873 a 35-year-old Scot called Stuart was faced with one after being accused of attempting to obtain a wife in Liverpool "under false pretences".

Just before the wedding it was learned that the chap was already married and had three children in Edge Hill. He was also not the wealthy manager of a publishing company as he had claimed.

Newspaper reports described how Stuart had been lured on some pretence to the George Hotel in Bebington. There he was taken to a room filled mainly by young Liverpool men. The door was locked, a well-known local was chosen as chairman and the "court" went into session with "the fellow's heartless conduct" described.

Two young women then poured a pound of treacle upon his head and Stuart was pelted with bags of flour and treacle and a candle was stuck in his mouth. The "judge" sentenced Stuart to buy drinks for everyone, which he did until all his cash had been spent. "When he left, a crowd was waiting, and he had the greatest difficulty in escaping," commented the Western Gazette in their article entitled *"Lynch Law"*.

LYNCH LAW AT PEASLEY CROSS

Perhaps that case in Bebington inspired a similar punishment to a budding Lothario in Peasley Cross a year later. There was no mock court hearing involved – but the St Helens Newspaper comically reported the outcome in great detail, calling the affair "a somewhat remarkable and amusing instance of lynch law".

LYNCH LAW AT PEASLEY CROSS.

Pressure on our space last week obliged us to hold over a somewhat remarkable and amusing instance of lynch law which was administered at Peasley Cross, by residents of that neighbourhood. Some weeks ago a man who belongs to Manchester worked in one of our tailoring establishments. He was a married man, and ———— ————— ————, but it did not suit his lusts or his convenience to bring his family to St. Helens; and while he remained here he was therefore practically free from incumbrance. It does not seem, from many suggestive circumstances, that he succeeded in making himself popular amongst his fellow-workmen, but he was apparently endowed with the higher faculty of securing the admiration of the other sex. Having no physical or mental graces, it seems strange that this should be so, but a philosopher would set it

St Helens Newspaper May 2nd 1874

However, the names of the parties that were involved were omitted, as was the exact age of the girl at the centre of it all – although it sounds like she could have been in her mid-teens. The Newspaper on May 2nd 1874 explained the background to what occurred by describing how the married Manchester man had found work in a St Helens tailoring firm:

But it did not suit his lusts or his convenience to bring his family to St. Helens. He paid his addresses to a young girl who is not yet a young woman, and who resides with relatives at Peasley Cross, and he doubtless succeeded in awakening a sympathy in her heart.

After returning to his wife and children in Manchester, the man attempted to set up an assignation with his girlfriend in St Helens. But the "head of the family" – as the individual was described – intercepted his letter. The note contained a time on a certain evening when the man would arrive at Peasley Cross Station and he asked the girl to meet him there.

And he was met – but not by the girl. This is how the Newspaper comically described his reception committee:

> At the appointed hour the conspirators assembled at the tryst. When the train arrived and departed again, a light figure surmounted by a smirking face, bounded up the airy and graceful flight of steps which ornaments Peasley Cross Station, and emerged on the road. The new comer saw in a moment, by the faces, that he had fallen into a trap, and he would have retreated promptly had the chance been offered. But the frowning relative of the girl took possession of him, and the others laid hands on him, and he was a prisoner. Then commenced a comedy of the most amusing character.
>
> First he was subjected to that peculiar species of rough horse play, which is so very painful and inconvenient to the object who cannot resist it. His ears were boxed, his hair and ears pulled, his nose tweaked, and his clothes torn. He was thrown from one to another without ceremony, and to the delight of a crowd. He roared for mercy, but none was granted. Some ingenious person, with American recollections, suggested tarring and feathering, and although

the proposition was joyfully adopted, the ingredients were absent.

However, an adjacent shop supplied plenty of treacle and flour, and with these substances he was besmeard [sic]. A thick coat treacle was first laid on, and upon this the flour was poured and rubbed until the wretch gleamed white all over. A woman who took particular pleasure in the proceedings brought the tormentors a handful of soot, with which they decorated Lothario's cheeks, nose, forehead, and chin, until his face presented the appearance of the card known as the "five of clubs." To complete the joke and carry out the strict letter of lynch law, he was carried to a wooden fence, and mounted in riding posture on a rail, and as some of the wags shook the rail to give him a jaunt on it, the constant bobbing up and down of the "five of clubs" made the crowd shriek with laughter. No such grotesque sight had been seen in that region within the longest memory.

The population turned out to enjoy the spectacle, and on each accession there was an increase in the violent and boisterous merriment. Lothario's impotent rage had exhausted itself, and he sank into non-resistance. He rode on the rail in the mutest manner, the variant scarecrow that had ever been seen rising over a field-fence, and it is quite certain that his unhappy wife and children, had they seen him casually, would have laughed uproariously in great ignorance of his identity. At length it was felt that punishment enough had been inflicted, and he was permitted to depart.

He took to his heels at once, and ran in the direction of a pool a quarter of a mile off, to erase the fantastic decoration of his face at least. When his persecutors saw his object they thought it was only fair that they, who had dirtied him, should wash him, and they pursued him successfully. When the pool was reached he was washed to an extent that was hardly necessary. He was rolled in the water, scrubbed with tufts of grass, and generally reduced to the sorriest of plights before being finally allowed [to] depart from the scene. Some time afterwards he was descried [seen] hastening in the direction of St. Helens Junction, where he probably took [a] train for Manchester. It is not likely that he will again exhibit himself in St. Helens, and his fate will probably deter others as ill disposed.

SAVED FROM LYNCH LAW AT RAINHILL

What the newspapers referred to as "the principles" and "strict letter" of lynch law could be extended to a number of different types of offender. In June 1854 a St Helens painter called Charles Smith was charged with violently assaulting a railway porter called William Harper.

Smith admitted the charge but claimed that the porter had behaved in a very insolent manner towards his mother. The magistrates fined the man 20 shillings and costs and told him that he should have complained to the railway authorities instead of "administering Lynch law".

Twenty-five years later on July 12th 1879, the 7th annual athletic festival of the Rainhill Mutual Improvement Society was held on the village cricket field. The Prescot Reporter's subsequent write up of the event included this paragraph:

> The prohibition of betting, which the managers of the festival took every pains to notify, did not prevent the intrusion of one or two bookmakers, and one of these gentry having been detected in the act of "welshing" a confiding "backer," was seized and hustled by a number of people, and was

only saved from the rigours of Lynch law by the timely interposition of the officials and a policeman.

Then on October 19th 1893 after miners had attacked men undertaking safety work during a strike at Ashtons Green Colliery in Parr, the Manchester Daily Examiner wrote:

> Neither lynch-law nor mob-law can be tolerated, and unless the colliers control their passions and refrain from acts of violence their sufferings will be prolonged, because the chances of victory to their cause will be rendered still further remote.

COURT LYNCHING

As we have seen the moral outrage of the mob could be stirred by promiscuity within their community. If the target of their ire became involved in a court hearing, then concerned moralists – usually women and boys – often gathered outside the courtroom. And they could expect to receive some rough justice as they left the building.

Not that their "lynching" would likely cause the individual/s much more than a few bruises and loss of dignity. For one thing the town's main police station was right by the Town Hall court – whether in New Market Place or its replacement building in Corporation Street – and so protection was never far away.

On July 4th 1874 the St Helens Newspaper described how a woman called Dingsdale had accused Emma Atherton of assaulting her in Traverse Street in Parr. She was accused of pulling off Mrs Dingsdale's bonnet and shawl and throwing them to the ground and then pushing the woman down onto them.

However, in cross-examination what the Newspaper described as a "disgraceful story" was told. After fifteen years of marriage Emma Atherton's husband had left his wife to openly live with Mrs

Dingsdale and for the last ten months she'd been his lover – or "paramour", as the Newspaper put it.

Mrs Dingsdale's separated husband and "his new flame" had been walking along Traverse Street together when the woman saw red and committed the assault. Upon hearing the background to the case, the magistrates decided to dismiss the charge. However, that was not quite the end of the matter. The Newspaper added:

> When complainant and her man left the court they were mobbed, and had to run for refuge.

Not so fortunate with the courthouse lynch mob had been a chap identified by the St Helens Newspaper only as Gorse. When the young man appeared in St Helens Petty Sessions on April 18th 1870 he was heavily criticised by the Bench. That was through his repeated denials that he'd made a girl called Hasleden pregnant.

The young woman had died shortly after giving birth and there'd been strong evidence he was the father. It had been an affiliation or "bastardy" hearing in which Gorse was ordered to make maintenance payments to the guardians of his illegitimate child. But with no blood or DNA testing to prove paternity, he had chosen outright denial to try and save himself a shilling or two a week.

The St Helens Newspaper under the headline *"Mobbing an Obnoxious Individual"* described how a crowd of furious females had gathered outside the courtroom wanting to make their feelings on Gorse's behaviour known:

> The defendant wisely lingered awhile in the court, after his business there had ceased, in the hope, no doubt, that the crowd outside would soon disperse, and enable him to go home without being made the object of a popular and not very flattering demonstration. But there were a number of ardent females so impressed by his persistency in the case just decided, that they mutually agreed to await about the

entrance to the building until an opportunity offered of giving expression to their feelings in his presence. Mr. Gorse at length, fondly hoping for the success of his scheme, came leisurely down the sinuous staircase, and stepped into the street, only to find how cruelly he had deceived himself.

His appearance was no sooner observed, than a very wave of female humanity rolled against and around him with a characteristic uproar of angry voices. Bad names, curses, and strikingly negative compliments, were hurled at him with perfect prodigality, and more serious still, fists were brought into requisition to emphasise the torrent of language. He took the onslaught easily at first, stalking like an Ajax amongst the herd of his foes; but unfortunately for himself, he was clad in a more vulnerable material than the Homeric warrior was wont to appear in, and the repeated blows, falling on parts already irritated, gave him so much pain that he turned to bay [faced the women], and as a preliminary movement, overturned a pair of the graces in most immediate proximity by a couple of well-delivered blows of his fists. This action did not serve to lesson the clamour or allay the excitement, and the result would have been more serious but for the arrival of a policeman, who soon affected the release of the much-abused man.

CHILD ABUSE

The abuse of children through severe beatings or neglect was another reason for the unseemly juxtaposition of lynch law outside of a court of justice. On September 21st 1868, William and Ann Leather from Sutton *(seemingly of Robins Lane)* were charged at St Helens Petty Sessions with cruelly beating and ill-using a two-year-old child. Little Edith was the daughter of William, who had not long since married Ann.

She was a widow who had a family of her own. Although the evidence showed that Ann's 11-year-old daughter Louisa had also struck the child, it was clearly the stepmother that had been responsible for most of the appalling abuse.

Superintendent James Ludlam had examined Edith after she had been taken to the police station and – according to the St Helens Newspaper – had "found the back black and covered with bruises, and its legs and arms in the same state."

Dr James Ricketts told the hearing that he had examined the little girl at his Cotham Street surgery and she had been a "mass of bruises on all parts of her body, except the stomach and chest". He said he considered that the use of a thick stick would likely have caused the bruises.

The magistrates decided that the child should be looked after by her grandmother, and ordered the parents to pay her 2s 6d per week maintenance. The hearing was then adjourned for a month to see if their wishes were carried out.

The Newspaper then described how as William and Ann Leather had exited the building an angry crowd had set upon them, believing the couple had been too leniently treated:

> During the hearing of the above case, a large crowd, principally composed of women and boys, held an indignation meeting in the market-place, and evidently came to the determination of giving unequivocal evidence of their feeling of disgust at the offence of which the prisoners were supposed to be guilty. At the same time the court room contained a large number of people of the same class, who frequently manifested their bias during the investigation.
>
> It would appear as if they were displeased at the leniency of the magistrates, for when the accused were leaving the court, after being released from custody, an excited crowd

pressed out of the doors along with them, and down the stairs to the street. The stream of people pouring into the market-place drew the attention of the women outside, and the moment the Leathers were observed a shout of indignation was set up. The female, who appeared the particular object of regard, went boldly up to the crowd, and attempted to make her way through, but, some one, having opened the ball by striking her bonnet, she was hustled about from side to side, cursed at, and threatened with all sorts of desperate usage. Dreading the fulfilment of some of the threats, she hastily, and with some difficulty, made her way to the police office, where she was joined by her spouse, who had been separated from her in the street.

After a few minutes they emerged in company, and the crowd began to give fresh evidences of hostility. One woman fastened upon Leather, secured a grasp of his hair, and maltreated him woefully, without his having the power to retaliate, from the threatening pressure of people round. Meantime, his wife found herself surrounded, and dashed from one to another in the most unmerciful manner. She fought at bay, striking here and there, but numbers conquered her, and she was borne back and forward.

Getting an opening at last she made a rush for a grocer's shop, but a hospitable gentlemen, standing in the doorway, pushed her back amongst her enemies, who surrounded her again. In this condition, and while receiving such usage, she was pushed and dragged along Naylor-street, and towards Church street. Finding it impossible to get home without serious danger, she got back to the police office, and accompanied by her ill-treated partner, remained there until the storm blew over.

THE HUNT FOR THE MAN THAT EXPOSED HIMSELF TO A CHILD

My final example in this chapter does stretch its theme a little. Although the term lynch law was not mentioned in the newspaper reports, there were some of its expected aspects. The public fury over a perceived wrong showed itself in the form of a furious mother who attempted a citizen's arrest on a man accused of exposing himself to her daughter on two occasions.

And although the police led the subsequent hunt for the offender, there were a number of men with them who represented the

A CROSS-COUNTRY CHASE AFTER A COLLIER.

On Saturday forenoon, shortly after ten o'clock, the police at St. Helens received information that a man named Henry Hesketh, a collier, had acted indecently towards a girl named Mary Ann Baldwin, 12 years of age. The offence was committed near a bridge which, in a line with Talbot-street, crosses a brook at right angles, and thither Inspector Whiteside and Sergeants Wood and Berry proceeded, but by the time they arrived they found that the man had made his escape across an adjoining cricket field, and by this time had a mile start. The officers, as soon as they got fairly on his track, went off in hot pursuit, the excitement being heightened by the joining in of several men and boys, and even women. The route taken by the culprit was evidently in the direction of Rainford, and the pursuers, with Sergeant Wood in advance, gradually gained on the man as they approached Eccleston. The fugitive then beat across Millbrook-lane, near Millbrook House, and crossing another field he came out at Longbarrow, which is the boundary between Rainford and Knowsley. It now became a race, as it were, for life, and Hesketh was beginning to get winded, for as he passed Mosbro' Hall his pursuers were still gaining on him, until at length they lost his trail by his diving into a plantation between Mosbro' Hall and Rainford. Twice the plantation was "beaten" by the police and their rustic assistants,

Prescot Reporter March 27th 1875

aggrieved public. There were also boys amongst the band who dashed up trees to keep their quarry in sight. The searchers were the Lancashire version of the American posse seen in many a Western film, without the horses!

The serious incident that led to the chase occurred just after 10am on Saturday March 20th 1875. Mary Baldwin of Lowe Street in St Helens had been despatched by her mother to bring home her little brother from where he'd been playing with friends. The 12-year-old's errand meant she had to cross a bridge that spanned a brook in Talbot Street. At one side of the bridge sat on a pile of stones was Henry Hesketh and as Mary walked past him the man exposed himself to her.

After collecting her brother and a little girl, Mary needed to pass the same place on the return trip home. As she did so the 38-year-old miner repeated his offence and also asked the child to go with him. But, instead, Mary dashed home and told her mother what had occurred. That led to the woman going to the bridge with her daughter where they found Hesketh still sitting there. At this point I'll let the St Helens Newspaper of March 27th 1875 take up the rest of this remarkable story:

> She seized him and accused him of his atrocious conduct, when he offered her half-a-crown to say nothing more about it, and when this was indignantly refused, he threatened to throw her over the bridge. Entreaties and threats were alike unavailing to the enraged mother, who would listen to neither, but sent her daughter in search of a policeman. The prisoner, finding matters were now getting rather hot for him, at once wrenched himself clear of Mrs. Baldwin, and made off across the old cricket field as fast as his legs would carry him. In the meantime the daughter had fallen in with Inspector Whiteside and Sergt. Wood in Liverpool road, and they at once went off to the place already named to find that the prisoner had got nearly a mile start of them. They at once gave chase and were shortly afterwards joined by Sergt. Berry; several men and boys also joining in pursuit.
>
> The fugitive now "made tracks" in the direction of Eccleston, from where he crossed Milbroke [sic] lane, near Milbroke House, and then started right across a field to Longbarrow, which is the boundary between Rainford and Knowsley. Hence he made past Mossbro' Hall, and bore on to Rainford, his pursuers "driving him to cover" in a plantation between the two. Those in pursuit now made sure they had their man properly caged, and so he was, as they beat about and searched the place twice to no effect, but P.C. Sheriff, who had come by another route, saw a rabbit spring up from one of the hedges and take across the plantation.
>
> Looking down in the direction whence the rabbit had issued, he there saw the prisoner, who was sitting with his legs

down two separate rabbit holes, as far as he could get them, and his head and shoulders crouched under the hedge, he at the same time being evidently "pumped out." To secure and handcuff him was, as may be expected, but the work of a moment, and the whole party returned to St. Helens where they arrived shortly after 2 o'clock, after a chase of about seven miles. We may state that for once in a way the boys who joined in the pursuit were of considerable use to the officers, as they every now and then climbed up trees in the track, and were thus able to keep the prisoner in sight when those on the ground could not see him, as he "dodged" them in the undulating land over which he led them. The Bench considered it a very bad case, and committed the prisoner to gaol for two months.

The Story of The St Helens Circus

"I am sure most of you will remember St. Helens when it was a much smaller place when they had not so much smoke and had not got so far advanced as to have a circus every night."

A little known fact is that for around ten years in the late 19th century, St Helens had its own dedicated circus building. The St Helens Circus – *aka Cullen's Circus, the Circus Of Varieties, Transfield's American Circus, The Gaiety, Gaiety Palace and Lucas's Hippodrome & Circus* – in North Road was the largest meeting place in town with a capacity of up to 3,000 people. Although all sorts of other theatrical events and gatherings were held at the venue, its primary purpose was as a home for the exhibition of clowns, acrobats, horses and other animals.

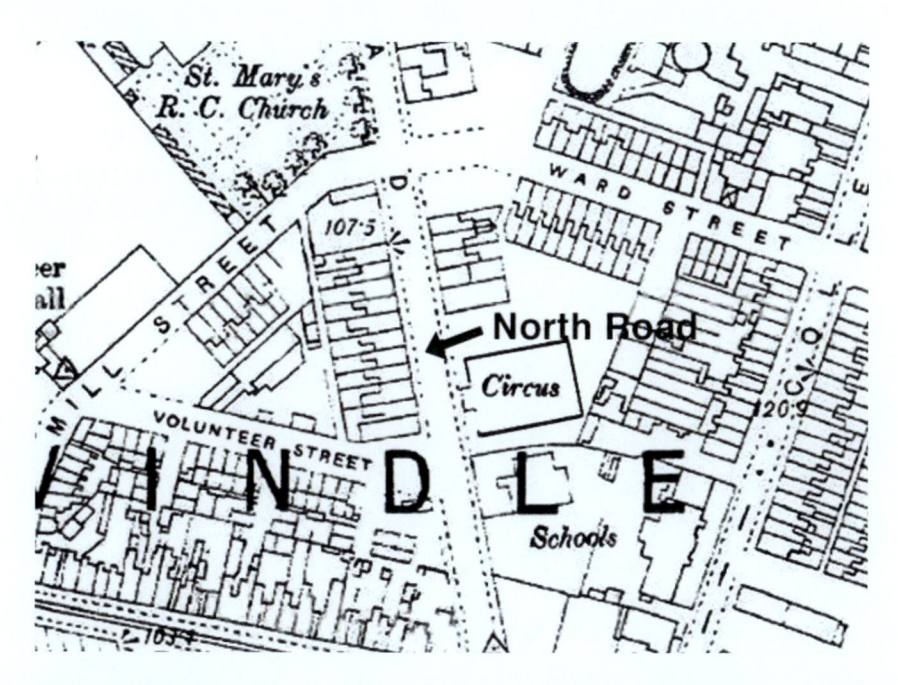

Sadly there are no known photographs of what was a huge wooden structure. But we can see from this map that The Circus was situated close to the junction of North Road and Volunteer Street in St Helens and adjacent to "Lacey's" Cowley School *(where Central Modern would later be built)*. Its building took place in 1882 and on July 29th of that year, the theatrical paper known as The Era described the forthcoming attraction:

> **CULEEN'S CIRCUS** – This place of amusement is announced to open for the season on Monday next. It is to be hoped Mr Culeen will have a successful term, as apparently neither energy nor money has been spared in the construction.

Then on August 5th 1882 the St Helens Examiner published this report on the new venture:

> On Monday evening another source of amusement to the St. Helens public was opened in North-street, in the shape of a circus. It is a substantial and capacious wooden structure, erected at considerable cost by Mr. Thomas Culeen, an experienced and successful circus manager. There have been large attendances during the week, and the entertainment provided is of the best character, as there is a full complement of clever and skilful riders, witty and amusing clowns, and well-trained horses and ponies.

On the 12th The Era gave its take on the newly opened Circus:

> **CULEEN'S CIRCUS** – This establishment, which is stated to have cost £1,000, was successfully opened on the 31st ult. in the presence of an audience whose number and enthusiasm augur well for the future success of the enterprise. The building, which presents a very comfortable appearance, is 100ft. long and 75ft. broad, and affords seating accommodation for 3,000 persons. The ventilation so far seems perfect, and ample means of ingress and

egress have been provided. A full and efficient company has been engaged, who secure much applause in the varied and interesting programme nightly presented. The band, under the leadership of Mr Prideaux, is a capital one.

The only other venues capable of holding large numbers of people in St Helens at that time were the Assembly Room of the Town Hall and the Volunteer Hall – but these were eclipsed by the huge Circus. A week later The Era wrote:

> **CULEEN'S CIRCUS** – The large and talented company engaged here continues to attract good audiences. The specialities during the past week have been Storelli, the royal musical entertainer; the "Lancers' Quadrilles" on horseback, steeplechasing, and the first appearance of Master T. H. Culeen, equestrian marvel.

The latter was Thomas Henry Culeen, the young son of The Circus's proprietor who already ran a circus in Burnley. The family surname varied in newspaper accounts between Culeen and Cullen, although the former seems the correct version.

In 1881 a dedicated circus building had opened in Sankey Street in Warrington and this along with Culeen Snr's experience in Burnley, appears to have been the inspiration for the St Helens venture.

At Warrington the building had also been used for drama, meetings and even church services and in North Road in St Helens they attempted to follow that same model. On September 2nd 1882 the Examiner newspaper provided the latest update:

> **CULLEN'S CIRCUS, ST. HELENS** – This circus, which has now been established something like a month at St. Helens, has met with a very successful reception. On almost every night it has been filled to repletion, not only in the cheaper portions, but also those which are more costly and select.

> The entertainment provided is of a high class, and on the whole notably free from vulgarity. During the present week there has been a representation of "The Brigands," adapted from the opera "Fra Diavolo," and has on each occasion been witnessed by a large and well-pleased audience.

The Era's report stated that gymnasts and a juggler had also been highlights, with the theatrical journal adding:

> There is but little diminution in the attendance here, thanks to the sound policy of an ever-changing programme.

However, for much of August the town's Theatre Royal – then housed in the building known more recently as the Citadel – had been closed for renovation and The Circus faced no competition.

On October 28th The Era again reviewed the past week's entertainment:

> **CULEEN'S CIRCUS** – The first appearance in this town of Nimrod (equilibrist, juggler, and musical genius) has during the week stirred the enthusiasm of the patrons of this establishment. Madame Gartner (a graceful and accomplished equestrienne) also made her first appearance, and was well received. Among the other items were Van Barr (a clever trapeze artist), Mr Vernon (who introduced two very cleverly-trained ponies), Persivani and Aseiky (excellent knockabout clowns), and an equestrian spectacle entitled the Egyptian War, which, being well put into the arena and acted efficiently throughout, sent the habitues home in high glee.

The Circus became the talk of the town and in November 1882 at a Town Hall dinner for the old folk of St Helens, the Mayor Richard Pilkington quipped:

I am sure most of you will remember St. Helens when it was a much smaller place than at present when they had not so much smoke, and so much dirt; at any rate, they had not got so far advanced as to have a circus every night!

On November 11th the St Helens Examiner suggested that drama and circus acts were being combined in North Road:

CULLEN'S CIRCUS – This excellent circus still maintains undiminished the popularity which it has enjoyed since it came to St. Helens, and during the past week large audiences have been delighted by the production of a beautiful equestrian spectacle, entitled "Joan of Arc," written and arranged by Mr. J. F. Scott. The part of the famous maid is taken by Miss Georgina Webster, a splendid performer, and she is ably sustained by the rest of the large company. All the other accessories necessary to a popular circus are provided, and as a result Mr. Cullen reaps the benefit of his enterprise and management in large and delighted audiences.

CULLEN'S CIRCUS, ST. HELENS.

On MONDAY EVENING, APRIL 9TH, 1883, The Members of the Liverpool Gymnasium will give a Grand ATHLETIC TOURNAMENT AND DISPLAY OF GYMNASTIC EXERCISES, In aid of the Gymnasium Prize Fund, Under the distinguished patronage of HIS WORSHIP THE MAYOR OF ST. HELENS (Lieutenant-Colonel Gamble, J.P.), The St. Helens Cricket Club, the St. Helens Bicycle Club, and the Gentry of the District.

The programme will include Dumb Bell, Bar Bell, and Indian Club Exercises, to musical accompaniment; Horizontal Bar, Irregular Bars, Vaulting Horse, Boxing Exercises, Running Maize, High Leaping, &c., &c. Also, a Fancy Bicycle Riding Competition between T. D. McKenzie and other well-well-known competitors.

Doors open at 7-30; to commence at 8 o'clock.

Admission :—Reserved Seats, 2s ; Second seats, 1s ; Gallery, 6d. Tickets may be had from Mr. McKENZIE, Druggist; and Mr. FOREMAN, Printer.

Advert in the Prescot Reporter of March 31st 1883

However for some reason – probably financial – The Circus closed in mid-November of 1882 and did not properly reopen for eight months. However, a gymnastics and athletics tournament was held at the venue in April 1883 and in June Casey's Clowns combined appearances at The Circus with playing cricket matches at Dentons Green. The St Helens Examiner wrote:

> The play of the clowns was not of a particularly impressive kind, though considerable amusement was caused by some of the more comical members of the team.

After its lengthy period of hibernation, The Circus fully re-opened in July 1883 and the St Helens Examiner described the first night:

> **CULEEN'S CIRCUS, NORTH-ROAD**. – This circus was reopened on Monday evening by Mr. Culeen, and performances have been given during the week in the presence of very large gatherings. The programme of entertainment is varied and well-selected, and seems to be greatly appreciated. The acrobatic and sleight-of-hand feats in particular are such as to win particular admiration. The clowns, who are so important an adjunct to establishments of this kind, are also well up to their work, and ensure a plentiful supply of laughable incidents.

However, the incident that occurred in the building a fortnight later was far from laughable. A boy called James Harrison from Lord Street in Gerards Bridge in St Helens died at The Circus while attempting to ride a live mule.

During the performances it had become a regular feature for boys to be invited to attempt to ride a frisky mule. The animal had been specially trained to throw its riders by putting its head to the floor and kicking up its hind legs. The 12-year-old had accepted the invitation and was predictably thrown off the mule. James was then seen to stagger to the barrier in front of the reserved seats and shortly afterwards he collapsed and died. A lad named John Magin told James' inquest that his friend had been thrown off twice and on attempting to remount, the mule had kicked him in the stomach. Another youth named Gregory said he did not notice any kick but said he had witnessed James staggering with his hand grasping his chest.

Thomas Cullen, the owner of The Circus, said he was present at the time of James' death and was positive his mule did not kick him. Dr Arthur Jamison thought that the boy's demise had been caused by a "form of apoplexy brought on by over-excitement" and added that he was "perfectly sure" that death was not the result of a kick or any other violent act. However, no post-mortem examination appears to have been carried out.

The inquest jury returned a verdict of death from natural causes – which they thought had been caused by a "fusion on the brain brought on by excitement". Some of the jurors remarked that the public ought not to be allowed to ride the mule. However, the Coroner pointed out that as the jury had not attached blame to anyone, they could not make such a recommendation but must instead leave the matter up to the proprietor, adding:

> Mr. Culeen has to cater for the public, and the public are never satisfied unless something extraordinary is being done. I am quite sure Mr. Culeen will do his best to protect the public, but, if they will have dangerous things done, I think the public are more to blame than the proprietors.

I'm not sure modern-day health and safety inspectors would agree with that statement! But despite the tragedy, performances continued and on September 29th 1883 The Era wrote:

> **CULEEN'S CIRCUS** – The newcomers here on Monday were Ling-Look, who has caused no little sensation in his entertainment of sword swallowing and fire-eating, and the Brothers Lero, very clever gymnasts, hat throwers, and acrobats. The bare-back riding of Master T. H. Culeen on

four ponies and of Mr A. Wells on four horses is exceedingly good, and secures loud applause. Signor Andrea proves to be an extremely clever juggler; Madame Pablo and Mause display their equestrian abilities with success; while the humour of Ferns, Pablo, and Rodway produces great mirth.

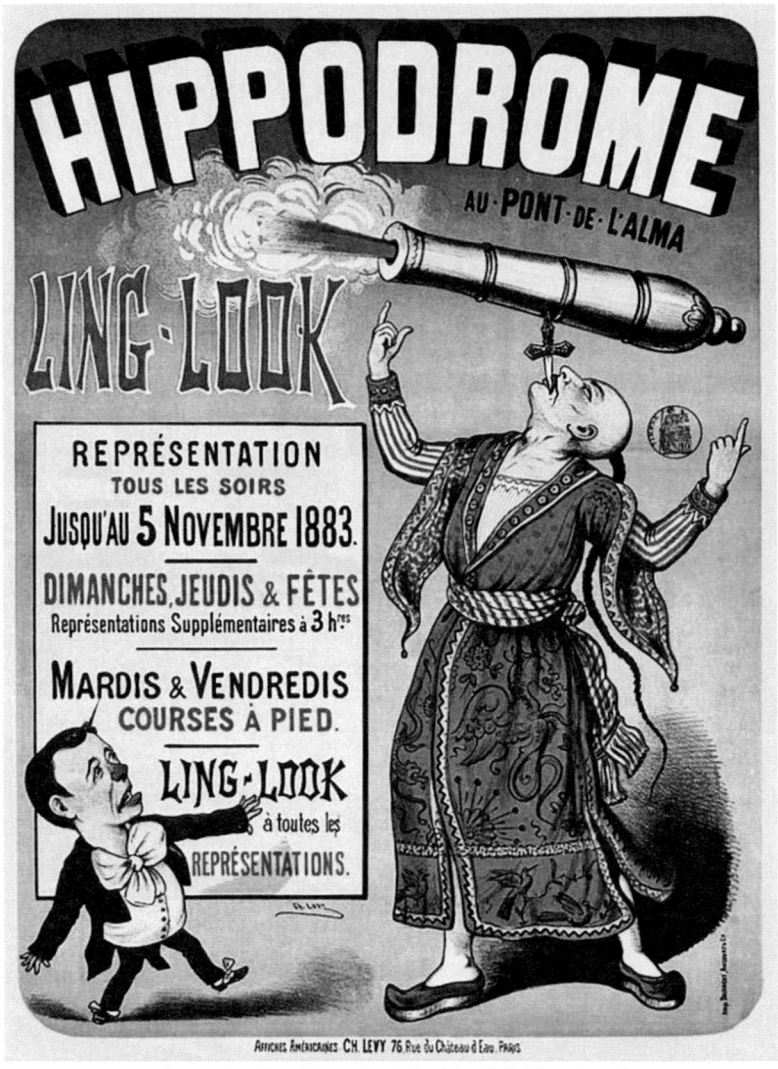

A poster for the remarkable Ali Ling Look

Ali Ling Look's party trick was to balance a cannon on a dagger that had been rammed down his throat – and then fire off the cannon. Although after the tragic events of December 1881, party invites were probably few and far between!

At a show in Brighton the Chinese sword swallower had blown the head off a 15-year-old boy that was sitting in his audience. Ling Look was subsequently charged with manslaughter but after a lengthy period in custody was acquitted at trial. The Yorkshire Gazette wrote at the time of the incident:

> A Chinaman, named Ling Look, gave an acrobatic and juggling performance on Tuesday night at the Oxford Music Hall, Brighton. One of his feats consisted of balancing a small cannon on a sword held in his mouth, and firing it in that position. The cannon was directed towards the upper gallery, and when it was fired the charge struck a boy who was seated in that part the building, and killed him, the upper part of his head being blown away.

Ling Look, who couldn't speak any English, continued performing after the trial – but presumably cut out his cannon firing. When he appeared in St Helens a review said the Chinaman caused "no little sensation in his entertainment of sword swallowing and fire-eating" – although clearly not as much as he caused in Brighton!

CULEEN'S CIRCUS,
NORTH-ROAD, ST. HELENS.
Sole Proprietor - - THOMAS CULEEN.

CROWDED HOUSES NIGHTLY!
IMMENSE SUCCESS!!
OPEN EVERY NIGHT!!!
ANOTHER GRAND CHANGE OF PROGRAMME!
ANOTHER GRAND CHANGE OF PROGRAMME!!
ANOTHER GRAND CHANGE OF PROGRAMME!!!
Commencing MONDAY, 27th August.
DICK TURPIN, or Bonny Black Bess. Special Engagement of TED CROUEST, England's Greatest Jester in the title rôle. First appearance of FUNNY PABLO, son of the original Pablo Franque. The Stock Company comprises FUNNY CLOWNS, Clever EQUESTRIAN PERFORMANCES, &c., &c.
Grand Day Performance every Saturday at 2-30.
Prices of Admission:—Reserved Seats, 2s.; Boxes, 1s.; Pit and Promenade, 6d.; Gallery, 3d.
Doors open at 7; to commence at 7-30. Half-price to Boxes and Reserved Seats at 8-45.   243

CULEEN'S CIRCUS,
NORTH-ROAD, ST. HELENS.
Sole Proprietor - - THOMAS CULEEN.

NOVELTY TRIPS THE HEELS OF NOVELTY.

BRILLIANT SUCCESS.
CROWDED HOUSES.
SPLENDID HORSES.
CLEVER ACROBATS.
AMUSING CLOWNS.

CONSTANT CHANGE OF PROGRAMME.

Grand Day Performance every Saturday at 2-30.
Prices of Admission:—Reserved Seats, 2s.; Boxes, 1s.; Pit and Promenade, 6d.; Gallery, 3d.
Doors open at 7; to commence at 7-30. Half-price to Boxes and Reserved Seats at 8-45.   246

Adverts in the Prescot Reporter of August 25th and September 15th 1883

At the end of October 1883, The Circus closed for a fortnight to undergo "extensive alterations and embellishment" before reopening under new management as a music hall. The venue was now owned by Edwin Trevanion of the Adelphi Theatre in Liverpool and renamed 'Trevanion's Theatre of Varieties'.

Instead of circus acts performing in a ring, there was now a series of ventriloquists, comics, singers and dancers. There were also, sadly, black entertainers performing grotesque parodies of "negroes" with exaggerated mannerisms.

On January 3rd 1885 The Era stated that Edwin Trevanion was severing his connection with the theatre and it would be consequently closing down. Despite what was stated to be large audiences regularly in attendance, admission fees had been kept low to bring in the punters and the running costs were high.

There was no bar or other refreshments available and so such additional revenue streams were denied to the owners. But there were plenty of new proprietors waiting in the wings convinced they could make the venue pay.

This is Dan Leno who many consider the finest music hall act in the Victorian era. He seemed to agree, as in the 1890s the London-born comedian and dancer styled himself as *"The Funniest Man on Earth"*. Well, modesty never got you anywhere in show business!

On October 3rd 1885 The Era described how the 24-year-old Leno had been top of the bill at what was now called The Gaiety in St Helens. The theatrical journal added: "His clever dancing has caused quite a furore". Two months earlier Messrs. Alvo and Newby had taken over the

Circus building and renamed it 'The Gaiety'. Its previous owners had decided to run the custom-built circus building in North Road as a music hall and its new bosses chose to continue this policy. But it was a short-lived venture as the huge wooden building came with large overheads and at the end of October 1885 the theatre was again closed.

Henry Finch – who ran a pub in Salisbury Street in St Helens – became the next to have a crack at trying to make the venue pay. So on November 9th 1885 'The Gaiety Palace' opened its doors – but Finch was another theatrical impresario with a short shelf life.

On January 30th 1886 the Liverpool Weekly Courier wrote about a dispute that had played out in St Helens County Court. An act called the Sisters Phillips and the Brothers Lorenzi – who described themselves as *"The Comical Boys and the Curious Girls"* – demanded £5 off Henry Finch. A contract for the troupe to play six nights in North Road for the sum of £10 had been agreed – but Finch had only paid half their fee.

The hearing was told that Finch was filing for bankruptcy because of his losses sustained during his brief tenure of the venue. During the week in question nine other artists had been performing along with the Sisters Phillips and the Brothers Lorenzi.

I doubt they'd all have been paid as much as £10 for their week's work; but with other costs including wages for theatre staff and leasing fees – it's easy to see that the pennies paid for admission would not prove sufficient income to make the enterprise a going concern.

A Mrs F. Charsley then took over the running of 'The Gaiety Palace of Varieties' – still operating it as a music hall. In early April 1886 the Carles with their troupe of performing pigeons appeared at the theatre. Their performance was described as a "really first-class and wonderful entertainment". Later in the month there was yet another change of ownership and it was decided to return the building to its original core purpose – as a circus.

That was how the building had been designed with a ring and much open space to accommodate all the horses and clowns. I expect that arrangement had not suited music hall turns, particularly in the days before microphones and amplification.

So Transfield's American Circus featuring a flying gymnast, female jester, horizontal bar performers, a lady juggler on horseback, a bare backed equestrienne, equilibrist and clowns returned to North Road. The Era wrote:

> This place of amusement has been reopened by Captain Transfield. Extensive alterations and new decorations have been carried out at a great expense, so as to render the building as comfortable as possible. The opening took place on Good Friday to a large and appreciative audience.

However, Thomas Transfield became unwell and his illness led to his reign in North Road being another brief one. In March 1887 Wallace Revill acquired The Circus, renaming it 'The Grand Circus of Varieties', three years after the theatrical impresario had taken over the Theatre Royal in St Helens. That was still situated in the building on the corner of Milk Street and Waterloo Street in the premises that in later years became known as the Citadel.

Having decided to build a new luxury Theatre Royal in Corporation Street, this notice was published in the St Helens Reporter on May 4th 1889:

> **THEATRE ROYAL & OPERA HOUSE, ST. HELENS** – Note. – Mr. Wallace Revill having entered into an arrangement to Sell the above property, the public are respectfully informed that the LAST DRAMATIC PERFORMANCE in the present Theatre will positively take place on SATURDAY EVENING, MAY 4th, 1889. Pending the erection of the New Theatre Royal and Opera House, at Corporation-street (which will be erected on Fire-proof

principles, with all the latest improvements at cost of over £10,000), all Dramatic and Variety Contracts entered into by Mr. Revill will be fulfilled, and business carried on as usual at the CIRCUS OF VARIETIES, North-Road.

The Salvation Army would, incidentally, ultimately be the ones who would buy the old building and call it the St Helens Citadel. As to the new Theatre Royal constructed on "fire-proof principles", that would open in Corporation Street in 1890 but burn down nine years later. So much for fireproof! However, in the interim the theatre moved lock, stock and barrel to North Road with circus acts now taking a back seat.

The Salvation Army Citadel

As previously stated the venue had been built to suit the largely visual circus performers with a ring and open space to accommodate the movement of horses and clowns. However, in the pre-amplification days you really had to be sat near the front of an auditorium to fully appreciate a dramatic show with dialogue, such as a play. Music hall turns with musicians, singers, visual performers and loud comics were far easier on the ear.

This is alluded to in this report in the St Helens Reporter of September 14th 1889:

> The Grand Circus and Theatre of Varieties is this week dedicated to a programme of a various description – a programme much more adapted to the building than the legitimate or illegitimate drama. It is great strain on the attention to sit in one of the remote tracts of the Circus and endeavour to follow the action of a drama as revealed by the

utterances of the performers. It is much more agreeable to watch a variety music hall performance.

When the new Theatre Royal in Corporation Street opened in August 1890, The Circus appears to have become disused. That was until February 1892, when on the 13th of that month the St Helens Examiner published this piece:

> The large and commodious building known as the circus in North-road St. Helens, has latterly been undergoing extensive alterations and decorations and it is understood that it will be shortly opened with one of the best circus company's in kingdom. There has been no institution of the kind in the town for some years and there is every prospect that the new venture will prove successful. The interior of the building has been almost entirely transformed and a splendid "ring" and all the surroundings of a high class circus have been provided. The opening of the new place of entertainment is already eagerly looked forward to.

Fred Lucas had leased the building off its owner Wallace Revill and circus acts were once again the primary form of entertainment on offer. A fortnight later under the headline *"A New Circus At St Helens"*, the Examiner wrote this article:

> Next Monday night will witness the opening of Lucas's Hippodrome and Circus, North-road, St. Helens, and as far as present appearances indicate, the new place of amusement will undoubtedly be one of the finest and most comfortable circuses in the provinces. The building has been entirely renovated and decorated, and all the seats from top to bottom have been admirably re-arranged so that every visitor will be afforded an uninterrupted view of the performance. The structural alterations have been of an extensive character, and an immense sum of money has

been laid out in order to provide every convenience and comfort for such a building. And under the personal direction and control of genial Mr. Fred Lucas everything will he done to maintain its character at the highest pitch. The Company engaged for the opening will certainly compare more than favourably with any company at present in the country, for variety and efficiency of performance. The attractions are many. There are no less than over twenty artistes of acknowledged ability and fame, and they have been selected from the best circuses in Europe and America. They include every variety of performers, lady and gentleman riders, gymnasts, acrobats, vaulters, Arab tumblers, and the best of humorous clowns. Then there will be a stud of splendidly trained horses, in addition to which an engagement has been made for a series of performances by the well-known performing elephant "Gipsy" from the Royal Aquarium, London. Special attention has been paid to the selection of the band and Mr. F. Godfrey will be the musical director.

The St Helens Examiner later wrote how the new venue had been crowded each night during its opening week. The chief attractions had been a performing elephant called Gipsy, "marvellous feats of horsemanship", a big boot dance, the "comicalities of the clowns", performances on flying rings, an exhibition on stilts and "daring performances on pianoforte wire".

On March 26th 1892 the Examiner published another update. However I would caution readers that 'Lucas's Grand Hippodrome' was by now advertising heavily with the paper and so the Examiner was unlikely to say anything negative about their client:

THE CIRCUS AT ST. HELENS. The circus and hippodrome in North-road, St. Helens, continues to prove the most popular place of entertainment, apart from the Theatre

Royal, in the town. Since its opening a few weeks ago some of the best equestrian talent in the kingdom have given their performance and there have been some remarkably crowded houses, testifying in that respect, the splendid character of the entertainment. An exceptionally strong programme has been arranged for next week, including the attendance of Mr. James Newsome and family, with their well-known stud of horses, ponies and mules. The performing elephant, "Gipsy," from the Royal Aquarium, London, is again visiting the circus, and will undoubtedly as on its last appearance in St. Helens, be one of the attractions of the week.

LUCAS'S GRAND HIPPODROME.
NORTH-ROAD, ST. HELENS.
Now Open for the Season.

DAY PERFORMANCE every Saturday, Doors open at 2 o'clock; commencing at 2.30 p.m. Children half-price.
CELEBRATED COMBINATION of CIRCUS STARS.
BRILLIANT GALAXY OF TALENT.
The Place to spend a Happy Evening of Wonder and Joy, with Everlasting Reminiscences!
STARRING ENGAGEMENT for Six Nights Only of DR CLEMENT,
The KING of ARIEL PARALLELS, Introducing a most Novel Performance on Suspended and Parrelled Bars.
Great success of Mr. CLAUDE RANDELL, in his Newmarket Jockey and Hurdle Act.
MDDLE. VERA, will introduce her two Beautiful Arab Steeds Tandem (without reins).
FRANK JENNINGS, in his great Bareback Trick Act, &c.
MISS MARIE REIVES, Introducing the Highly Trained Horse " Lucifer."
Special Engagement of FRED LITTLE, MUSICAL CLOWN. Great success of the Singing and Talking Clowns.
MISS AGNES and F. L. STEVENSON, in their Marvellous Entertainment, entitled the "Enchanted Lady."
Doors open at 7 o'clock; commence at 7-30.
Carriages may be ordered for 10-15.
PRICES of ADMISSION: Front seats, 2s; Second seats, 1s 6d; Side, 1s; Promenade, 6d; Gallery. 4d.
Box office open at the Circus between the hours of 10 o'clock and 3 o'clock daily, when seats may be secured.
Early doors at 6-30; 3d extra to all parts; Gallery 2d.

LUCAS'S GRAND HIPPODROME.

NORTH-ROAD, ST. HELENS.

Now open for the Season.
GREAT ATTRACTION FOR THE HOLIDAYS.
EASTER MONDAY, APRIL 18TH, and during the Week
Grand production of the Celebrated Circus Performance

TURPIN'S RIDE TO YORK.

FULL COMPANY OF TALENTED EQUESTRIANS

NEW CLOWNS.

EXHIBITION NIGHTLY OF

DEEMING'S LION.

This LION was brought by DEEMING, the Rainhill Murderer, from Africa, and sold to Mr. Wm. Cross, naturalist, Liverpool.
The Place to spend a Happy Evening of Wonder and Joy, with Everlasting Reminiscences!
Doors open at 7 o'clock; commence at 7-30.
PRICES of ADMISSION: Front seats, 2s; Second seats, 1s 6d; Side, 1s; Promenade, 6d; Gallery. 4d.

Adverts in the St Helens Examiner of March 5th and April 16th 1892

Frederick Deeming – the infamous Rainhill murderer – was still five weeks away from being hung for the shocking crimes that he had committed against his own family when the Examiner published this piece on April 16th 1892:

> The enterprising and energetic proprietor of the popular circus and hippodrome, North-road, St. Helens, Mr. Fred Lucas, has arranged an exceptionally attractive programme for the holiday season. Undoubtedly one of the most prominent features will be an exhibition of the famous lion cub, known as Deeming's Lion. This animal was brought by the notorious Rainhill murderer from Africa and was sold by him to Mr. Wm. Cross, the well-known naturalist, of Liverpool. At an enormous expense Mr. Lucas has arranged for an exhibition of the lion at St. Helens, on the night of Good Friday, Saturday, Easter Monday, and every evening during next week. The animal will be exhibited during the ordinary interval in the evening's programme at the circus.

We have already seen how there had been a death at The Circus in 1883 and on November 29th 1892 another incident took place that could have had a similar outcome.

Although the consequences turned out not to be serious, it is extraordinary that what were described as "wild, vicious, and nervous horses" were being tamed at the venue in public.

Local horse dealers and proprietors of horse-driven vehicles had provided the animals for them to be subdued by a renowned tamer called Professor Norton B. Smith. Michael McGhee, a grocer from Liverpool Street, had supplied a particularly wild horse.

The St Helens Examiner described how as Smith was handling it, spectators threw lighted crackers into the ring which caused the animal to panic:

> This caused considerable excitement and there was a stampede, the people running in all directions out of the way.

Luckily there were no injuries and in order to prevent a re-occurrence, a rope was put round the ring to prevent the wild horses from getting out.

Five months later Fred Lucas – The Circus's former lessee and manager – opened a theatre of his own in Corporation Street *(although then part of Shaw Street)*.

This was called the People's Palace and was situated on the site that the Hippodrome would later occupy. As a result Wallace Revill, the owner of the Theatre Royal and The Circus, fell out with Fred Lucas. At a court hearing in April 1893, Revill's solicitor stated that there was no room for two such places of entertainment in St Helens.

The People's Palace

His client, he claimed, had been unable to make both the Theatre Royal and The Circus pay and so it appears that Revill had closed down the St Helens Circus to concentrate operations on his grand new theatre in what we know as Corporation Street.

The huge Circus building that accommodated up to 3,000 persons would soon be demolished and the Ordnance Survey map of 1908 shows that houses were now occupying the site in North Road.

It certainly had a short and troubled life after being launched only in 1882. However, thousands of our ancestors were entertained in The Circus and it played an important role in the development of leisure and entertainment in St Helens.

Conmen And Imposters In St Helens

"The defendant is one of the biggest liars and hypocrites the police has had to deal with."

In Volume 1 of *'Hidden History of St Helens'* I relate the activities of James Smythe, the so-called "Colorado millionaire" conman who came to St Helens in 1910. James Scowcroft – the landlord of the Wellington Hotel in Naylor Street – ended up in America penniless after falling for the lies of the smooth-talking Smythe.

Not all deceptions that have been committed in St Helens over the years have been on his scale. Some seemed hardly worth the imposter's while with little financial gain made. But, of course, making money was not the conman's only motivation. They clearly enjoyed the respect their phony exalted status gave them and the power they held over those they conned.

And so this chapter is devoted to the activities of some of these liars and imposters who enjoyed conning the people of St Helens – even if financially they derived little benefit.

THE SHAM GERMAN NOBLEMAN

I'll bet Annie Brownley was mightily impressed when on April 10th 1888 a German man called Fritz von Weissenberg turned up at her Claughton Street home in St Helens seeking lodgings. The visitor claimed to be a wealthy nobleman who owned a mansion with 24 rooms, as well as a warehouse in Leeds. The German accent would, of course, have been a big help to von Weissenberg in convincing the 53-year-old widow that he was the real thing.

Mrs Brownley agreed to rent her noble lodger some rooms and later that day he showed her a bundle of papers that he passed off as money. In fact they were advertisements for Dunville's Irish whisky made up to look like bank notes! Four days later after becoming suspicious of her new lodger, Mrs Brownley asked von Weissenberg to pay the 15s 9½d bill that had built up during his short stay. That prompted the 39-year-old to pick up his hat and walk out of the house, never to return.

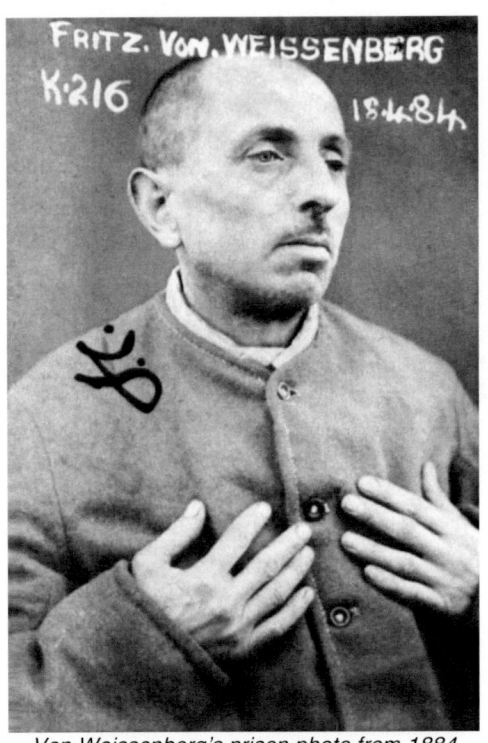

However, in making his swift departure from Mrs Brownley's Claughton Street home, von Weissenberg left behind a bundle of papers. These contained the fake bank notes as well as details that showed he was a convict on licence. And so Mrs Brownley went to the police and the imposter was arrested in Liverpool.

Not only had von Weissenberg cheated his landlady but he had also failed to report his presence in the town to the St Helens police, as required by his early release from prison. That had been from a five-year sentence imposed on

Von Weissenberg's prison photo from 1884

him in London for cheating a baker out of the huge sum of £600. Then the man had claimed to be Baron von Weissenberg, a friend of the Duchess of Albany and a relative of Prince Bismarck.

Upon appearing in court in St Helens, Weissenberg insisted that he did have a large house and had not intended to cheat Mrs Brownley – but was committed for trial at Liverpool. On May 10th 1888 at the Liverpool Spring Assizes, Fritz von Weissenberg was sentenced to eighteen months in prison. The judge said that what he had done in defrauding a widow had been a cruel thing.

DEAF AND DUMB IMPOSTER

Street beggars knew the public would treat them more sympathetically if they had some form of infirmity. And so it was not uncommon for them to carry cards falsely claiming to be deaf and dumb or blind. Under the headline *"A Begging Imposter At St. Helens"*, the St Helens Examiner on May 9th 1885 described how William Ogden had been charged with "soliciting alms" in Duke Street and Church Street.

The middle-aged man had claimed to be deaf and dumb and when taken to the police station had continued the pretence so successfully that he was released with a warning – presumably in writing. That was at a time when beggars could expect to receive 7 to 14 days in prison.

However, Ogden was later found gesticulating to persons in the street and back at the police station admitted it was all a con. The Examiner wrote:

> It was eventually found that he was an imposter, and in the dock he pleaded guilty in a clear voice. He had admitted being sent to prison for begging in other towns. Alderman Harrison committed him for seven days with hard labour.

SWINDLING A WIDOW AT ST HELENS

The Liverpool Weekly Courier's introduction to their report of August 13th 1887 headlined *"Swindling A Widow At St. Helens"* is a bit on the cruel side. They wrote: "An instance of the ease with which some domestic servants of even middle-age are duped transpired on Wednesday at St. Helens."

The unnamed victim can hardly be blamed for being taken in by a smooth-talking young man that had seen her advertisement seeking a position as a general servant in a household and had decided to exploit her situation.

The fraudster had called at the woman's home and passed himself off as the son of a horse dealer living at Heath Cottage in the district of St Ann's in Eccleston who had a vacancy for a servant. He invited the 35-year-old to accompany him to meet the "old gentleman" to see if they suited each other. The newspaper takes up the rest of the story:

> On emerging from the house he very confidentially informed her that he had a number of accounts to pay, and pulling out a quantity of what appeared to be half-sovereigns and silver – the genuineness of which is doubted – said he was afraid he had not enough to pay all. This was immediately followed by his coolly asking if she could lend him some money until they arrived at Heath Cottage. The woman was caught by the bait, and taking a sovereign from her pocket handed it to him, and he then asked if she had any in the house she could fetch. She turned back, procured another sovereign, which, it is understood, constituted her "all," and gave it to him.
>
> They then came down to the end of Bridge-street, and seeing a tram ready to start for St. Ann's he said that would go to the door of his father's house, and they might as well ride. He went to the top and she got inside, but she was surprised on getting to a street corner to see him hurriedly jump off the car. She shouted to him, whereupon he waved his hand, said he would be back in a minute or two, but disappeared up a side street, and was not again seen by the woman. It is supposed that the man, who was tall and slender, and attired as horse dealers or racing men generally are, had one or two accomplices at hand, and that he belongs to a gang of professional swindlers.

The heartless scam does not at first sight appear to have been a particularly fruitful one as it resulted in only two sovereigns (i.e. £2). However, that was more than a week's wages for most people at that time and was seemingly all the money that the victim possessed. If the confidence trick was repeated two or three times a week – perhaps, in neighbouring towns – then it was easy money for the swindler.

GIGANTIC SYSTEM OF FRAUD

Of course, anyone could be taken in by a conman, as was shown in 1862 when Francis Jackson fleeced lots of St Helens traders. That was after he had first taken around twenty Liverpool businessmen to the cleaners in what the Liverpool Mercury called a "gigantic system of fraud".

While working his fraudulent schemes in St Helens, Jackson obtained goods to the value of £5 from Porter's drapers in Church Street; a watch costing five guineas from a Mr Butler; a harness off a Miss Johnson; a pair of boots from a Mr Mort – the list of cheated business folk went on and on.

COMMITTAL OF A NOTORIOUS SWINDLER.

At the St. Helen's Police Court, yesterday, before Messrs. R. Daglish and W. Pilkington, jun., an aged and respectably-attired man, who gave the name of Francis Whittall Jackson, and his son, Septimus Jackson, a boy about twelve years old, were charged with obtaining a large quantity of various articles from tradesmen in the town by false pretences and with intent to cheat and defraud. Several witnesses were examined, and from their testimony it appeared that the elder prisoner is a plausible fellow, who has for some years carried on a gigantic system of fraud, which eclipses the nefarious transactions of the notorious Gilmour. A gentleman from Mr. Mactaggart's establishment, Bold-street, in this town, gave the prisoner a very unenviable character, and enumerated about 20 Liverpool firms who have been victimised by the rogue, some to the extent of above £50. Jackson's *modus operandi* was this. He first contrived to obtain an introduction to his intended dupe, to whom he would tell a very plausible story. Sometimes he would represent himself as a traveller

Liverpool Mercury May 21st 1862

Jackson's technique was to obtain an introduction to a trader and after flattering them would order goods on credit. Instructions were given for the items to be sent by train to Rainhill Station where his supposed friend the stationmaster would have them delivered to his nearby home.

But one cautious tradesman decided to accompany his goods and found that the stationmaster at Rainhill knew little of the man. He also discovered that porters carrying the transported goods to their supposed destination were usually met on the road and their parcels taken from them by a man claiming to be the recipient.

That led to Jackson being taken into custody with the Mercury calling him a "scoundrel" and adding: "It is gratifying to find that the career of so clever a rogue has been arrested." The St Helens magistrates on May 20th 1862 said it was "one of the most extensive swindling transactions that had been brought before the public for some time" as they committed Jackson for trial at the Kirkdale Assizes, where he was sent to prison for a year.

THE SHAM BAILIFF

Many firms employed collectors to visit clients and collect moneys owed for goods or services. However, sometimes after an individual had been sacked or had otherwise left their job they'd continue collecting money from unsuspecting persons and pocket the cash. As a result notices were often placed in newspapers advising the public that such-a-person was no longer in the employment of such-a-firm.

James Ovens had been more than just a collector. He'd been employed as a bailiff working for St Helens County Court. As Ovens was described by the St Helens Examiner as "a cripple living at Pocket Nook, who pushes himself about the streets in a wooden carriage", that seems to have been an unlikely job for him to have done. And for reasons not disclosed Ovens had in the summer of 1886 been relieved of his position — but then decided to go into private enterprise.

A SHAM BAILIFF AT ST. HELENS.
At the Town Hall, on Wednesday, before Dr. Gaskell, James Owens, a cripple living at Pocket Nook, who pushes himself about the streets in a wooden carriage, was brought up charged with "acting under a false colour and pretence of the process of the County Court of Lancashire, holden at St. Helens." Mr. Garner (from the office of Messrs. J. O. and W. Swift) prosecuted, and stated that on the 26th May a judgment was obtained by Messrs. Price and Sons, furniture dealers, against Benjamin Scott, of 38, City, Windle, for goods sold and delivered, for him to pay £1 18s by monthly instalments of 4s. Mrs. Scott seemed to have made her payments regularly, and as late as the 23rd August paid an instalment. The same evening the prisoner called upon her and said he had brought her trouble, and that unless she paid him a sovereign he would "clear her house out." She said she had that day paid an instalment, but he repeated his threat, and called up the road to two men who were standing there. Mrs. Scott became terrified, and, thinking they were really bailiffs and had come to clear the house under a warrant from the County Court, she procured a sovereign. He (Mr. Garner) would call evidence to prove that prisoner was not an official of the St. Helens County Court, and that he had no right to make people believe he

St Helens Examiner September 11th 1886

A furniture dealer called Price and Sons had sold some goods to Benjamin Scott and his wife Ellen in Windle City. As the couple had not been able to make the repayments, a court judgment had ordered them to pay the balance of £1 18 shillings by monthly instalments of 4 shillings. Those payments were regularly made with one having taken place on August 23rd. But later that same day James Ovens turned up at their house claiming to be a bailiff and demanding more money, as the St Helens Examiner newspaper described:

> The same evening the prisoner called upon her and said he had brought her trouble, and that unless she paid him a sovereign then he would "clear her house out." She said she had that day paid an instalment, but he repeated his threat, and called up the road to two men who were standing there. Mrs. Scott became terrified, and thinking they were really bailiffs and had come to clear the house under a warrant from the County Court, she procured a sovereign.

The £1 gold coin was borrowed from a niece but in the end Ovens only took 4 shillings with Ellen Scott telling the court:

> I gave him 4s. because I was afraid of his taking the things and for the sake of quietness, because he made such a row in the neighbourhood.

The fact that Ovens ultimately turned down the sovereign and offered to instead accept four shillings from Mrs Scott suggests that financial gain was not his motivation. The sense of his importance as a court official empowered to make such financial decisions appears to have inflated Ovens' ego, which must have been badly punctured by his dismissal.

But as the 31-year-old was no longer a bailiff he had no right to take any money whatsoever and certainty no right to issue a receipt using County Court paper. Ovens had also accepted two shillings from a Mary Rawlinson in Parr and faced a charge of:

> Acting under a false colour and pretence of the process of the County Court of Lancashire, holden at St. Helens.

It was a serious offence and in November 1886 in spite of pleading guilty at Liverpool Assizes, James Ovens was sentenced to nine months in prison with hard labour.

THE SHAM TRAVELLER

In mid-September 1900 a well-dressed man claiming to be employed as a travelling salesman for Lever Brothers turned up at the home of Richard Pollitt in Atherton Street in St Helens. He was described as having "charmed the family" with his stories of the wonders of Lever's soap works and the village of Port Sunlight.

A SHAM TRAVELLER AT ST. HELENS.

Last week a well-dressed man, who said that he was a traveller and a representative of Messrs. Lever Bros., soap manufacturers. Port Sunlight, visited St. Helens and obtained accommodation at the house of Sergeant R. H. Pollitt, 73, Atherton-street. He charmed the family with his stories of the wonders of Messrs. Lever's works, and stayed until Monday morning, when he suddenly disappeared. It was then found that a gentleman's watch value five guineas, a lady's watch of smaller value, and a sum of money were missing from one of the bedrooms. Information was given, but up to Tuesday the whereabouts of the missing "gentleman" had not been ascertained, nor had the missing watches or money been recovered. Messrs. Lever Bros., on being communicated with, have replied that no person of the description given is in their employ.

Nantwich Guardian September 15th 1900

The St Helens Reporter of September 14th 1900 wrote:

> He made himself very agreeable and disarmed any suspicion by the glib manner in which he could converse on everything relating to the great soap works and the village.

After several days he disappeared along with two watches and a sum of money – and Lever's said they had never heard of him.

A LIAR AND A HYPOCRITE

> *"The defendant is one of the biggest liars and hypocrites the police has had to deal with. There is not a good point about him."*

Those were the words of the Chief Constable of St Helens, Arthur Ellerington, in describing Henry Davies to the magistrates on May 22nd 1917. After hearing details of the man's activities in St

Helens, the Chairman of the Bench, Ald. Henry Martin, declared the 26-year-old to be a "very bad lot" and a "wandering rogue".

WW1 was a fruitful time for conmen and fantasy heroes such as Henry or Harry Davies *(alias Burgess and Forrest etc.)* from Bootle. Ellen Johnson of Speakman Road in St Helens had given Davies food and lodgings after being impressed by the imposter. Calling himself Henry Forest, he claimed to be a well-off chap from Ireland that had obtained a good job at Pilkingtons through his father's personal connections with the glass firm.

Such itinerants that travelled the country pulling the wool over landladies' eyes needed a good cover story as to why they were staying in lodgings when supposedly well off. And paying a compliment to your victim was as good as it gets.

Davies told Miss Johnson that he detested hotels and very much liked the pleasant home that she had created. His lack of luggage was also easily explained by claiming it was in storage at Lime Street Station until he could obtain a house of his own. "Money is no object to me", the conman told his new landlady as he promised to pay her the large sum of 35 shillings a week rent.

Davies's fantasies included fighting in the Battle of Jutland and he gave vivid descriptions of the sinking of the ships. Davies also claimed his wartime experiences had led to partial memory loss – a ruse that allowed him to avoid answering embarrassing questions.

The 26-year-old said he had nearly broken his mother's heart when he joined the army as he'd been studying for the Baptist ministry. In reality he might have broken her heart by being a deserter from the army! However, the Chief Constable told the court that Davies's supposed religion did play a significant role in his deception:

> Before every meal the prisoner was sufficiently hypocritical to go through a fervent form of grace at the table. He was an expert at it, and could modulate his voice so as to give effect to the words.

| Harry Burgess, alias Harry Johnson, Phillip Dent, Henry Johnston, Harry Humphreys, Henry Davis, Henry Davies and James Forrest 150, Liverpool | 1891 Bootle | 5 | 6¼ | fr | fa | bl | heart with clasped hands, "LILY" underneath, l. forearm | False pretences and Larceny— Liverpool Sess. (Liverpool) | 2 yrs 30-7-1917 |

Harry Burgess aka Davies's record in Habitual Criminals Register 1918

Davies had also conned the secretary of the YMCA into lending him money and was said to have a string of convictions "in all parts of the country". The Chairman of the St Helens magistrates in sending him to prison for six months told Davies he was an "unmitigated rogue" and he said he was sorry they could not sentence him to a longer period of incarceration.

However, he assumed that when he came out of prison, the police would be waiting to take the conman back into custody for other offences alleged to have been committed. "I will see that he gets due attention", remarked the Chief Constable, before adding that even the suit Davies was wearing in court had been stolen.

A COMPLETE FABRICATION

One year earlier seaman Robert Hall had been charged with fraudulently obtaining food and lodging and stealing a watch. The sailor had turned up at Charlotte Hewitt's house in Woodville Street in St Helens on November 2nd 1915 dressed in naval uniform and wearing a war medal.

Hall claimed that he was on leave from HMS Lion, the Royal Navy's flagship battlecruiser and had been wounded by shrapnel while he had been serving in the Dardanelles.

A SEAMAN'S FRAUD.

Robert Edward Hall, alias Smith, a seaman, of no fixed abode, was charged at the Police Court on Saturday, before Mr. W. H. Leach (in the chair), and Mr. B. B. Glover, with obtaining by false pretences, food and lodgings. He was also charged with stealing a metal watch value 5s., the property of Charlotte Hewitt.

The Chief Constable stated that the complainant lived at 18, Woodville-street, and took in lodgers. Between eight and nine o'clock on the 2nd November, the prisoner called at the complainant's house and asked for lodgings. He was dressed in naval uniform, and he said that he belonged to H.M.S. Lion, now lying in at Cheetham, and that he had been wounded in the fingers through shrapnel while at the Dardanelles.

St Helens Newspaper February 1st 1916

However, Hall decamped with the watch after telling his landlady that he was going to draw £45 from St Helens Post Office.

On the following day Mrs Hewitt received a post card from Hall that had been posted at Wigan claiming he had gone to London to draw the money that was supposedly owed to him. The card read:

> I found a telegram at the post office instructing me to return to my ship. Therefore it is my intention to return to St. Helens, so will you meet me at the station to-morrow, 2-15 train. I have taken loan of the watch.

When charged by the police Robert Hall signed a statement that said:

> I plead guilty to the false pretences charge. I had no money to draw nor have I been wounded. I did not take the watch, but took the loan of it.

Although actually a seaman that had deserted, the rest of his story was a complete fabrication with the medal being a Boer War decoration bought from a pawnshop in Blackpool.

On January 29th 1916 in St Helens Police Court, Robert Hall was sent to prison for 6 months with hard labour. That was despite Mrs Hewitt telling the Bench that the stolen watch had only been worth 5 shillings and she had only lost 6 shillings in food.

ONE OF THE BIGGEST LIARS IN CREATION

John Galtry was another fantasist and opportunist keen to pretend he'd been heroic in battle. The young man from Scholes Lane had been doing well with his tall-tale-telling until he got carried away with his "fairy stories" – as the St Helens Newspaper dubbed them.

Galtry conned shopkeeper John Dagnall into believing he had been wounded in four places while serving in France and had spent time recovering in St Helens Hospital. He even had a genuine leg wound and walked with a limp.

Mr Dagnall from Arthur Street in St Helens took pity on the injured man and offered him work for several weeks. But Galtry's stories of his supposed wartime experiences got wilder as time passed. He claimed to have been bayoneted by a German soldier after he had given the man water — which led to him emptying his rifle into his ungrateful assailant.

The final straw was when Galtry claimed that the Germans had mounted the heads of babies on bayonets. At that point disbelief set in and the St Helens police became involved.

BOGUS SOLDIER'S FAIRY STORIES.

HOW HE KILLED THE GERMAN

At the Police Court, yesterday, before Councillor A Rudd and Dr. Dowling, a young man named John William Galtry, alias Smith, of Scholes-lane, was brought up on a charge of making certain false statements contrary to the Defence of the Realm Act, to which he pleaded not guilty.

The Chief Constable stated that John Dagnall, broker, Arthur-street, was standing at his door when he saw the prisoner, in civilian clothes, limping past with the aid of two sticks. He got into conversation with him, and the prisoner declared himself to be a wounded soldier, returned from France, where he had been for the previous fifteen months. He had been discharged from the St. Helens Hospital suffering from wounds in four places. Dagnall invited him into the shop, and prisoner showed him his leg which had been injured. Prisoner told Dagnall that his name was Smith.

St Helens Newspaper November 3rd 1916

Galtry had seemingly suffered a genuine injury in a coal mine but had never been in the army. In court on November 2nd 1916 he denied having made the statements attributed to him. Those included ones critical of British army officers, which placed him in defiance of the wartime Defence of the Realm Act.

Chief Constable Ellerington told the Bench that he was "one of the biggest liars in creation and a dangerous man" who at one time had shown extreme brutality to his wife.

Galtry was sent to prison for two months with hard labour for his Walter Mitty-like fantasies.

HE IS AN IMPOSTER – THAT'S THE LONG AND SHORT OF IT!

During WW1 many men in St Helens that weren't in the forces received a hard time from some ignorant folk – despite most having legitimate reasons for being at home. Those that had volunteered to serve before conscription was introduced but had been discharged after being wounded were the ones most aggrieved at being called a coward.

And so from July 6th 1916 men whose names had been on a War Office casualty list were allowed to sew a 2-inch stripe of gold braid on the left sleeve of their service jacket to indicate they'd done their bit and been injured. However, the concession did not extend to those with flat feet, such as Peter Davies. The native of Dublin had been discharged as medically unfit after just 75 days' service with the King's Own Royal Lancaster Regiment.

Davies was quick off the mark in faking the new stripe and on July 25th appeared in St Helens Police Court charged with unlawfully wearing a badge that resembled a military decoration. The 23-year-old said he had put the piece of gold braid on his sleeve because people had sneered at him as he walked through the streets. "He is an imposter, that is the long and short of it", was the Chief Constable's frank opinion in court. Davies was fined £2.

A LOATHSOME DISEASE

When Theodore Case appeared in St Helens Police Court on June 20th 1917 it was revealed that the soldier had stolen a bicycle belonging to John Lomax. The boatman at Taylor Park had stored his machine in the park's boathouse overnight. On the following morning when Lomax returned to his work he not only found the bike missing but chalked on some boards were the words:

We Have Laid Down Our Life's Blood For You,
And We Are Taking All We Can.

That same morning PC Thomas McHale saw Theodore Case dressed in an army tunic with a gold stripe on its sleeve. The constable asked to see his pass giving him permission to be on furlough – but Case did not possess one.

PC McHale then enquired about the bicycle that he had seen the man wheeling along the street earlier that day and Case's reply was: "You can go to hell!"

By then the machine had been sold to a man in Dunriding Lane and eventually Case admitted deserting from the King's Liverpool Regiment. He had also never spilt any blood – or even left the country. However, the St Helens Chief Constable, Arthur Ellerington, did claim that Case suffered from a "loathsome disease".

But that was his tendency to send lots of letters to girls and women all over England that he did not know. "He is a thorough wastrel", commented Detective Inspector Roe. For these offences Case was sentenced to 6 months in prison. Later in the day he was brought back to court to receive a further 3 months for stealing billiard balls from Millbrook House in Eccleston.

A SMOOTH TALKING CONMAN

Neville Roberts was another smooth-talking conman that spun a yarn to a St Helens landlady in order to get free accommodation. On July 9th 1918 the 30-year-old appeared in St Helens Police Court charged with stealing a bicycle and obtaining food and lodgings by false pretences.

In fact he'd been quite a busy boy since deserting from an army hospital in Bristol five months before. Roberts was wanted by police forces in 24 towns for a total of 38 offences.

While in St Helens the man had claimed to be an inspector of munitions and had so impressed Annie Hardman of Hamer Street that she had allowed him to take lodgings in her home.

Roberts then took off without paying for his food and accommodation on a bike stolen from another lodger. This he sold in Haydock, where Sergeant Houghton arrested him.

It certainly would have been easy to identify the conman if his sleeves were rolled up. On his forearms Roberts had tattoos of two women's heads, a tombstone and a heart! The St Helens magistrates committed Neville Roberts to the Liverpool Assizes, where he was sent to prison for 9 months.

THE BOGUS BOBBY

The 1921 census shows that Annie Hardman's son-in-law was Police Sgt. Henry Latus and he and Annie's daughter Lillian were by then residing at her home. It sounds like the sergeant wanted to keep an eye on who was living with his in-laws in Hamer Street – and certainly no bogus bobbies would have been allowed to gain entry! That was unlike Abigail Crossland of Peter Street in St Helens whose home was invaded by Walter Plows.

The 25-year-old conned Mrs Crossland and her son Clarence into believing he was a new member of the St Helens police force when he took up lodgings with them in February 1921. Plows would even rise at 6am to leave the house early as part of his pretence to be going on duty. His explanations for not having a police uniform included a shortage of the force's special buttons used on tunics.

But the Crosslands were seemingly not suspicious until the time came for Plows to decamp – as such cons only had a limited life when too many questions started being asked and landladies wanted their rent.

Fifteen shillings went with the man – cash that belonged to Mrs Crossland's son – along with an unpaid bill for £2 food and lodgings. But claiming to have been a police officer was treated as a serious crime and on February 26th Plows received three months in prison with hard labour. Some criminals that had served with distinction in the war received a discount when sentenced.

However, those with a bad war record could receive a longer term. Walter Plows had certainly not been good in the army. As soon as his unit had been put on draft for foreign service, Plows had deserted and he had been on the receiving end of three court martials. This also appears to have been taken into account in the sentencing.

A MOST DESPICABLE THING

In St Helens Police Court on January 17th 1923 Jack Broadley pleaded guilty to a charge of attempting to obtain £1 by false pretences. The man from Accrington had claimed to be a warder at Walton Prison and had visited the wife of Thomas Dolan at her Lowe Street home. He was a bankrupt haulage contractor who had recently been sent to prison for hiding some of his assets.

Jack Broadley claimed to be a warder called Walker and had told Mrs Dolan that her husband would receive better prison food if she gave him money. This is not the first time I've read of such a cruel scam. It hardly seems worth it for such small pickings but Broadley told the police that he needed some cash for his train fare back to Accrington.

The Chairman of the Bench, Ald. Henry Bates, told the man that what he had done was a "most despicable thing". Broadley had a long criminal record and he was sent to prison for three months with hard labour.

A DASTARDLY TRICK

The first modern coin-operated vending machines date back to the 1880s – but do not appear to have become widespread in St Helens until the inter-war years. Anything new will invariably attract the interest of criminals keen to exploit any weaknesses and there were several possibilities with such dispensers.

One ruse was to insert counterfeit coins and in January 1931 John Ollerton from Park Road in St Helens received nine months in prison for forging and using phony money. The 21-year-old had been caught extracting cigarettes from an automatic machine in Westfield Street using homemade coins. And he claimed to have developed his money-manufacturing skills – which were praised in court for the quality of his coins – on a Government training course!

Alternatively, you could nick the whole contraption. In February 1934 two youths removed a machine from the outside of Albert Higham's shop in Kitchener Street in St Helens and eventually chucked it into the Windle Brook after stealing all its contents.

Conmen also exploited the interest in the new technology by claiming to be offering shopkeepers deals on such machines. In 1930 smooth-talking Harold Roberts from Park Road South in Newton-le-Willows went round St Helens' shops claiming to be a travelling salesman for Lyon's tea.

And he was offering traders that participated in his bogus scheme what appeared to be a very good deal. If shopkeepers allowed Lyon's to install machines outside their premises dispensing tea-related products, they'd receive a weekly rent of 10 shillings. There was also the prospect of 2s 6d commission on every £1 of goods that were sold.

Unsurprisingly Annie Woodward from Boundary Road was quick to sign up and wasn't put off by Roberts' demand for an advance payment of ten shillings. That was supposedly for reasons of insurance and would be refunded if the machines were removed.

A DASTARDLY BUSINESS

MAN WHO WENT ABOUT DEFRAUDING SHOPKEEPERS

Harold Roberts, an Earlestown man, was fined £5 or one month's imprisonment, at St. Helens, to-day, on charges of defrauding shopkeepers.

Roberts had obtained 10s from a Mrs. Woodward, of Boundary-road, on making an arrangement with her to bring three automatic machines and place them in her shop. He obtained 7s 6d from a Mrs. Seddon in the same way.

Defendant pleaded guilty, and Superintendent Cust told the bench that defendant was a native of Earlestown and was apprenticed at the L.M.S.

Liverpool Echo November 6th 1930

But after the conman left the shop with Mrs Woodward's ten bob nothing further was heard. Enquiries were made but Lyon's said they had no knowledge of Harold Roberts and weren't in the

91

machine dispensing game. Although ten shillings was not very much to lose, these were hard times and with plenty of other shopkeepers in St Helens, Prescot, Liverpool, Earlestown and Wigan losing similar amounts, the total swindled added up.

On November 6th 1930 Harold Roberts appeared before the St Helens Bench charged with obtaining money by false pretences. The Chairman Thomas Edmondson said he was guilty of a "dastardly trick". Although only fined £5 and ordered to repay 17s 6d that he had obtained from two St Helens traders, Roberts would have to serve a month in prison if in default of payment and faced further charges in other courts.

And finally, this notice was published in the newspaper known as the Police Gazette on February 22nd 1918 seeking information on two wanted con artists. As gambling was illegal, few victims would probably dare report their loss to the police.

68.—St. Helens (*Borough*).—For stealing £7 15s. (confidence trick), 16th inst.—TWO MEN: 1st, age 28 to 30, ht. 5ft. 7 or 8in., full face, h. brown, clean shaven, gold-filled tooth rt. of upper jaw; dress, navy blue knap overcoat, belt at back, tight fitting blue serge suit, bowler hat, wearing a military discharge badge; 2nd, age about 26, ht. 5ft. 5 or 6in., c. fresh, long thin face, decayed teeth, clean shaven; dress, lt. raincoat, dk. suit, brown trilby hat, soft collar. Both of smart appearance. The first-described accosted complainant and asked for assistance in locating "Bradshaw's Agency" (non-existent). At this juncture No. 2, pretending to be a complete stranger, appeared, and on being appealed to point out the office. All then walked in that direction. No. 1 then explained that his object was to put £100 on the winner of a chess match between England and Ireland, of which, although he had received the information, the bookmaker was still in ignorance, and in return for courtesy shown offered to make bets for both. No. 2 advanced £1 Treasury note and was shortly afterwards handed the supposed winnings, the aggrieved party then followed suit and arrangements made to meet again, but nothing more was seen of the swindlers.

Warrant issued.

Information to the Chief Constable, St. Helens.

John Shaw Menzies – The Violent St Helens Vet

"He is a violent-tempered man, and when drunk, or disturbed by outside matters, went home and thrashed his wife."

This veterinary infirmary and shoeing forge was sited in Ormskirk Street in St Helens where Griffins Picture House *(aka the Scala)* would later be built. The building was owned by John Shaw Menzies, who for around thirty years from 1875 was a well-known man in the town.

As a veterinary surgeon Menzies was at times contracted to care for horses belonging to St Helens Corporation, as well as those owned by many distinguished persons. One might imagine that a vet that cared for animals would be a kind soul – but Menzies had a very violent temper. Most of his brutality was aimed at his wife

Ellen. But when in a drunken temper anyone could be Menzies' victim. On January 10th 1890 the veterinary surgeon appeared in court charged with assaulting Thomas King. He was the ostler at the White Hart Hotel in Church Street in St Helens whose job was to look after their customers' horses.

The court heard that Menzies had been drinking in the White Hart and had gone into its back yard – probably to use the outside lavatory.

The White Hart on the corner of Church Street and Hall Street pictured in later years

The St Helens Examiner described what the prosecuting counsel claimed had occurred next:

> The defendant entered the yard and without any provocation made use of brutal and offensive language to King. He then deliberately struck him behind the ear, and knocked him to the ground. Not content with that, Menzies exhibited a degree of cowardice which they would scarcely expect to find, by again knocking King over when he attempted to rise. King was so seriously injured that he had not been able to attend work since, and it would be three or four weeks before he would be able to do so.

The defence case was that Menzies had attacked King as he'd thought that he was a stranger who was interfering with his pony. Although the yard was unlikely to have been well lit, if what Menzies claimed had been true why did he not ask questions first before beginning his brutal assault? The magistrates fined the veterinary surgeon £5.

> [A CARD.]
> # JOHN SHAW MENZIES,
> ## VETERINARY SURGEON,
> (Member of the Royal College of Veterinary Surgeons, London)
> ### ORMSKIRK STREET, ST. HELENS.
> RESIDENCE :—38, ORMSKIRK STREET.

Advert in the St Helens Newspaper of October 1875

John Shaw Menzies had been born in Prescot in 1853 and he began his veterinary practice in St Helens about 1875. Four years later his premises in Ormskirk Street were extended to include a shoeing forge for horses.

> # SHOEING FORGE.
> ### J. S. MENZIES, M.R.C.V.S.L.,
> ## VETERINARY SURGEON,
> ### ORMSKIRK-STREET,
> ### ST. HELENS,
>
> RESPECTFULLY announces that he has made extensive improvements and additions to his Premises, in Ormskirk-street, having healthy and comfortable accommodation for a number of horses.
>
> J.S.M. has now OPENED a SHOEING FORGE, where horses can be carefully and scientifically shod under his personal superintendence. Only steady and experienced workmen will be employed.   s15 r&stf

Advert in the Prescot Reporter of April 19th 1879

Menzies had married Ellen Gee of Bolton in 1877 and the couple had eight children. In December 1883 one of their boys came close to being killed when what the Prescot Reporter described as a "gale of a most fierce character" struck St Helens.

About three o'clock in the morning one of the chimneypots on the Menzies home in Ormskirk Street was blown through the roof and landed on a bed in which a son was sleeping. However, somewhat miraculously the boy escaped with only a slight bruise on his cheek.

It would be an understatement to say that the couple had a difficult marriage. In court papers filed in 1894 Ellen claimed to have received eighteen different beatings – or serious threats of violence – from her husband over the previous sixteen years.

But as was often the case with battered women, she felt powerless to do anything about her situation until February 1890 when the then 38-year-old took her husband to court. The St Helens Examiner described the hearing:

> At the Police Court, on Friday afternoon, before Alderman Harrison and Mr. Walmesley-Cotham, John Shaw Menzies veterinary surgeon, was summoned for assaulting his wife, Ellen. Menzies did not appear nor was he represented. Mr. J. P. Mearns who appeared for the complainant stated that the defendant, by not appearing, showed his usual cowardice. He was supposed to be a respectable man, in a good position as a veterinary surgeon in the town, and he was summoned on a charge of assault committed on his wife on Saturday night. The parties had been married, about 13 years, and the whole of the complainant's married life had been one of patient suffering from beginning to end. The parties had had eight children, and five of them were living. Mrs. Menzies had put up with the brutality, and uncalled for and unprovoked treatment so long that she asked their

worships to grant her a judicial separation with the custody of the children and also to grant her a weekly allowance. She had put up with the treatment so long principally on account of her eldest boy being a cripple.

On Saturday night the defendant came home. He cursed, threatened, and frightened the life out of her and the children. He then made her go from one room to another, and as she left the room, as he ordered her about, he kicked her seven or eight times, and threatened to put an end to her. The children were all screaming, and running about the house terrified, and it was not until about two o'clock in the morning that he cooled down. Mrs. Menzies was then called and gave evidence in support of Mr. Mearns' statement. She added that she had suffered from her husband's ill-treatment since a fortnight after the marriage. Twice she had left her home and returned on his promising to amend. Margaret Yates, a servant, was also called, and Mrs. Menzies, in reply to another question by Mr. Mearns stated that she had been to see a doctor, who had found marks about her body. The marks were caused by her husband's violence.

The Liverpool Weekly Courier in their account of the hearing said Mrs Menzies had told the court the ages of her five children were twelve, ten, nine, six and three. She had also stated that her husband was earning at least £600 a year – which was then a very considerable sum. The Courier also quoted the prosecution solicitor in saying:

> He was a violent-tempered man, and when drunk, or disturbed by outside matters, he went home and thrashed his wife.

The Bench imposed a fine of £5 and costs on Menzies for the assault on Ellen and granted her a separation order in which he was ordered to pay his wife £3 a week. The court was also told that the veterinary surgeon had been convicted on three previous occasions for various offences over the past year.

One of those cases had been in April 1889 when Menzies had been brawling outside the Fleece Hotel in Church Street with a boilermaker called Stephen Pennington. Although police in St Helens dealt with fights on a daily basis, for one of the combatants to be a professional man earning over £600 a year was far from being an everyday occurrence.

The Fleece Hotel in Church Street

PCs Patterson and Kilpatrick told the court that the incident had attracted quite a crowd. They described finding the two men struggling together and making a lot of noise and after separating them ordered both to go home. However, they said they twice needed to return to the place to pull the men apart after their fighting had resumed.

Both Menzies and Pennington had been charged with committing a breach of the peace by fighting but that's where the similarity ended – as they told diametrically opposite tales to the Bench. Menzies claimed the incident had begun after Pennington had pushed a little boy selling matches against the wall:

> I told him he was a coward, and he struck me, and I closed with him in self-defence. After the constables had separated us he struck me again, and if I had not defended myself I should not have been here to tell the tale.

That last claim provoked laughter in the courtroom, with those on the public gallery seemingly preferring Pennington's version. The boilermaker at Daglish's foundry in St Helens said the trouble began as he came out of the Fleece. Menzies stopped him and wanted to know the names of the men that he was with.

After telling him who they were, Pennington claimed Menzies called him a liar, seized him by his vest and struck him. The Bench ultimately decided to bind both men over in the sum of £20 to keep the peace for three months.

In October 1890 Menzies was given the benefit of the doubt by the magistrates on another charge after appearing in St Helens Police Court accused of being drunk in charge of a horse and carriage – despite damning testimony from a constable.

PC Turton stated that he had seen the vet at 2:30am driving his horse and carriage up and down North John Street and Ormskirk Street in St Helens:

> I watched him for five or six minutes driving about at a very dangerous rate. He lashed the horse and ran on the parapet several times and nearly collided with the lamp posts. The defendant ultimately attempted to get out of the carriage near his forge, but fell on his back.

Menzies' acquittal of the charge led to this report being published in the Widnes Examiner of October 18th 1890 which suggested that the vet had received preferential treatment because of his professional status:

> If one policeman can prove that a labourer is drunk, how many police officers are required to prove that a veterinary surgeon is intoxicated? The answer is, that nobody can tell, after the hearing of a case bearing on the point at St. Helens, on Monday. P.C. Turton swore that he saw Mr. Menzies, veterinary surgeon, drunk whilst in charge of a horse and carriage, and P.S. [police sergeant] Charlton and P.S. Hudson corroborated; but, as sundry witnesses who were called, expressed another opinion, the case was dismissed. Wonder if Mr. Menzies, if he had been a carter, would have got the benefit of the doubt?

Although he got off that charge, Menzies was convicted of "furious driving" in his horse and trap two years later. That was after he was spotted by PC Hall going like the clappers down Croppers Hill into Westfield Street. For that offence in September 1892 he was fined ten shillings.

The separation between Ellen and her husband did not seemingly last for long and she had returned home by at least August of 1890. It was very common for violent husbands to promise that they would reform and it seems that Ellen was persuaded that it would be best for her family if she gave her spouse another chance. However, the abuse continued and in July 1894 Ellen Menzies took the rare step of filing for divorce.

As stated earlier, her petition cited 18 different acts of violence – or threats of violence – made against her by her husband between 1878 and 1894, with many assaults involving kicking.

Five of the alleged instances of violence had occurred after Ellen had returned to her husband in 1890. Here are some extracts from the divorce petition:

12. That about the 30th July 1885 (soon after your Petitioner's confinement) at St. Anns St. Helens the aforesaid John Shaw Menzies was very violent, dragged your Petitioner out of bed and forced her downstairs in her night dress, struck her with his hand and kicked her.

13. That about the 13th July 1886 at St. Anns St. Helens aforesaid John Shaw Menzies pushed your Petitioner into the yard when it was raining and struck her violently several times

until her face was quite out of shape, bruised, and black.

21. That about the 22nd May 1894 at 7 Westfield Street aforesaid John Shaw Menzies was very violent, threw a hammer through the kitchen window and smashed it, threw a chair at your petitioner, ran after her into the Nursery, swore at her and pushed her head violently against the window frame and struck her twice on the shoulders.

Since the divorce there were very few news reports that mention Menzies and he died on June 25th 1905 in St Helens Hospital at the young age of 53. His death certificate suggests that he was still a practising vet in Ormskirk Street at the time of his passing, with the cause of his death stated as diarrhoea and asthenia.

I've not been able to find any obituary in the local newspapers, which, perhaps, suggests that since the divorce and its revelations, John Shaw Menzies had lost much of his respectability in St Helens.

The St Helens Newspaper's Beat Group Column – "Teen Topics"

TEEN TOPICS

In November 1963 a weekly column called 'Teen Topics' began in the St Helens Newspaper. It focussed mainly on the local beat scene with updates on the town's many bands. But the column also covered teen fashion and general pop news, including the singles that were the best sellers in St Helens' record shops.

The Beatles sudden rise to fame had inspired a wave of local talent who rehearsed in church halls and the like – with some playing guitars made in school woodwork classes! Most groups were short-lived but a few obtained record deals and some played at the Cavern Club in Liverpool and / or at the Star Club in Hamburg.

Group name and personnel changes were also common. This was at a time when people still talked of the Hit Parade and bands were called "beat groups". At one point the Newspaper even felt the need to explain what "fab" was short for! In this chapter I'm reprinting extracts from the column along with a few relevant stories from the Newspaper's news pages. The reprints, wherever possible, include each article's original headline and some images.

TEEN TOPICS – NOVEMBER / DECEMBER 1963

GED BACK WITH THE INCAS

One of the top South-West Lancashire beat groups – The Incas – have reinstated their vocalist, after protests from fans. The group's followers were angry when they learned vocalist "Ged" White had been sacked by the group because of his alleged lack of style.

A couple of weeks ago, a number of teenagers, all supporters of the group, inserted an advertisement in the personal column of the Reporter, demanding "Ged" be given his old job back, or an explanation for his dismissal.

This week the Reporter learned the fans had been granted their request. Ged was back in the line-up, when the group appeared on stage at a local dance hall. Their manager, Norman Thomas, head boy at Cowley boys' grammar school, admitted Ged had been dismissed because his style did not suit the group. However, he has been reinstated following the fans' protest.

But Ged must vary his style. Before the sacking, he sang ballads and rarely moved from his position at the centre of the stage, it was complained. His place was taken by Martin O'Brien, formerly of The Fire Flights, another local group.

In contrast, Martin moves about the stage, putting rhythm into each song and giving his fans something to scream about. Now that Ged has been given his old job back, there is no singing-spot for Martin and he has been asked to leave. Fire Flights fans are now left wondering if he will be offered his old job back.

ELECTRIC SHOCK GUITARIST SAVED BY SWIFT ACTION

But for the swift action of a 16-years-old Haydock youth, a local pop group's practice session on Tuesday night might have ended in tragedy. The Vardells were half way through a number when rhythm guitarist Nigel Parr jumped forward and caught a falling microphone. He received a severe electric shock which burned his arms and travelled across his chest.

Other members of the group hesitated, but Colin Gange, 373, Clipsley Lane, remained cool, and scrambled over the furniture to disconnect the electric socket. Nigel (aged 15), was rushed to St. Helens Hospital where he was treated for burns. He was detained in hospital for observation until Thursday when allowed home.

His father, Mr. Joseph Parr, 7, Forsters Road, Haydock, said: "Colin's action certainly avoided a terrible accident. If he had been just a little slower it could have been fatal. Everyone in the room panicked when Nigel received the shock, but Colin decided that cutting off the electricity supply was, of course, the best thing to do." Mr. Parr later discovered that a wire had been torn loose in the microphone, possibly in the fall.

MOTHER BLAMES JUKE BOXES

A woman whose 16-year-old son was summoned for drinking under age, told St. Helens Juvenile Panel on Tuesday: "It's these jukeboxes in the pubs. They're enticing young people inside." The boy, an apprentice sawyer, admitted drinking 5 pints of bitter beer in a local hotel on 25th October. Fining him £5, Coun. J Woodcock, chairman, said: "They were expensive pints, weren't they?"

NEW GROUP, NEW GIMMICK AND NOW A NEW DISC

A black-cloaked figure with a dagger, stalking across a stage lit by the eerie glow of candelabras, a dark form rising from a coffin – this is just a part of the act of a beat group with a difference, in which versatility is the keynote.

The group, Cadillac and the Playboys, have been together for a year. During that time they have made a record (to be released in the New Year), played in theatres all over the country, done cabaret in some of the leading night clubs

Cadillac and the Playboys in November 1963

in Britain, and appeared at that now almost legendary Cavern Club. The group have formed themselves into a limited company

(Mike Cadillac Ltd.) following the example set by The Beatles, and other leading show business personalities.

Led by Mike (aged 21), who lives at 22, Chapel Street, and a former trainee engineer with I.C.I. Ltd., the group consists of Kevin Lang (21), bass guitar, Stuart Fahey (19), lead guitar and George Allen (20), drummer.

Their many acts include impersonations of Johnny Ray, Shirley Bassey, Benny Hill, "Screaming" Lord Sutch, and many others. With their new record ready for release, a trip to Hamburg and a possible tour of America in the offing, the future looks rosy for these new faces.

"BIGGER" BEATLES IN TOWN

A ten-minute Pathe News colour and Techniscope [widescreen] film report featuring The Beatles is to be released by Pathe News. Cinemagoers will be able to see it at the ABC and Capitol cinemas next week, beginning on Sunday.

POP SHOWS

Watch out for a great new programme "Top Of The Pops," starting at 6:35 p.m. tomorrow on BBC TV. An ITV company have at last signed on two teenage advisors for the very popular weekly show "Ready Steady Go."

KNIGHTHAWKS BREAK-UP

At a time when rock groups are being manufactured as speedily and mechanically as incubator born chicks, comes news of one brood – The Knighthawks – which has tumbled from the roost. Two members of the group are going into temporary retirement, a third is joining another group, and the remaining member is entering the theatrical managing business. Hatched two years ago, The Knighthawks only took their entertaining seriously twelve months later. During that time they have gained considerable popularity.

Their rather brief career began at St. Anne's Youth Club, Sutton, where they appeared once weekly. But as they improved, bookings in higher rock circles were obtained. Reason for the break-up is mainly lack of rehearsal time.

FREE USE OF HALL

In order to keep young people off the streets and to keep them occupied, the Clock Face Miners Sports Committee have lent their hall, free of charge, to anyone who can play an instrument and wants to form a group, or is a follower of the "beat" craze. The hall, which has been empty for two years, has been completely re-decorated for the teenagers and the committee have spent more than six months in making the preparations.

Said Mr. Morris, 56, Leach Lane, Sutton, a committee member who piloted the idea: "We have had to delay the opening of the club due to last year's bad Winter. The pipes had burst and all the wallpaper had peeled off."

The teenagers are keen that this scheme should develop, as they have spent much of their spare time in helping to install the snack bar, the six loudspeakers and many other things which have made the hall appear so attractive. The club nights, which are every Monday and Thursday, could prove to be very popular. As one of the members pointed out: "There is nothing like this club anywhere in the area."

CHRIS AND THE AUTOCRATS

A priest, a star Rugby League wingman, and an amateur boxing referee, are just three of the many people who have helped to bring Chris and the Autocrats – five of the youngest purveyors of the Liverpool Sound – to the electric atmosphere of some of the top clubs and dance halls in Lancashire. The Autocrats (all born in St. Helens, and average age 16½) drifted together, rather than formed, two years ago, when with cheap equipment they searched high and low for somewhere to practice.

"We couldn't very well play in our houses the noise we made," quipped Gerald the rhythm guitarist. But finally, with the aid of a priest, Father P. Murphy, they were able to rehearse in Sacred Heart church hall. As soon as the group's playing grew better, they were joined by youngsters attracted by the sound of a big beat. Eventually, however, the group decided to look for somewhere else to practice.

When the electric current at last began to flow through their guitars again, it was from the sockets of the Ring O'Bells public house, the licensee of which at that time was Tom van Vollenhoven eager to help the boys in any way he could. Long hours of practice and painstaking care with every song, enabled the lads at long last to start to "do the clubs", the period which seems to be the testing time for many of the rock groups of the present day.

Portico Labour Club, Parr and Hardshaw Labour Club, the Plaza Ballroom, all served to enhance the reputation the group was earning for itself. During one of their first bookings at a club, they met the then little-known, but now famous Beatles, who were confident that the habit of copying the Shadows' footwork gimmick and guitar style by the groups was very soon going to die next, and their (the Beatles') music would replace it. At that time it was a couple of weeks before the release of "Love Me Do," and we all know where they went from there.

But enough of the group's history, what of the lads themselves? Beginning with the drummer, we have John Richmond (aged 20), who is the driver of the van. John, who lives at 9, Banner Street, is tall and dark, works with the St. Helens Corporation as a bricklayer, and was educated at Sacred Heart. Bass guitarist is 15-years-old David Banks, 134, Morley Street. Rhythm guitarist Gerald Knight (16), 36, Rivington Avenue, is an apprentice fitter and turner with a local engineering firm, and ex-pupil of St. Theresa's R. C. school.

Eighteen-years-old lead guitarist, John Yates, Argyll Street, works at Pilkington Brothers Ltd., and was educated at Central Modern School. Vocalist Chris Richmond has a likeness to Paul McCartney in both looks and voice. Aged 16, he works at the local brewery and used to attend Sacred Heart R.C. school. He is John's brother, and lives at the same address.

THE FIRE FLIGHTS

The Fire Flights – Jimmy, Alan, Trevor, Colin and Mart have known the ups and downs of the semi-professional entertainment world, but still managed to emerge with their popularity unscathed, and a place in the semi-final of a talent contest that could win them a lot of cash, and what is more important, a recording contract.

The group was formed three years ago, long before the Mersey beat caught the limelight of the national scene, when lead guitarist ALAN SCOTSON, now aged 20 and a male nurse at Rainhill Hospital, used to play his guitars in rooms above the York Hotel, kept by his father, in Nutgrove Road.

Alan had three guitars, and soon he invited his friend, rhythm guitarist, COLIN ASHCROFT, 3, Lonie Grove, now aged 19, and an apprentice electrical engineer, to help him make use of them. As their proficiency increased they decided to start a group and were joined by 17-years-old apprentice engineer, TREVOR BOLD, 162, Albion Street, who plays the bass guitar.

The drummer and vocalist came in the persons of JIMMY LYNCH, 5, Patterdale Drive, an 18-years-old apprentice butcher, and fair-haired ALAN BIRCH, the original singer with the group. A once-a-week stand at Holy Cross Hall led to appearances at the majority of clubs and dance halls in the area.

It came like a bombshell to the fans when Alan Birch decided he could no longer sing with the group. Courting and rehearsals did not mix. It was as simple as that. For a while the boys "did a Beatles" by singing while playing, and then MARTIN O'BRIEN arrived on the scene.

TEEN TOPICS – JANUARY 1964

MAGNETIC APPEAL HERE

A rhythm and blues group which are little-talked-about but proving extremely popular, are the Cordelles. They have a magnetic appeal over members of such clubs as the famous Cavern in Liverpool, where they have been a regular feature for many months, and the JungFrau, Three Coins, and Twisted Wheel clubs in Manchester.

The Cordelles as pictured in Teen Topics in January 1964

Managed by John Lewis Enterprises, they came into existence last May, when bass guitarist Terry Marsh (aged 20), 9, Melbourne Street, and lead guitarist Kenneth Blackmore (aged 17), 101, Ruskin Drive, pupil of Cowley boys' school, the only members of the Citroens, decided to change their name.

Settling on the title of The Cordelles, they were joined by rhythm guitarist Norman Finn (aged 15), 44, Irwin Road – another Cowley boy – and 16-years-old David Chisnall, 46, Irwin Road, a pupil of Grange Park technical school. With these two former members of the Cheetahs, the melodious quartet was complete. The group practise behind locked doors in the Plaza ballroom, a venue at which they have grown accustomed to playing.

Wherever they travel they receive enthusiastic applause from audiences who admire their professional style of performance. The boys are all accomplished musicians. Their charm, talent and ability enables them to conquer even the most unreceptive of audiences with their "swinging" act.

STRANGE NAME – GREAT GROUP

With a name like "The Psycho Five" something like a horror quintet out of a Hitchcock thriller might spring to the imagination – but the members of this strangely named group are far from horrific. The boys (they are a quartet at the moment, their lead guitarist leaving them a short while ago) are down-to-earth and entirely realistic about their past, present and the most important, their future.

Their basic training was received while playing with other groups. Quite recently the boys won a talent contest at the Riverside Club, Tarleton, which realised them £50 in prize money plus a terrific amount of prestige.

SWEPT COUNTRY

Ever since The Beatles first appeared at Liverpool's now legendary Cavern Club, there has been a revolution in teenage fashions. This change has not been gradual, but has swept the country in a matter of months – evidence of the tremendous impact made by The Beatles. You might ask how this fabulous group have influenced your wardrobe, and just how it all started.

Not so many months ago there came to our notice a newly-found group who were struggling to find fame and fortune. At that time The Beatles lacked the polish they now have. They wore black leather jackets and had hair styles which were not in keeping with the tastes of most young gentleman of the time.

At first there was a great deal of criticism about this 'off-beat' look and in some quarters there still is. However the group had an obvious effect on teenagers and throughout the entire country black has been the most popular colour and polo-neck sweaters and leather jackets have captured the imagination of most young people.

Teenage hairdressing has made a startling change. Barbers in St. Helens agree that there has been a definite tendency towards the "Beatle cut" which has been especially asked for by the younger set of teenagers – the 12 to 14-year-olds. This trend in fashion has led to the names and photographs of the Beatles being boldly printed across the fronts of sweaters and skirts, indications of the admiration for the Liverpool group.

Having prints on garments is not enough for the fans. They also have bracelets, necklaces, and medallions, covered with Beatle portraits and signatures. It is becoming increasingly obvious that to look feminine and attractive is not "with it." Most of today's teenage girls appreciate the long tight pants, black duffle coats and bags slung carelessly across the shoulders.

The boys also have a cult of their own – beatle jackets and long pointed shoes with shiny gold buckles. They too have their skin-tight pants and more often as not the general appearance of the two sexes is very similar. How long can this last? Some people might say "as long as the Beatles do." We'll have to wait and see.

MEET 'THE SCREAMING SKULLS'

A terrifying film perhaps springs to mind when we hear the name of a comparatively new group in St. Helens, The Screaming Skulls. It was, in fact, at the pictures that the group found their name. They adopted it about six months ago when they saw a film called "The Screaming Skull" – a horror film, of course!

The lead guitarist, 16-years-old JOHN GLOVER, 41, Hope Street, agrees that they must be one of the youngest groups in St. Helens. The rhythm guitarist, 15-years-old BRIAN WHARTON, 2, Kitchener Street, admits that, like many other groups, they have had their embarrassing moments. He remembers one night when nothing seemed to go right. They were appearing at St. Patrick's Youth Club, Greenbank Crescent.

Fans were twisting and shaking and generally having a high old time when – calamity! The drummer, 16-years-old ALLAN MORROW, 63, Campbell Street, was playing without a care in the world when one of his cymbals fell with a resounding crash.

A little later the electric lead snapped on John Glover's guitar, and he had to retire to fix it. This left the drummer doing a solo. By this time, the dancers were doing a slow handclap. The fourth member of the group, 16-years-old, JIMMY YATES, 52, York Street, who plays bass guitar, says they can now laugh about the night of mishap. Manager of the group, MR. GRAHAM EDGERTON, 88, Peter Street, says: "We have been helped and encouraged by the fact that Mr. E. Jenkins, manager of the Star Hotel, Liverpool Road, has let us use his room to practice in. Sacred Heart Church have also lent us St. Patrick's Youth Club hall." The group have had to work hard for the success that has come their way. Equipment has cost them £250.

THE INCAS

Uncrowned kings of the local pop scene – the Incas rhythm and blues group – have a chance to crash the international scene when they visit Hamburg, the Mecca of Liverpool groups, in April. The month's stay at the famous Star Club is a culmination of years of sheer hard work, frustrated by some disappointments, but also encouraged by success after success.

All but one member of the group are ex-pupils of Grange Park Technical School where the then Vigilantes were born. Together with three other pupils, Terrence Broughton and Robert Martin made guitars and entertained at various school functions with a Shadows instrumental type of act.

Joined by Alf Anslow, the drummer, the group, with home-made guitars, hammered out their tunes, while gaining the experience which shows so much in their act today. After the five had left school their number was gradually whittled down to the existing members, who were joined by John Grogan.

Playing the clubs and dance halls in the area, they were approached by Ged White – no longer with them – enquiring whether he would be suitable for vocalist. He was. When their present manager Norman Thomas, took over in May 1963, he achieved the feat of making a booking at the Cavern, alongside Gene Vincent and the Hollies. That booking was the first of many at this now legendary "shrine."

In contrast to the humble equipment with which they started, their total poundage today is £1,500 worth of the BEST in amplifiers, guitars and drums. Each member has three different stage suits, one gold satin, one dark brown, and one in green mohair. At £17 per suit, their success is obvious.

The group have a newly-formed fan club run by two teenage girls which, in its infancy, has over 100 members. Later on, membership cards will be printed and the official Incas fan club will be in operation.

TEEN TOPICS – FEBRUARY 1964

THE RELUCTANT BEATLE

Walking along the road was a girl of nine, wearing a plaid kilt, red stockings and carrying a guitar almost as big as herself. Trailing wearily by her free hand was her younger brother. "You're George Harrison," said the little girl. "No, I am not," said the little boy firmly.

"Listen," the girl went on, with a plaintive note in her voice. "I am Paul McCartney and you are George. All you have to do is go, 'She loves me, yeah, yeah, yeah,' that's easy." Unfortunately, the little boy did not seem impressed with three words that have shaken the pop world. He refused to utter a sound. The little girl trudged off with her charge, still exhorting "Yeah, yeah, yeah."

THE HELLIONS

Slick salesmen of the St. Helens rhythm and blues sound are the Hellions, a group with the "old-school-tie" look. Three former pupils of Cowley boys' school in the group are rhythm guitarist Harry Allcock (aged 19), 104, Harris Street, a clerk at the Town Hall; lead guitarist Laurence ("Lol") Hordley (aged 20), 4, Ainsworth Road, a quantity surveyor; and drummer Victor Bellard (aged 19), 22, Barton Street, a clerk at the B.I.C.C.

Completing the group is vocalist Barry Kelly (aged 19), 394, Watery Lane, an apprentice with a television firm. The Hellions (every member of the group has an "l" in his name) started to practice at the Police Club in Bishop Road, moved to a local cafe, and soon had an enthusiastic following.

CRAZY ABOUT BEATLES

Confirmation of the Beatles' popularity in the United States comes from a regular Reporter reader in Grand Rapids, Michegan [sic], U.S.A. Joan Gibbs, whose parents live in Recreation Street, writes that the kids in Grand Rapids are as crazy about the Beatles as are the kids in St. Helens. Joan sends her best wishes to all her friends in St. Helens and we are glad to be kept in touch with the American "pop" scene.

ROLLING STONES GATHER MOSS

The long-haired Rolling Stones are gathering a host of fans locally, and their records have been enjoying heavy sales. Their latest release, an E.P., features the slow r-and-b number, "You'd Better Move On." This record is not only well liked by teenagers, but by mothers and fathers as well. It should soar into the national Top Ten.

BEGAN WITH OWN-MAKE GUITARS

The Whirlwinds are four very talented lads. In only twelve months, they have reached a standard of performance which normally takes years to attain. The idea of forming a group was born at Rivington Road school when the boys decided to try their hand at guitar playing, and spent £12 each on constructing three guitars during their woodwork lessons.

Having made the guitars, they set about learning to play them, and with their knowledge of music, were soon quite expert. The drummer, Johnny Roberts (aged 17), 2, Nutgrove Avenue, Thatto Heath, received help and advice from his father, who was once drummer for a professional dance band. Glyn Hourihan lead guitarist (aged 17), 18, Boundary Road, had piano lessons for many years, and took as easily to the guitar as he had to the piano.

Morris Scott, rhythm guitarist (aged 17), 42, Princess Avenue, Windlehurst, enjoyed playing the harmonica from being very young and plays the piano accordion and trombone. Bass guitarist Ray Stockton (aged 17), 161, Windleshaw Road, has certificates to prove his skill at the trumpet and flugal horn. They have played at Olympia, where they met comedian Jimmy Saville and at a big dance in Huddersfield.

ADULT VIEWS ON "POP" STARS

This week Teen Topics decided to seek adult views on some of today's leading "pop" stars. Parents in particular are in a good position to air their views on beat groups, because their children are usually "beat-mad." And it seems that many parents are themselves beat fans, judging by their comments. Here are some comments:

GERRY MARSDEN: "He is the kind of boy I would like my daughter to bring home."

THE BEATLES: "They are wonderful performers, but why does everyone scream?"

THE ROLLING STONES: "I don't mind listening to them if I don't have to look at them. It is time they visited the barbers."

THE SEARCHERS: "I like their clean cut appearance and their songs, because they are not very loud."

BILLY J. KRAMER: "He seems to be a quiet, likeable boy."

BILLY FURY: "I enjoy listening to him singing ballads."

BEST SELLER – BY A GIRL

"Anyone Who Had A Heart," by Cilla Black, was the best selling record [in St Helens] last week. Down to slot two were The Searchers and "Needles and Pins," followed by Gerry and the Pacemakers, with "I'm The One." Also selling well are "Diane," by

The Bachelors; "I'm the Lonely One," by Cliff Richard and The Shadows, and Jim Reeves, with "I Love You Because." However, the new Dave Clark single, "Bits and Pieces," is not selling as well as "Glad All Over" did.

TEEN TOPICS – MARCH 1964

THE PRICE OF BEING POPULAR

One of St. Helens' top groups, the Cordelles, has broken up. The boys were becoming "too successful." It came to the point when they had to choose between turning professional to make show business their career or pursuing their present jobs to the best of their ability. They chose the latter course.

FOR BEAT FANS

Members of Sutton Methodist Youth Club are hoping to publish a magazine entitled "The Local Beat Scene" in the near future. They think it would be of interest to all teenagers and beat groups and if anyone is interested they should contact Miss Janet Haines, 48, Forest Road, Sutton Manor.

THE BEATLES STILL ON TOP

The Beatles are still firm Number One favourites locally, judging by this month's teenage survey. The Rolling Stones collected the next highest number of votes, followed closely by The Searchers. The Dave Clark Five got a surprising number of votes, considering that the group have been under fire a great deal locally.

CUTTING DISC SOON – THE FEDERAL FIVE

A group on the way up, the Federal Five, are due to make a demonstration disc for a recording company in the near future. They practice at the Primrose Hotel in Park Road and have over £1,000 worth of equipment. The boys have a chance of a summer season at a holiday resort, and if it materialises, it could be the start of something big for them.

The Federal Five as pictured in Teen Topics in March 1964

The group is led by 19-years-old Lambert Clayton, 42, Higher Parr Street, known as "Shirt" to his friends. The group's vocalist is John Crenan, 6, South John Street, aged 17, and an apprentice electrical engineer.

The group's first booking was at the Co-operative ballroom and they recall practising for hours on end to get the numbers off correctly, and went on stage "bleary-eyed." One of their favourite bookings is at Christ Church, Haydock, where they can be seen regularly.

INCAS FAN CLUB

The Incas fan club is now well under way, and the membership has reached a total of more than 150. Printed cards and photographs are available for every member.

CAVERN NEWS

Work on the extension of the Cavern Club, Liverpool, is going ahead but an unexpected problem during the past eight weeks has been the locating of a "missing" drain! This has baffled experts, and now owner Ray McFall is trying to find a water diviner, and there is even talk of bringing in an X-ray machine to solve the problem!

LECTURER PRAISES BEATLES

The Beatles came in for some praise during a lecture last week at Pilkington's new Theatre Royal, St. Helens, by David Attenborough. "Until the Beatles came along," he said, "people had forgotten what singing and dancing was about. You never find people in Africa or South America who are prepared to sit and watch. They want to join in. The Beatles are four lads who have said to themselves, 'This is fun! Let's join in!'"

SOBBING TEENAGERS LED FROM CINEMA

Sobbing teenagers were led from the auditorium during a stage show at the Wigan ABC cinema on Friday. The show starred Billy J. Kramer and the Dakotas, but the tears flowed during an act by America's Gene Pitney. Billy, however, attracted his share of screaming, as did the rest of the star studded line-up – Cilla Black, The Escorts, the Remo Four and The Kinks. Teenagers from all over South Lancashire flocked to Wigan to see in person their record idols. Two packed houses marked the success of the one night stand.

HELPING HANDS

The Psycho Five, who were recently joined by the Cordelles' former rhythm guitarist, Norman Finn, have decided to offer their services, free of charge, to the now struggling Zephyrs Club, Sutton.

THE BEATLE LOOK

Bench chairman, Mrs. R. Houghton, did a double-take at a 17-years-old Liverpool youth who appeared for a motoring offence at St. Helens Magistrates' Court on Friday, and said: "I thought at first we'd been honoured by the presence of one of the Beatles."

The youth, Robert Bernard Stephenson, 6, Bleesdale Avenue, Aintree Village, just peeped through his hair and smiled. He pleaded guilty to driving a car in Peasley Cross Road without due care and attention and was fined £8.

DO A BEATLES

Since the beat boom started earlier last year, numerous groups have appeared on the local scene, each determined to "do a Beatles." Many have faded away, while others have gone from strength to strength.

In fact, at the moment, there are probably more groups in the town than there have ever been. There are the Kirkbys, the Newtowns, the Comets, the Cellarmen and a host of other line-ups, all commanding a large following of fans.

HEAVIEST SALES OF WEEK

Billy J. Kramer and The Dakotas enjoyed the heaviest record sales locally last week, with "Little Children". There are no prizes for guessing next week's best selling record. It is certain to be "Can't Buy Me Love," by The Beatles. This disc has notched up advance sales of almost one million. *[Author's Note – A few weeks earlier Teen Topics had written: "Not much chance of success for Billy J. Kramer's 'Little Children'."]*

THE CORDAYS

When they made their first appearance at the Cavern Club, their lead guitarist was in hospital, but that did not prevent The Cordays from making a hit. In existence for three months, these five boys who are pupils or ex-pupils of Prescot grammar school, have already had an invitation to play at Hamburg's Star Club. But for two of the boys this would have meant missing work, and the fact that they turned down the offer indicates that, though ambitious, The Cordays are not star-struck.

THE CHEETAHS CAST OFF SPOTS

The Cheetahs have cast off their spots and assumed a new identity as the Triffids – this enterprising Sutton group found their name clashing with that of another act. The lads have more than £1,300 worth of equipment and have built up an established act as a polished and versatile beat group.

Managed by 21-years-old Nicky Richards, 341, Robins Lane, the group have become a regular feature at all the local clubs and have achieved a terrific following of satisfied customers. The group, who wish to thank all at the East Sutton Labour Club, have yet to fill their great ambition – a booking at the Cavern.

LOCAL GROUP AT PARIS NIGHT SPOT

A number of the North's top pop groups have been travelling abroad and reaching fame and fortune. The Classics, who a year ago were St. Helens' greatest group, are no exception. Remember them? For many months the boys seemed to have faded into obscurity but then this is understandable as they have not been in St. Helens – but in Paris! They are resident at a famous night spot and draw capacity crowds every night. The group comprises Les Stocks, Stan Gibbons, Johnny Densen and a Liverpool drummer, Les Watkinson.

BEATLES BACK AT NO. 1

The Beatles are back as Number One favourites of the week. Their latest (and some say their greatest) "Can't Buy Me Love," enjoyed the heaviest sales locally last week. The song, penned by John

Lennon and Paul McCartney, shoots straight to the top of the national Hit Parade on the strength of almost one million advanced orders. Also selling well are The Bachelors with "I Believe," The Escorts with "Dizzy Miss Lizzie" and "I Know," by Chick Graham and The Coasters, and "Little Children" by Billy J. Kramer and The Dakotas.

TEEN TOPICS – APRIL 1964

HAVE GIRL VOCALIST

A group with a difference has been formed in St. Helens. They are the Navigators, and are the only group in the town with a female vocalist. They have been in existence just over a month and practice at Lowe House Boys' Club, but despite their newness to the entertainment world, have managed to secure many good bookings. Eighteen-years-old Nita Kay is the first girl in St. Helens to try her luck in a hobby which for so long has been dominated by males. Nita, who works in a local store, makes an impression with both sexes when the group plays at their venues.

ARDENT FANS

A group practising at Carr Mill Community Centre are in the opinion of their fans "one of the best groups in town." The group – Dave and the Buccaneers – certainly have four ardent fans in Diane Hackay, Linda Pennington, Rita Matthews and Diane Moore. They wrote to us to make sure we knew about their idols.

SURPRISE CUSTOMER

Surprise visitor to the Golden Moon Chinese Restaurant, Duke Street on Saturday was Millie, the latest arrival on the "pop scene." While she was eating her evening meal, eager teenagers waited at the Plaza Ballroom where the Jamaican girl was doing a one-night stand. So far, in her short career, Millie has had few records to her credit, the second however "My Boy Lollipop" has stormed into the charts and reached the number ten position.

Travelling from London where she had appeared on the Television programme, 'Ready Steady Go,' Millie appearing with The Embers sang eight songs at the Plaza before moving on to Liverpool to appear at the Cavern the same evening. The sixteen-years-old singer loves Britain and when asked about St. Helens she told the Reporter "it seems a real nice place and the teenagers are very friendly."

TEEN TOPICS – MAY 1964

TOWN SPOT FOR HAYDOCK GROUP

One of the few Haydock groups, the Vardels, are making quite a name for themselves in the area. They have had a number of engagements and are looking forward to playing tomorrow at the Royal Raven Hotel, St. Helens. The group, all from Haydock, are comprised of Eric Garnet, Nigel Parr, Colyn Gange and Kenneth Wiswell.

LENNIE AND THE TEAM MATES

If talent plus personality rates a place in the beat world, 1964 should see the rise to fame of Lennie and the Team Mates, a local group who have plenty of both. Led by vocalist LENNIE SINCLAIR, 5, Raleigh Avenue, Whiston, a 19-year-old who is so full of rhythm he even seems to walk with a beat, the group was one of three chosen to represent Merseyside in a beat contest in Bristol recently.

Merseyside won, of course, but it says something for Lennie and his Team Mates that when Merseyside is bursting at the seams with beat groups, they should have been chosen. Let us meet the Team Mates. Rhythm guitarist is RONNIE LYON (aged 28), 28, Weyman Avenue, Whiston, who is an underground mechanic at Sutton Manor Colliery. Then there is blond TERRY HUYTON (aged 17), 17, Princess Avenue, St. Helens, on lead guitar. A former pupil of Grange Park technical school, Terry now works at Pilkington Brothers Ltd.

LENNIE EVEN SEEMS TO WALK WITH A BEAT

Group comic is BOB UNDERWOOD (aged 21), 44, Nelson Avenue, Whiston. Bob, who had his first guitar when he was 13, plays bass guitar. And still at school is the drummer, 15-years-old HAROLD BARROW, 39, Bewsey Street, St. Helens, who goes to Cowley grammar school.

The boys speed away each weekend to different one-night spots. So far these have included shows in the Midlands and Wales as well as around Merseyside, and they can switch their style to please teenagers and their parents alike. That is why they are thinking of turning professional. Said Ronnie Lyon: "We're versatile enough to please everyone. We choose our numbers according to where we are playing." They change their suits as well, with Beatle suits for the beat world, and flamenco pink jackets with black lapels for clubland. Listening to Lennie swing from a fast beat number into a sentimental ballad, it is obvious why his rich rather husky voice has gained him plenty of teenage fans.

TEEN TOPICS – JUNE 1964

OPEN-AIR BEAT

Manager of the Triffids beat group, Mr. E. Williams, has written condemning the Parks Committee decision not to allow his group to give open-air performances in St. Helens parks during the Summer.

Referring to the disorder at similar concerts elsewhere, he says, "It seems a shame that the pleasure of so many should be spoiled because of the acts of vandalism caused by just a few." The group have had one open-air booking, however, at a barbecue at Christ Church, Eccleston, on Saturday night, and there were no reports of trouble.

The Triffids in Teen Topics in June 1964

DISPELLED A RUMOUR

A spokesman for a local record shop this week dispelled the rumour that P. J. Proby's "Hold Me" had been withdrawn from the sales counters. The record, he said, was still selling "and selling well."

BEATLES BOOKED AT WIGAN

Great news for Lancashire beat fans – The Beatles and the Rolling Stones are to appear in separate one night stands at the A.B.C., Wigan, later this year. This follows the success of a one night stand starring Billy J. Kramer and the Dakotas.

GUITARS AND THE GOSPEL

A group with a difference, the Victors, recently played at the National Covenanter Rally in Birmingham Town Hall to an audience of more than 3,000 people. The guitar group, practising Christians from St. David's, Carr Mill, find this the best and most entertaining way of spreading the Gospel.

WOULD RATHER PLAY AT PLAZA THAN CAVERN

"We'd rather play at the Plaza than at the Cavern." This outspoken comment came from a Liverpool group who were playing at a fete at Mossborough Hall [in Rainford] on Saturday. The group, the Citadels, come from Liverpool and hope to turn professional in about six months. They say that they would rather play at the Plaza, St. Helens, than at the "over-rated and much publicised Cavern," Liverpool.

The boys, Ricky, John, Tony, John and Tony, commented: "The Cavern caters now for an extremely young audience, whereas at the Plaza you get a much maturer type of person and the atmosphere in consequence is much better." The group who have played a couple of times at the Cavern, once with the Hollies, say that at the Cavern fees are hardly enough to cover the cost of travel. The club's proprietors, the boys say, seem to consider that the "honour" of playing there is payment in itself.

DEVOTED FOUR

Local beat group, the Screaming Skulls, have earned themselves four devoted fans. Eileen, Joyce, Barbara and Jennifer wrote to say how they came to idolise the group. The girls were at a local youth club, when they heard a "terrific beat" coming from the hall. On entering they saw the group pounding out a "fab" number. The rhythm guitarist was playing the maraccas and the drummer "had them going with his movements".

TEEN TOPICS – JULY 1964

SURVEY PUTS STONES ON TOP

A Teen Topics teenage survey in the town centre at the weekend reveals that the Rolling Stones now top the Beatles in popularity locally. In third place are the Hollies, followed by Merseybeats (4), Dave Clark Five (5), Four Pennies (6), the Animals (7), the Mojos (8), the Searchers (9) and Manfred Mann (10).

TESTING TIME

Open air beat shows in the town's parks will go on after all. The Town Council ruled this on Wednesday after the Parks Committee said they would wait on reactions to similar performances in other towns. Now, teenagers in St. Helens have a chance to prove to their elders just how responsible or irresponsible they can be.

One or two people could spoil it for hundreds. At a recent beat show in Kirkby held on a school playing field, with several top groups, fights broke out in the latter part of the evening, and the organisers have decided not to hold any more shows.

POPULAR HERE

The Addicts, local beat group who secured a recording contract with Decca in May, are selling their record, "Here She Comes" very well locally. A spokesman for a local record shop said that although the record had made no impact nationally, the sales in this area had been very strong, and were only just beginning to fall off, two months after its release. The single is backed by "That's My Girl."

TWO WEEKS' RUN FOR BEATLES FILM?

The fabulous Beatles first major film, "A Hard Day's Night", will be showing at the A.B.C. Cinema, Bridge Street, next week. And if it has a successful run, which seems very likely, it will be presented for a second week. "A Hard Day's Night" will be followed by Cliff Richard's "A Wonderful Life".

FAN CLUB IS GROWING

A group with a growing fan club are The Hammers, who have played at most of the top Northern entertainment centres. Group line-up includes drummer Allan Glenn (aged 19), from St. Helens and 22-years-old Peter Shoesmith, an ex-professional, who plays lead guitar and also comes from St. Helens. Peter, in his professional days, has backed Screaming Lord Sutch.

TEEN TOPICS – AUGUST 1964

BEST SELLING RECORD LOCALLY

Best selling record locally last week was "Do Wah Diddy," by Manfred Mann which displaced The Beatles' "Hard Day's Night." Other records that are selling well include "Tobacco Road," by the Nashville Teens, "I Found Out the Hard Way," by the Four Pennies, "I Wouldn't Trade You for the World," by The Bachelors, and "The Crying Game," by Dave Berry.

TEEN TOPICS – SEPTEMBER 1964

FIRST RECORD

Released last week was the first record of local pop group, The Five Nites, who present "Let's Try Again" and "With a Loving Kiss," both penned by Warrington dance band leader, Eric Pepperell. Members of the group are 23-years-old bass guitarist Tony Bennet, 161, Wargrave Road, Newton, Ron Pickard (aged 21), of

Warrington, who plays lead guitar, Alan Taylor (19), of Dallam, Warrington, the vocalist, Gordon Marsh (21), drummer, and Geoff Taplin (21), rhythm guitar, both of St. Helens.

FROM DANCING TO DISCS

After an eight week's Summer season in Cabaret at Newquay, a sixteen-years-old St. Helens girl, Kathy Martin will be cutting her first disc within the next few days. Kathy, better known locally as Christine Murphy, of Rose Avenue, Sutton, will make the record within a few days of her seventeenth birthday later this month.

As a dancer she won 380 medals and 56 trophies, but last October Kathy finished with dancing to concentrate on a singing career, and has already appeared in many parts of the country.

TO PLAY AT GARDEN PARTY

Rising in the popularity polls in the St. Helens area are the Screaming Skulls. The boys have been chosen to play at a Blind Society garden party at Windle Hall on Thursday, along with another group The Hideaways, and Terry Gore and His Jazzmen.

Listening to them will be many celebrities, including Bob Wooller, the Cavern club's disc jockey; Ray McFall, owner of the Cavern, and Beatle George Harrison's mother. On Wednesday the group appeared at a Sutton club where they were well received.

STEADY PROGRESS

A local group, The Reflections from Grange Park, are now meeting with more success in the music world. Since rhythm guitarist Roy Burt, 56, Springfield Road, returned to the group after a month's absence, the group have been giving steadily improving performances. Last week they played at the Paradise Club in Wigan and on Sunday at Warrington's Heaven and Hell Club. The foursome are looking forward to great things within the next few months.

ODD ONE OUT?

A quote from Mrs. Molly Voliner, a former St. Helens girl now living in America but visiting her mother, Mrs. Elizabeth Simms, at 21, Barton Street: "The Beatles seem a grand bunch of boys. If they would just get their hair cut, I guess they would be all right."

ON TOUR

Little Eva, who is over in this country for a three weeks' tour of theatres and ballrooms, is scheduled to appear at the Plaza Ballroom, Duke Street, on Friday. Little Eva is well-known for her records, "Locomotion" and, "Turkey Trot."

"OPPORTUNITY KNOCKS" FOR WHIRLWINDS

A local group, the Whirlwinds, seem to be making their voices heard in the world of pop music. They have had an offer to cut a demo-disc for Decca which will probably be made in October. We have good news for you girls, the group will be starting a fan club in a few weeks.

They may further their chances of success with the possibility of appearances on "Opportunity Knocks" and "Scene at 6.30." They have the talent to go far, judging by the already famous names they have appeared with, including Mike Berry, Wayne Fontana and Shane Fenton.

TEEN TOPICS – OCTOBER 1964

THE TAKERS IN LOCAL TOP TEN

It's happened again. The Takers – formerly the Undertakers – have crashed into Liverpool's own top twenty but so far have not made any impression on the national charts. All their records have made the Merseyside charts . . . and their latest "If You Don't Come Back" has arrived at number 18.

NEW TITLE BRINGS LUCK

News from the local "pop" scene - The Federal Five have changed their title. They are now called The Streamers. The new name certainly seems to have brought the group luck. This month they have an audition for a show in Germany – a big step in the right direction! Another change has recently been made. The boys have a new vocalist in John Crehan, of South John Street, St. Helens.

TEEN TOPICS – NOVEMBER 1964

SUCCESS TOUR

News of the Screaming Skulls from their rhythm guitarist Johnny Glover. In a letter to Teen Topics, Johnny says that lately the boys have been playing out of town and have been enjoying success at clubs, including the Heaven and Hell, Warrington. While at a venue in Woolton, Liverpool, there was a rather disturbing incident. "We were playing all night," says Johnny, "until screaming girls took our maraccas [sic], tambourine and drum-sticks. They refused to give them back, so we let them keep them."

GROUP HAS NEW LOOK

One of the town's top groups, the Incas, has a new look. New man Les Williams was formerly a member of popular local group the Triffids and joins the group on solo guitar. The new vocalist is Martin O'Brien. Martin, who used to sing with the Fireflights and the Federal Five has proved a great favourite with beat fans in St. Helens and the Incas have made a wise move in acquiring his services. They are, by the way, believed to be the only group in the town with a 12-stringed guitar.

TEEN TOPICS – DECEMBER 1964

FROM STRINGS TO KEYBOARDS

One of the oldest groups in St. Helens – the Fireflights – have now become "The System." The dramatic nom-de-plume heralds a new line-up. Bass guitarist Trevor Bold who has been with the group since its early days has relinquished his bass guitar for an electric organ. This should be a stunning new feature of their act. Their new bass guitarist is ex-Federal Five man, Mike O'Brien.

BEST GROUP

The Coroners as pictured in Teen Topics in December 1964

Local group The Coroners have made another fan. Carole O'Hare, 38, Windermere Avenue, Clinkham Wood, wrote to us, "At a recent night at the Plaza, The Coroners filled in for another group in the top spot, and I must say they are the best group I have heard for some time. I think that more people should have the pleasure of hearing them. Has the group a fan club?" asks Carole. If not she would like to start one.

WHY OUR 'STARS' ARE NOT SHINING

St. Helens is famous for many things. Its top-of-the-table Rugby League team and its glass are among them. Yet the town has never hit the national highspots by producing a pop singer or group of any renown *(writes a staffman)*. The nearest we have ever come to that claim to fame is Frances Lea of the Vernons Girls, and June Leslie, vocalist with Bob Miller and the Millermen.

NEWSPAPER & MIDWEEK REPORTER,

★ TEEN TOPICS

Why our 'stars' are not shining

The reason is not lack of talent. It is lack of originality. Of all the beat groups that have sprouted like mushrooms in the town over the past two years only one ever had that original touch. They were Cadillac and the Playboys with their "horror" act and even this can be regarded rather quizzically when set against the act of Screaming Lord Sutch and the Savages.

When the Shadows did their footwork routine the groups followed suit. When the Beatles came along everybody bought high-heeled boots, grey thatched haircuts and attempted to harmonise. Even this is old hat now. The Rolling Stones have been on the beat scene for quite a time and their influence is being felt. Groups wear their hair shoulder-length, dress like and try to mimic the Stones.

Never do the local groups make attempts to utilise their talent. They merely follow a pattern set by better and more popular groups until the fans are sick of seeing the same old performance. How can our local groups expect talent scouts or agents from record companies to realise their true worth when they all look like carbon copies of each other?

If only some of the established groups would break free from the old "pop" tradition that all the part-timers look like dulled imitations of the stars; perhaps St. Helens would be able to boast of a record at No. 1.

UNTRUE

Popular group the Screaming Skulls have moderated their horrific title to the mere spine-chilling Skulls. Teen Topics learned this in a letter from rhythm guitarist Johnny Glover, who would also like us to dispel ugly rumours that their lead guitarist "Flingell" Eric Mercer is a drug addict.

"He is no such thing," says the letter, "it takes him all his time to take an aspirin." The idea arose, it seems, because "Flingell" is fond of jumping up and down on stage, and lying on his back and rolling his eyes.

By now the St Helens Newspaper's Teen Topics was becoming irregular and the column soon ended. The paper itself had become part of the St Helens Reporter Group and served as their mid-week edition until Nov. 1980 when the Newspaper ceased publication.

"Dear Sir" – A Collection Of Curious Correspondence Part 2

In 'The Hidden History of St Helens Vol 2' I transcribed some letters that were sent to the town's newspapers during the 19th and early 20th centuries. This chapter is devoted to a second batch of correspondence. Usually signed with a pseudonym, these can provide more insights into the social life of St Helens than the newspapers' own reports from that time.

THE FAST WALKING CRAZE

This photograph was published in the St Helens Newspaper in June 1903 and shows Corporation clerks at Dentons Green taking part in what the paper described as the new "walking craze". Fast-walking races *(aka pedestrianism)* had a long history in the town. However, such matches usually only comprised a couple of athletes competing against each other for money, with much betting taking place on the result.

The new *(and seemingly short-lived)* walking sport involved a group of amateurs competing in walking races for fun. On July 10th 1903 the Newspaper published this letter in which the author supported the craze and felt that the new electric trams in St Helens were making townsfolk lazy:

> Sir – I was glad to see a letter from C.R. in last Saturday's issue of your paper, advocating that as a town we should begin to recognize "Walking" as a branch of Athletics. One of the most pathetic signs of the times is to see strong, healthy young men and women patiently waiting for the [tram] car at the various penny stages along the tram lines. Our grandparents thought nothing of a 20 or 30 miles walk, and they were a sound-winded, strong-limbed race of people. Physicians tell us that there is now growing up in our large towns a new type of individual, the superficially smart young man, well groomed, and keen witted, but without the backbone and stamina of his ancestors. Walking is the healthiest and cheapest form of exercise that anyone can indulge in, and I for one would welcome a movement which would take advantage of the present "walking craze" to organize it into a standard and recognized form of recreation.

A CHURCH YARD DISCRACE

It appears there is nothing new as regards complaints of churchyards not being well cared for. This letter was published in the St Helens Newspaper on August 9th 1870 criticising the state of the graveyard at St Thomas's Church:

> **ST. THOMAS' CHURCHYARD** – Sir, Allow me through the medium of your valuable paper to call public attention to the above yard, which is daily becoming more and more disgraceful to the neighbourhood. What are the feelings of those who have relatives or friends lying within the precints

[sic], pen cannot describe. As they view the sod – sod did I say? Pardon the mistake. As they look at the stones and other rubbish scattered over the grave of the cherished one, can it be wondered at if they are seen turning away in tears?
– **VERITAS**

BLOWING UP OF FISH

During the 19th century the St Helens water supply was sourced from Eccleston Hill and from Whiston. On January 11th 1879 this letter was published in the Prescot Reporter protesting about proposals to dynamite fish and suggesting an alternative:

THE FISH IN THE WATER RESERVOIRS. – To the Editor of the Reporter and Standard. Dear Sir, – Could you kindly spare room for a few lines in next Saturday's Reporter, just to draw attention to an oversight in the management of the Corporation dams at Eccleston. I hear, on what I consider good authority, that it is the intention of our worthy engineer, Mr. Gaskin, to destroy the fish in the above dams by an explosion of dynamite. Now, I think that would be a very grave error. Why not let the fishing to lovers of "the gentle craft" at, say £1 per annum per rod? Something of the sort is done in other towns – the Warrington Water Company, for instance, who, I understand, realise a nice income from it, besides benefiting their friends. The above seems to me a practical way of keeping the fish within bounds, and of affording fresh air, and innocent amusement to plenty of lovers of the angle. – Yours respectfully, **BOGIE**. St. Helens.

THE DRUNKEN SOLDIER IN CHURCH STREET

We've all grown up familiar with the Territorial Army *(or Army Reserve as it's now known)*. However, in 1870 the idea of a military force comprising part-time volunteers was still a bit of a novelty, as the 47th Battalion of the Lancashire Rifle Volunteers had only been formed in St Helens ten years before. Not all of its members were well-disciplined and some would call in the pub after exercises and get drunk. On August 9th 1870 the St Helens Newspaper published this letter critical of one particular part-time soldier who had indulged too much:

> Sir, On Sunday last, in passing through Church-street, I observed one of the 47th Rifle Volunteers in an advanced state of intoxication, carrying his rifle and side-arms. I suppose he had been camping on Saturday night, and had taken more than he could carry with safety, for he instantly got at loggerheads with a passer by, and after a few minutes of fierce wrangling he pulled out his bayonet, fastened it to his rife, and very rashly struck at the other with it. If it had not been that the other quickly stepped aside, and grasped the weapon with his hand (thus cutting his finger and thumb) he would certainly have been seriously wounded. I hope if his commanding officer sees this he will deal with the volunteer in the manner such unmanly conduct deserves; for, however he may have been attacked by the other, he was surely not justified in striking an unarmed man in such a cowardly way. I remain, Sir, yours, &c., **L, St. Helens**.

THOSE WERE NOT THE DAYS?

Reflecting on the past in the St Helens Reporter of May 3rd 1946 was someone adopting the pseudonym "Regular Reader". Their letter commented on a photo of a Conservative party gathering in 1909 that the paper had printed in its previous edition. The letter was published under the headline *"Those Were Not The Days?":*

> The photograph in Friday's paper of the garden party at "Woodlands" is interesting, but the heading, "Those were the days," is, in my humble opinion, unfortunate. As a reminder of Tory pomp and power it may bring back nostalgic

memories for some people, but I remember that in those days more hungry, dirty, barefooted children could be seen in an hour's walk round St. Helens than could be found in the whole of England to-day. Not that St. Helens was alone in this respect, by any means. None the less, in those days, only as far back as 1909, little orphan apprentices were in our glass factories as a matter of course. Boys of tender years were worked 13 hours a day – and night, too – for a mere pittance. As regards adult employment, it was plentiful enough for those who could survive in the atmosphere of our chemical works and glass houses. One had to be strong! The weakest went to the wall, or the workhouse, and stayed there. The scales of relief were not as generous as they are to-day. Old age pensioners were more neglected then than now. As regards food, in my own experience it is better and more fairly distributed to-day, even under rationing.

I am quite sure my children have had a better time in that respect than I had, even though my parents were hard-working and respectable. They had not always the means to feed and clothe us as they would have wished. As regards the town itself, there were districts, like Smithy-brow and Peasley Cross, where our wartime gas masks would have been invaluable when the "chemic" works poured their stink out. The housing situation was not so bad then; there were more slums, and more pubs, one at every corner, and in between as well. No; St. Helens is a better place now than ever it was, and I maintain that the Conservative party has done little to bring this about. "Those were the days" are dead and buried, thank God! – **REGULAR READER**

The comments created a storm of protest mainly because of the accusation that the Conservatives had done nothing to improve matters. It was pointed out that St Helens actually had a Labour MP in 1909!

THE NOISY PEASLEY CROSS STREETS

Also reflecting on the past in the St Helens Reporter was Arthur Jones. On October 4th 1974 he recalled how very noisy life had been in the Peasley Cross streets of his youth. It must, at times, have been a bit loud inside his home, too. The 1911 census shows eight persons living at 150 Peasley Cross Lane, with father Andrew employed as a chemical labourer. By the 1921 census times had become hard with Andrew listed as an out of work copper smelter and his sons Arthur and Henry unemployed chemical labourers. This was Arthur's letter to the paper:

> Having been born in Peasley Cross, St. Helens, in the year 1901, may I recall the days of my youth before the introduction of noise abatement. We lived in Peasley Cross Lane behind French's butcher's shop. At the top of the lane next to us was a pawn shop. I wonder to this day how men slept who were on shift work as during the early mornings a policeman would come rattling at shop doors to see that everything was secure and shine his oil lamp up at the windows. With the pawn shop being next door, I suppose special attention was paid to those premises, but I must have been wakened every night. After that came the knocker-up with his big pole tapping at the bedroom windows around 4.30 in the morning, and then the rattle of clogs going to work in all directions as many people had to walk as far as Sutton Manor and Clock Face collieries. And as there was no Welfare State I always, as a boy, thought the clogs used to say as they went along "I'm bound to go, I'm bound to go." It was either work or starve, and many went to work feeling ill.
>
> Later we had the clanging of the tram cars on rails and the clatter of the points as the trams entered the loops. One car would come from Dentons Green, while the other came from

the Sutton junction, to and fro all day long. The last tram from the junction always went pell-mell [hurried manner] down Peasley Cross Lane around 11.30 p.m. It was a gradient of about 1 in 12. No one had any consideration for the working man in those days as regards noise. Everyone who sold their wares in the streets shouted "coal," "light cakes," "muffins," "cockles and mussels" and "milko." Tramps would knock at the back doors asking for tea etc., that was a common sight. The hurdy-gurdy man playing his favourite tunes, vehicles drawn by horses, and the man shouting "whos lad" or "gee up."

The corporation came round about 2 in the morning once a week to empty the old-fashioned middens and open lavatories with the pails instead of the flush toilets. They would come round with what we called in those days "Aunt Sallies" drawn by shire horses. The full pails were placed in cubicles at the sides of the vehicles and clean ones put in their places. Where they took them to be emptied we never knew. All I know was that at each house they smothered the middens and toilets with chloride of lime. It was an age of noise. However, we all pulled through as there was no option in those days." – **ARTHUR JONES**, Wrexham

THE DEADLY ST HELENS CANAL

Over the years many hundreds of people have perished in the waters of the St Helens / Sankey Canal. These deaths could be by accident or design – with the former mainly through stumbling into deep water in the dark. There was very little in the way of protective fencing and those walking home from the pub were particularly vulnerable. A correspondent in the St Helens Newspaper on April 12th 1870 with the initials "J.E.P." was concerned about one of the worst stretches of waterway which was near the Navigation Inn:

The Navigation Tavern or Inn by the side of the St Helens / Sankey Canal

Sir. – May I beg a corner in your paper to make known the dangerous and improper state the canal is from the Navigation Bridge to the east end of the canal. Scarcely a week passes over but there is some one found drowned (in the portion I name), and I am not the least surprised at it, for there is nothing whatever but a loose chain hanging down, which is not protective whatever, but only a sham, to keep people from falling in.

And near the Navigation Inn and the railway bridge there is nothing whatever for protection to keep strangers from falling in, if they are not acquainted with the road, and especially on a foggy night. I understand the canal is leased to the railway company, and I would suggest the Town Council of St. Helens should compel the railway company to have a fence built – say about four feet high right along from the Navigation Inn Bridge to the Railway Bridge, west. If something of this kind was done we should hear very little of people being found drowned there, except they got over the railings and wished to have a duck. Hopefully this may be the means of stirring some one up whose duty it is to protect the public from such unprotected places as these. – Yours truly, **J. E. P.**, St. Helens.

QUARRY ACCIDENTS

The canal was not the only place of danger. Towards the end of the 19th century St Helens became pockmarked with old pits, quarries and other disused workings. Often these were situated in places where lighting was poor and with little fencing surrounding them, many accidents took place – particularly at night.

In 1883 Robert Davies from Elephant Lane was discovered lying at the bottom of an old stone quarry in Thatto Heath. The young man had been dashing to the railway station to catch a train into St Helens. As a sovereign had gone missing from his clothing, foul play was at first suspected.

However, after Robert's inquest had been held the money was found secreted within a pocket. It was then realised that he must have fallen into the almost 70ft. deep pit. Consequently In the Prescot Reporter of November 10th 1883, this letter was published criticising the fact that no one authority appeared to take responsibility for the safety of such places:

THE QUARRY ACCIDENT AT THATTO HEATH. To the Editor of the Reporter. Sir, – Permit me through your paper to call attention to the accident at Thatto Heath, where a young man, and a steady man, lost his life. As a sovereign has been found in the clothes he had on, there seems to be a strong supposition that he walked into the quarry. Then we come to the question. Should such danger to the public remain, or whose duty is it to protect the public? Had the quarry been occupied by any person or company, would they not have been considered neglectful, or even made liable for damages? Surely to this case there must be neglect in some quarter. I think that it is an obligation upon the public authorities to protect the people from danger, and the roads have a distinct department, who have the responsibility. They can, if an individual has dangerous property, interfere. Who are the people to interfere when they don't do their duty?

The corporation have fixed lamps in the Rainhill-road, but taken care to fix them as far as they could from this dangerous spot. Now, had that poor man a right to go that road, to cross Thatto Heath? I think he had every right; and going from the station, out of the gas light, to where his club was held, it would be his road; but as there was no light at the quarry, he missed a few yards. There is a public road the other side of the heath, which is a disgrace to any public body having control of it. – Yours respectfully, **N. P.**

A TIMELY DISGRACE

With the time of day available now in a vast variety of forms, including cheap watches, mobile phones and even microwaves, there is no great necessity to have a traditional clock in the house. And the public ones on display in St Helens tend to have stopped – but nobody seems to mind!

However, it was very different in 1870 when many people did not own a timepiece and only a handful of places – such as some churches – had clocks. And during dark nights in St Helens, these would be impossible to see. On December 31st of that year this letter was published in the St Helens Newspaper:

> Sir, It is very much to be regretted that St. Helens does not possess a public illuminated clock. The want of it has been long and deservedly noticed, and I am sure that the majority of the ratepayers would approve of such an undertaking. Is it not a standing disgrace to the town and corporation of St. Helens that the town should be so utterly without an illuminated clock? Other towns of no greater importance – such towns, for instance, as Wigan, Warrington, and Runcorn are in possession of illuminated clocks, and even Widnes stands before us in this matter. Then, I ask again, is it not a perfect disgrace to a town of the size and importance of St. Helens that it should be so far behind in this respect? Those who know St Helens are aware how inconvenient it is to those who are not in possession of a good watch to ascertain the correct time at night. – **A. Ratepayer**

It seemed that Ald. James Radley read the letter, as in August 1873 an illuminated clock donated by the coal magnate was installed on the parish church's tower. The Newspaper described it as a "remarkable work of art" with four dials, each 5 ft. in diameter, bearing "massive gilt hands". The paper added that all the metal used in the clock's works had been "lacquered by a patent process, so as to more effectually resist the action of the St. Helens atmosphere".

HELPING CHILDREN WITH TERRIFIED EYES

In May 1903 John Pennington was undertaking some work in the heavily built up Greenbank area of St Helens around Bold Street, Mount Street and Sandfield Crescent. The builder from Greenfield Road witnessed many poor children that had never left the district and seen the beauty of the countryside. And so Pennington raised some cash and organised an outing to the rural areas of Eccleston.

There the sight of a stream was apparently so new to the kids that some were described as apprehensive when invited to cross the shallow water to pick flowers. Other trips to other nearby places were also organised but soon he ran short of money and decided to hold a fundraising bazaar. On August 28th 1903 the St Helens Newspaper published this revealing letter from Mr Pennington concerning the children that he was trying to help:

> Sir, I have decided to hold the "Poor Children's Bazaar" on Saturday, September 5th, at 2 p.m. I am sorry that my effort to brighten the lives of the helpless ones has not met with that response from the general public which I anticipated. Have we, I would ask my friends, no duty towards these children, whose pinched faces and terrified eyes appeal to us for help and sympathy? God grant they may not always appeal in vain. Summer after summer their hopes are dashed to the ground until no hope remains. Can we expect these unhappy, helpless little ones to carve a way in life for themselves, when no hand is outstretched to help and guide them, no effort made to foil the evil influences of their gutter life?

THE RAINFORD RURAL PANDEMONIUM

In November 1871 Thomas Haslam, the licensee of the Black Bull in Church Street in St Helens, organised a race between two youths at the Royal Oak Park in Manchester. One runner was identified as R. Sefton of Rainford and the other as W. Woodcock from St Helens. The contest over 150-yards was more about gambling than athletics and led to a Rainford man using the pseudonym Nemo having this critical letter published in the Liverpool Mercury:

> Gentlemen. – On a former occasion I called attention, through the medium of your columns, to the disgusting exhibition at Rainford commonly known as the election of lord mayor. I would now bring before you another phase of

rural life equally as revolting as the previous one. For the last month or so, various rumours have been spread about a foot race, and the large amount of money that was staked on the event. Yesterday the race came off (at Manchester, I believe); the Rainford champion won; consequently last night the people were jubilant, the grog trade flourishing, and the whole place little better then a "rural pandemonium."

Now, this is my complaint. Ought a man to be allowed to hold a license – who gets up these obnoxious exhibitions for the sole purpose of selling his liquors? For in all these races a publican is invariably the prime mover, and the real object is to benefit his house. It was lamentable last night to see boys, girls, and even babies, who could barely lisp, discussing about the odds, the amount won by their fathers, and in one case a promising youth of seven regretting that his father had not enough upon the event. I cannot close this letter without asking – Where are the police? What are their duties? And if they do not put down nocturnal rows, what redress have the respectable inhabitants? Yours, **NEMO**.

That letter does generate curious mental images of babies in their prams discussing betting odds! Exactly what Mr Nemo meant about the election of a lord mayor at Rainford (which has never had one) I am not quite sure – but clearly he was against the drinking that went on at such events.

THE STURDY ST HELENS WATCH

On January 21st 1872 thousands of St Helens folk lined the town's streets to watch the funeral procession of James Ramsdale. The hugely popular railway guard from Shaw Street had been described as "literally cut to pieces" as a result of a shunting accident near St Helens station. A fortnight later the St Helens Newspaper published this letter from fellow guard George Butcher about Mr Ramsdale's watch:

To the editor. Sir. – In your insertion of the fatal accident to the late guard, J. Ramsdale, you stated that the watch worn by him was the one worn by the late Inspector Needs, who met with his death on the railway under the same melancholy circumstances, on the 4th of February last. I beg to inform you and the public that such is not the case, as Ramsdale was served with his watch, No. 1, years before Mr. Needs came to St. Helens, and had always retained the same until the day of his death. It was the first watch made by Mr. Butler, of Church street, for the old St. Helens Canal and Railway Company. It was given to Ramsdale by Mr. Cross, and has been in his possession from then until now. In the late accident the glass of the watch only was broken, while coins, keys, knife, tobacco box, &c., in his pockets, were broken and smashed in all shapes. I am, sir, respectfully yours, **George Butcher**, Guard St. Helens.

That's the robust quality of a St Helens watch for you – able to withstand being run over by a loco engine! Although Prescot is rightly credited as the centre of the country's watch movement-making industry, there were actually more individuals scattered around the St Helens district making timepieces than in Prescot itself. The vast majority of these made only part of the watch movements, which were then sent south for other craftsmen to complete – although some finished watches were also made.

DEAR LIVING

I expect St Helens folk have always moaned about the cost of living. On August 30th 1873 a letter was published in the St Helens Newspaper complaining about rises in the price of food and its quality. When 20 to 25 shillings was the working man's average weekly wage, a few extra pence on staple foods could upset the family budget. The letter was published under the pseudonym "A Poor Working Man" and headline *"Dear Living"*:

To the Editor, Sir, – The inhabitants of this town, after two or three years of suffering from the high price coals, butter, butcher's meat, and other domestic necessaries, cannot be well prepared for the approaching winter. These commodities, have been advancing in price with a rapacity fit only for Hotentots, nor do I think the class of people whose hearts allow them to run up such prices for the above articles are at this present moment a whit [sic] better. There can be no such scarcity of butcher's meat, as to demand 1s. a lb. for very inferior beef, perhaps an old bull, many of which are weekly imported to private slaughter houses, which ought to be abolished. The same may be said of our Mutton; and Butter fares no better, for the rubbish at 1s. 2d. a lb. in shops, has no more of the sweet taste of butter, than a sperm candle. Putting all together it is frightful to glance at the approaching winter, with no apparent sign of any relaxation in the horrible state of our markets. If the poor working men of town and country do not take action, and try to alleviate their present state of suffering, famine in disguise will sweep away many families, or bring them into a low and delicate state of health. Let meetings be called in all available places, and societies for protection, organised. – **A POOR WORKING MAN**, St. Helens, Aug. 27th.

A CAUTION TO PRESCOT FIRE BRIGADE

The term "playing" was regularly used by St Helens newspapers in the context of fire brigades distributing water onto a blaze. However, this letter that was published in the St Helens Weekly News of February 15th 1862 reckoned that the Prescot Brigade did too much of another sort of playing:

Sir, As you are always both ready and willing to insert anything in your valuable and very widely circulated paper that tends to promote the good and well being of your neighbourhood and district at large, I beg to ask you to caution the Prescot Fire Brigade, upon their next trial of the fire engine, (which I believe is arranged to take place on Shrove Tuesday afternoon next) not to have any ridiculous nonsense during the trial, by dousing men, women and children, thereby bringing considerable odium and contempt upon themselves. – Yours, **A. Z.**, Prescot, Feb. 10, 1862

The letter led to this reply from the paper's editor:

In compliance with the request of our correspondent, we caution the Prescot Fire Brigade against playing the silly pranks alluded to. We are informed that, at the late fire at the asylum, they were more than an hour in getting their engine to play, and then only through the assistance of Bell, the superintendent of the St. Helens Brigade. Now if this be the fact, and we state it on Bell's authority, it will be quite as well for the Prescotonians on "Pancake Tuesday," to perfect themselves in something else than squirting water on unoffending and perhaps admiring women and children.

The fire at Rainhill County Asylum had broken out in their workshops on January 27th 1862 and caused a considerable loss of property. Several thousand persons congregated at the scene of the blaze which could be witnessed for several miles.

CRIMEAN AND INDIAN HERO

There is a long history of soldiers having served their country in wartime but feeling discarded upon returning home. On October 30th 1875 the Prescot Reporter wrote of the case of Thomas Dutton. The 45-year-old resident of Snig Lane in Prescot had undertaken military service in India and in the Crimea but was discharged after being paralysed down one side. Sgt. Dutton was subsequently awarded an army pension of just tenpence a day, which was cancelled after three years. The Reporter in their article did not ask for charity for Dutton but wondered if any reader was prepared to offer him any light work. On November 6th 1875, the paper published this letter from a vicar in Ilfracombe:

> The case of Thomas Dutton, referred to in your paper of the 30th ult. as a Crimean and Indian hero, and who has for some time lived in Prescot in very needy circumstances, and as having endured many privations, has touched my heart with sorrow to think that his gallant services, extending over 11 years and 230 days, have been so ill requited by the government and the people at large. When we remember what noble deeds were accomplished, and hardship untold was borne, by those who so well sustained our British arms in the Crimea and throughout the Indian mutiny, surely our sympathies will at once manifest themselves – if we are able – by liberal contributions towards any of those who unfortunately stand in need of our assistance; and in this case especially are the people of Prescot called upon to relieve, as they so well know how to do, one who is altogether worthy of their support, as being for some time in the town, paralyzed on one side, discharged with a miserable pension of 10d. a day for three years only, holding a good conduct certificate, and being a sober reliable man, of a very retiring disposition, as testified by the editor of this paper. I, for my part, feel much pleasure in helping him or any one in Prescot, if deserving – by forwarding £1 as a general starting fund, or if not that, as an incentive for some sympathizing gentleman to give him, as you suggest, light and regular occupation, he being, notwithstanding his affliction, suitable for it. Why not sink a fund for him, and give him light employment as well?
>
> I am, Yours, &c., **REV. FRANCIS DE LACY WHITE**.
> Ilfracombe, N. Devon.

Four Curious Cases Of Bigamy

"People must understand that men have no more right to sell their wives than to sell other people's wives, or to sell other people's horses or cows, or anything else."

INTRODUCTION

When the St Helens Petty Sessions were held on July 22nd 1871 an individual that the Liverpool Daily Post described as a "respectable-looking working man" applied to magistrate Henry Hall for advice on getting a divorce. The man explained that his wife had left him for a Liverpool shopkeeper and Hall's advice was that if he had £50 he should go to the Divorce Court – otherwise "let the matter remain as it is". The Post added that: "The applicant went away dissatisfied".

In the 1871 census Henry Hall describes himself as a "landowner and farmer" living in Dentons Green Lane in St Helens. If he had wished to divorce his wife Catherine, I expect Hall would have been able to find the necessary funds. But for working-class folk earning somewhere between 15 to 30 shillings a week, it was quite impossible to obtain £50.

The Church was against any changes being made to the divorce laws – despite the unhappiness that the existing arrangements often caused. In 1918 when plans were being considered for easier divorces for couples that had been separated for three years, the Vicar of St Helens drew a parallel with the downfall of the Roman Empire. Canon Albert Baines added that they would:

> …be running a great risk of national disaster if the country were to adopt such an iniquitous proposal.

There were some in authority who realised that things needed to change. Rigby Swift had been born in St Helens in 1874 and brought up at Hardshaw Hall – which later became Providence Hospital. Swift became MP for St Helens in 1910 and a judge ten years later. In their 1937 obituary, the Lancashire Evening Post described Sir Rigby Swift as "undoubtedly the most outspoken judge of his day", who'd called the divorce laws "wicked and cruel".

There were two main consequences of the inability of working class folk to get their marriages annulled. Many women became trapped with brutal or uncaring husbands and some men and women chose to take their chances and commit bigamy.

Rigby Swift (1874 - 1937)

There were, of course, different types of bigamous second weddings but most were the result of legitimate first marriages having long broken down. The main victim of bigamy tended to be the single woman who believed she had married a single man only for her hopes and dreams to vanish when the police came knocking on her door.

John Kinsella was an extreme example of someone who not only robbed his female victims of their futures – but also helped himself to anything valuable belonging to his wife. In 1918 The People newspaper dubbed Kinsella a "super-bigamist" and "arch-scoundrel" after he had been sent to prison for 7 years for bigamously marrying 13 women. The man had used matrimonial adverts to lure lonely ladies "of means" and then after marrying them, scarpered with their money, jewellery or furniture.

In sentencing Kinsella at Manchester Assizes, Justice Slater said:

I don't know how many women in the course of the last 24 years you have ruined by this abominable form of seduction and plundered after you have ruined them.

However, this chapter is concerned more with curious cases of bigamy where all the parties were fully aware of the existing marital arrangements. Some had strange ideas of how they were not breaking the law when taking a second spouse, with my first example quite a corker!

1) THE MAN WHO SOLD HIS WIFE FOR A QUART OF BEER WORTH SIXPENCE!

When Justice Denman sentenced Betsy Wardle for bigamy at Liverpool Assizes on November 13th 1883 he remarked:

> People must understand that men have no more right to sell their wives than to sell other people's wives, or to sell other people's horses or cows, or anything else.

The middle-aged woman had been arrested in Parr Flats in St Helens where she had been living with her second husband, George Chisnall. The couple had gone through a marriage ceremony at St Thomas's Church in Westfield Street in St Helens on September 4th 1882 after her lawful husband James Wardle had given his consent.

However, the man had insisted on two conditions. Wardle insisted that their child had to remain with him and he demanded a quart of beer as a sort of transfer fee. A paper was also drawn up cementing the deal – although not, of course, utilising the services of a solicitor who would, no doubt, have sent them all packing!

So on August 20th 1883 when Betsy Wardle appeared in St Helens Police Court to face the charge of bigamy, she insisted that witnesses would prove that her first husband had sold her to

George Chisnall. That to her mind meant she had not broken the law and had been fully entitled to remarry.

The acquiescence of James Wardle to her second marriage would have been a mitigating factor when it came to Betsy's sentencing at the assizes. But it did not alter the fact that the 25-year-old woman had committed bigamy and needed to face justice. Betsy told St Helens magistrates that her lawful husband was "idle and would not work". She said sometimes he would take off for two or three weeks leaving her and their child "to do what we had a mind".

The woman had spent ten days in custody on remand but the St Helens Bench granted her bail until the next hearing at Liverpool Assizes. Being remanded on bail was not a common practice by magistrates and was recognition that her offence was in all probably committed through ignorance. That said the bail and sureties totalled £40, which was very high – almost the figure needed for a divorce, although the bail and surety money was redeemable.

> **EXTRAORDINARY CASE OF BIGAMY.—SELLING A WIFE.**
> Betsy Wardle, aged 25, was indicted for having, at St. Thomas's Church, St. Helens, on the 4th September, 1882, married George Chisnall, her former husband being then alive. — Mr. Shand prosecuted. — The prisoner having pleaded guilty, Mr. T. Swift, who appeared on her behalf, said she instructed him that her husband sold her for a quart of beer—(laughter)—and she seemed to have been under the impression that the transaction was a legal one, and entitled her to marry again.—His Lordship: That is not what she said before the magistrates. She said then that he was an idle fellow and would not work ; that when she left him she took the child, and he said if she would let him have the child he would not trouble her any further ; and that he said he would sell her for a quart of beer. —Prisoner : He did so, my lord.—His Lordship : Is there anyone here who knows that?—Prisoner : Yes ; Alice Roseby and Margaret Brown.—Margaret Brown,

Prescot Reporter November 17th 1883

In reporting on the Liverpool Michaelmas Assizes hearing in St. George's Hall, the Prescot Reporter and St Helens General Advertiser of November 17th 1883 wrote:

EXTRAORDINARY CASE OF BIGAMY – SELLING A WIFE. Betsy Wardle, aged 25, was indicted for having, at St. Thomas's Church, St. Helens, on the 4th September, 1882, married George Chisnall, her former husband being then alive. Mr. Shand prosecuted. The prisoner having pleaded guilty, Mr. T. Swift, who appeared on her behalf, said she instructed him that her husband sold her for a quart of beer – (laughter) – and she seemed to have been under the impression that the transaction was a legal one, and entitled her to marry again. Margaret Brown, having been called, said she was present at the second marriage. She knew that the first husband was alive. The prisoner told her that he had sold her for a quart of beer, and Chisnall showed her a paper to that effect. – His Lordship: Where is that paper? – Prisoner: It has got away, sir. – His Lordship (to witness): It purported to be a paper written by Wardle, saying he had sold her for a quart of beer? – Witness [Margaret Brown]: Yes. – His Lordship: And you believed it? – Witness: Yes. – His Lordship: And you thought it right for her to marry again? – Witness: She asked me to give her away, and I did so. – His Lordship: You helped her to commit bigamy. Take care you don't do such a thing again, or you will get into trouble.

Alice Roseby was next called, and said she saw Wardle drink a glass out of the quart of beer. – His Lordship: Who was the bargain made with? – Witness: With George Chisnall. – His Lordship: I am not sure that you are not guilty of bigamy, or of being an accessory before the fact. You must not do this sort of thing again. People have no right to sell their wives for a quart of beer or for anything else. George Chisnall, the second husband, a young man, having been called and asked by his lordship how he came to marry the prisoner, replied, "I bowt her." (Laughter.) – His Lordship: You are not fool enough to suppose that you can buy another man's wife? – Witness: Ay. (Laughter.) – His Lordship: How much did you give for her? – Witness: Sixpence. (Laughter.) – His Lordship: You are quite as guilty as she is. You are an accessory before the fact. You have committed bigamy yourself. Everybody has committed bigamy in this case. (Laughter.) How long have you lived with the prisoner? – Witness: Going for three years. – His Lordship: Do you want to take her back again? – Witness: Ay, and keep her if you loike. (Laughter.)

Mr. Swift, on behalf of the prisoner, expressed the hope that his lordship would not think it a case in which she ought to be punished severely. She seemed to have met with a bad husband in the first instance, and an ignorant one in the second. In reply to his lordship, the learned counsel said she had been out on bail. His Lordship said it was absolutely necessary that he should impose some punishment in order that people might understand that men had no more right to sell their wives than to sell other people's wives, or to sell other people's horses or cows, or anything else. It was not a legal transaction. So many of them seemed to be ignorant of this that it was necessary that he should inflict some punishment in this case, so that they might understand it. He then sentenced the prisoner to a week's imprisonment. At a later period of the day, Mr. Swift informed his lordship that the prisoner was apprehended on the 17th of August and was kept in custody until the 27th before being admitted to bail; so that she had already undergone a longer period of imprisonment than that to which his lordship had sentenced her. – His Lordship: I will consider that.

2) THE BIZARRE TURKS HEAD BIGAMY CASE

The Washington Inn on the left and the Turks Head on the right

In 1879 the Turks Head on the corner of Cooper Street and Morley Street in St Helens was at the centre of a bizarre case of bigamy. Although many St Helens men have entered into bigamous marriages over the years, William Harrison's case must surely have been unique.

Instead of wanting to start a new family with his second "wife" – as male bigamists usually do – the landlord of the Turks Head returned from the wedding ceremony in Liverpool to continue living with his first wife in St Helens. The middle-aged Harrison had participated in a sham marriage with his young girlfriend and declared he had no intention of ever seeing his new spouse again.

These days we hear of illegal immigrants taking part in such arrangements in order to remain in this country. However, Harrison's motivation was to provide his 22-year-old girlfriend with "marriage lines" – a piece of paper that would obviate her shame and legitimise both her and their illegitimate child.

After getting Elizabeth Holden pregnant Harrison thought he was doing the decent thing by going through a marriage ceremony with her. But he was trying to convert illegitimacy into a legitimate state by illegitimate means – and the law was not too happy about that!

Just whether Harrison's intent had genuinely been not to see his new wife again, I cannot say. But he did continue to see Elizabeth at her home at the Washington beerhouse in Lowe Street. That led to his real wife Margaret learning of her husband's liaisons.

As a result Margaret went to the pub to have it out with Elizabeth. A row occurred which led to a summons being served on the young woman. However, when the court case took place, Elizabeth foolishly produced her marriage certificate to show she'd been summoned in the wrong name. That got her off on a technicality but set the ball rolling on the far more serious charge of bigamy.

My first report comes from the St Helens Examiner of May 31st 1879 and concerns another court hearing in which Harrison attempted to get out of the deep hole he had dug for himself by claiming his original wedding ceremony might not have been legal:

> At the Liverpool Police Court, on Tuesday, before Mr. Raffles, William Harrison, of St Helens, was brought up on remand, from the previous Tuesday, charged with having, on the 21st of June 1878, feloniously married Elizabeth Holden, his wife, Margaret Harrison (to whom he was married at St. Mary's Roman Catholic Church, St. Helens, on April 22nd, 1866) being then alive. The prisoner is landlord of the Turk's Head Beerhouse, Morley-street, St. Helens, and the young woman Elizabeth Holden, is daughter of Mrs. Holden, of the Washington beerhouse [Lowe Street], St. Helens. Mr. Cleaver, barrister (instructed by Messrs. Cleaver and Holden), appeared to prosecute; and Mr. Riley, of St. Helens, defended the prisoner.
>
> Detective Strettle said he apprehended the prisoner on the 19th inst. The prisoner said the first marriage was illegal, as the askings had not been put up at Rainford, where he then resided. He also said that he was persuaded into the second marriage by Miss Holden's mother, to save her daughter

from shame. Theresa Shanahan, living at the Turk's Head, St. Helens, said that she was present at the marriage of her sister, Margaret Shanahan, with the prisoner, on the 22nd of April, 1866, and that person was still alive. The prisoner had been living with his wife up to the time of his arrest. Elizabeth Holden, residing at 28, Lowe-street, St. Helens, stated that she went through a ceremony of marriage with the prisoner, in the name of William Allen, at the registrar's office, Clayton-square, Liverpool, on the 21st of June, 1878. He had told her that his name was Allen, and not Harrison, but she knew that his name was over the public-house door as William Harrison. At the time of the ceremony she knew that he was the father of six children, but he told her that the woman with whom he was living was not his wife.

Cross-examined:- The prisoner had been in the habit of visiting her mother's house, and he was always known by the name of William Harrison. At the time of the marriage ceremony witness was expecting to be confined, and a child was born on the 16th of August last, of which the prisoner was the father. Witness did not live with the prisoner either before or after the ceremony of marriage. The prisoner gave as a reason for going through the ceremony a desire to save witness from shame. The prisoner was committed for trial at the assizes. Bail was allowed, in two sureties of £25 each; but as the prisoner did not find sureties he remains in custody.

Then on August 9th 1879 under the headline *"A Peculiar Case of Bigamy"*, the Wigan Observer described the hearing that had taken at the Liverpool Assizes:

William Harrison (42), who was described as a publican, pleaded guilty to a charge of having, at Liverpool, on the

21st June, 1878, feloniously married Elizabeth Holden, his former wife being then alive. Mr. Cleaver prosecuted, and Mr. Addison represented the prisoner. Mr. Addison said he desired to make a few remarks on behalf of his client. The facts were as peculiar as those of any case of the kind that had ever come before his lordship. It appeared that the prisoner lived in St. Helens and had a public-house there. He was a man of apparent respectability, and was married to his first wife in 1866. He had known the young woman Holden since her school days, and, owing to misconduct on his part, she became enceinte [pregnant]. It was agreed by them that, in order to hide Holden's shame, they should get married at a registry office in Liverpool, in the name of Allen. That was done, and the girl became possessed of marriage lines, which she could show when her child was born.

After the sham marriage the prisoner returned to live with his first wife, and that led to the present proceedings. One consequence of his conviction for felony now would be that he would have to forfeit his public-house, and would be incapable of ever again holding a licence. His lordship remarked that the state of the law in that respect ought to be altered. Mr. Cleaver said the prisoner had sold all his furniture, and had not left even a bed for his children. His lordship, taking all the circumstances of the case into consideration, thought that a sentence of one month's imprisonment would be sufficient.

That was pretty generous as the average sentence for bigamy was then 6 months. But Harrison was clearly being given a discount for his chivalry to the young woman – although he doesn't appear to have treated his own family very well.

As predicted William Harrison lost the licence to run the Turks Head but the magistrates agreed to transfer it to his wife Margaret.

She wanted nothing more to do with her deceitful husband and in December 1879 took William to court. Since his release from prison Harrison had pestered Margaret to take him back and had issued threats. The court bound him over to keep the peace for twelve months, with Harrison having to find £50 and two persons prepared to pay sureties of £25 to guarantee his good behaviour.

As regards Elizabeth Holden, the 1881 census shows the then 24-year-old still living in Lowe Street at her mother's beerhouse. However, it appears that Elizabeth's 3-year-old child Minnie is being brought up as her sister. But her mother Sarah Holden was 57 and it seems unlikely that such pretence could have been maintained for long – especially as the landlady also had another "daughter" listed on the census in 10-month-old Matilda!

3) THE CERTIFICATE OF FREEDOM

My third example bears a similarity with the Betsy Wardle case – although the bigamy does not involve any women being sold for a tanner! But a deal was again done with a piece of paper facilitating the transfer of affections. The arrangement was once more based on the belief that if the first husband gave his permission for the second marriage, then bigamy was not being committed.

During and immediately after WW1 prosecutions for bigamy went through the roof. The saying "absence makes the heart grow fonder" certainly did not apply to all couples. Lonely soldiers' wives leading dull lives back home would have relationships with men who had not gone to war. And married soldiers a long way from home took up with other women and after making them pregnant felt compelled to marry them.

Bigamy was so widespread that at Liverpool Assizes in July 1919 more than a third of the cases heard involved bigamous weddings. The presiding judge, Justice Salter, declared that the crime was "shockingly prevalent" and "very cruel" to women. David Mitchell from Fishpond Cottage in Rainhill was one of the men that the judge harshly sentenced, committing him to prison for twelve months after bigamously marrying a young Thatto Heath woman.

> # REMARKABLE BIGAMY CHARGE.
>
> ## YOUNG ST. HELENS COUPLE INVOLVED.
>
> ## A WIFE'S "CERTIFICATE OF FREEDOM."
>
> ## DISABLED SOLDIER'S STORY.

Headlines in the St Helens Reporter of December 22nd 1922

But although males were responsible for most of the offences, women committed bigamy as well during the war and Mary Latham's crime was unusual. The 24-year-old believed she possessed a "certificate of freedom" that entitled her to wed for a second time without bothering with a divorce – which was now a little easier and less expensive to obtain than it had been in Betsy Wardle's day.

Mary appeared in the dock in St Helens Police Court on December 19th 1922 to face the charge of bigamy, alongside William Atkinson who was charged with aiding and abetting. The pair had been living together as man and wife in Woodville Street, off Shaw Street, in St Helens after going through a marriage ceremony at Prescot Church.

Atkinson denied having known that his "wife" was already married. However, Chief Inspector Roe had witnesses to prove that he had been informed on three separate occasions that Mary had a husband. He was Edward Latham and was the first to give evidence in court. Described as a "disabled soldier", the 28-year-old said he'd married Mary at St Thomas Church in Westfield

Street in St Helens in January 1916. Edward explained how he had joined the army three months later and his 18-year-old wife had moved in with her mother at her home in Doulton Street.

Whenever he was on leave Edward said he had lived with his wife and he insisted that the couple's relationship during those times had been a happy one. The last time he had seen Mary had been in early November 1917. However, letters that he subsequently mailed to her from France went unanswered. That was until September 1918 when Mary wrote that she'd given birth to a child.

As he had not seen his wife for ten months and two days, Edward told the court that he knew the child could not possibly be his. Upon being discharged from his military service, Edward went to live at his parents' home on Burrows Lane in Gillars Green. Sometime later he explained that he had received a letter from his wife inviting him to go and see her.

At the meeting Mary had asked him if he objected to her getting married again – as she felt she had a chance of happiness with William Atkinson. Edward told her that he had no objection and agreed to compose a letter putting his consent in writing. That was the "certificate of freedom" that Mary made much of in court – but which, of course, counted for nothing.

Margaret Powell was the mother of Mary Latham and she told the hearing that when William Atkinson came calling at her house she'd said to him:

> What do you want coming after my daughter for? You know she is married. You cannot have her.

Mrs Powell added that upon learning that her daughter was pregnant, she had ordered her to leave her home. And a brother of Mary gave evidence of asking Atkinson if he knew his sister was married. He said the man had replied that he did know and would stand by Mary and take care of her and their child. In cross-examination the brother admitted that both he and Atkinson had been a "little bit wild" during their conversation.

The hearing was also told how upon her arrest by the police Mary Latham had said:

> I would not have done it, only my husband, Edward Latham, told me he did not mind so long as I was happy. He gave me a letter giving me my freedom, and said he would never interfere. I knew my husband was alive, and Atkinson, whom I have since married, always made me happy.

The St Helens Reporter in their very lengthy account of the case added the following:

> The accused woman, Latham, asked by the Court if she had anything to say, referred to the certificate she had had from her husband giving her freedom, and said in view of that she thought she was free to marry again.

Mary Latham and William Atkinson were committed for trial at the Assizes but granted bail and on January 30th they were both sentenced to 14 days in prison. A very substantial discount was granted to Mary for her ignorance in believing she possessed a certificate of freedom.

And Atkinson – a glass blower at the Sherdley works of UGB – appears to have kept to his word to stand by Mary and take care of both her and their child. Not long after the court hearing Edward Latham obtained a divorce from his wife, which allowed William and Mary to re-marry.

When the marriage ceremony took place in 1925, the couple joined a very small number of persons that had bigamously wed and then subsequently made their marriage legal.

4) WHO IS SHE? A WOMAN'S CURIOUS PREDICAMENT

Before 1870 any money or assets that a married woman made or inherited legally belonged to her husband. That year the Married Women's Property Act allowed wives to own any personal income that they received and property that they inherited.

However, the legislation only went so far and a case heard in the St Helens Petty Sessions in 1879 revealed that a married woman's husband still owned her character. That meant that even if the couple was separated, the husband could publicly denigrate his wife and she could not sue him for slander.

In fact a wife's legal options were then quite limited. That was made clear in another case when a bigamous marriage was mentioned in passing. On April 1st 1873 a woman called Thompson sued a man named Gaskell in the St Helens County Court. Mrs Thompson told the judge that she had been employed by Gaskell as a domestic servant at 2s 6d a week. A paltry wage, although her keep would likely have been included.

Mrs Thompson said she had left the man's house after 23 weeks because Gaskell had wanted to marry her and she'd refused his offer. The woman claimed that her former employer owed her £1 16 shillings in back wages – but the questioning of her by the defendant's counsel brought out some extraordinary facts.

The woman admitted having had three husbands. Her first had been a man named Ward who had "disappeared"; the second called Thompson had died and the third husband named Sefton was alive and living with her.

This St Helens Newspaper in its report said: "The question then arose in court – who is she?" That was not so much an enquiry as to her name but as to her legal identity and rights. The judge said the woman must be the wife of either the first or the third husband, depending upon whether her initial spouse called Ward was still living. Further questioning elicited the information that Ward had been alive nine years before the hearing and had apparently re-married.

That meant both Mr Ward and Mrs Thompson *(aka Mrs Sefton)* had knowingly entered into bigamous marriages after parting. *"A Curious Predicament"* was the headline to the Newspaper's report on the proceedings. But there was no predicament for the judge.

Whether the first husband was still alive or not was irrelevant to the woman's claim for £1 16 shillings back wages. Whoever she was legally married to did not matter to Judge Yates. The fact was that she *was* married — and a married woman, he ruled, could not sue in her own name. So the case was nonsuited and dismissed.

The Public Hanging of A St Helens Painter – And The Death Of A Waterloo Hero

"It seemed as if every brothel, stew, and den of vagabonds had sent forth its inmates ... thousands hurrying forward in high glee, to see two human beings hanged by the neck."

This chapter describes the contrasting lives of two St Helens men with very similar surnames who lived during the first half of the 19th century. One called Buckley was a wife-killer who was hung in public to the glee of thousands of onlookers. The other named Bickley was a war hero who had a remarkable record of military service for his country – including being at Waterloo in 1815.

THE HANGING OF WILMOT BUCKLEY

In 1843 up to 30,000 people were drawn to Liverpool to witness a ghoulish event. The "gaping multitude" – as described by one newspaper – had travelled to Kirkdale Gaol on May 6th 1843 to watch a double execution take place. The high-noon hanging was of a Bolton woman who'd confessed to murdering her stepson and of a St Helens man convicted of killing his pregnant wife.

Wilton Buckley's public demise had not been expected. The jury at his trial felt the circumstances of the murder merited the commuting of his death sentence. The young painter's spur of the moment action in cutting his wife's throat had been completely out of character, occurring shortly after he had attended church.

Buckley and his wife Elizabeth had been living in two rented rooms in Mount Street in Greenbank, near Liverpool Road in St Helens. On the fatal evening the couple had been for one of their regular walks and had called for a glass of rum at the Bird i' th' Hand Inn in what many then called Combshop Brow. That was the last time Elizabeth was seen alive. Ninety minutes after leaving the inn her body was found in a nearby field. There were not yet any St Helens newspapers available to record the events of November 27th 1842. However, other papers covered the murder in great detail, including the Manchester Courier, who wrote:

> The excitement produced by this fearful event is very great in the neighbourhood of St. Helens, and hundreds have not only thronged the place where the body lies, but as many have applied at the police-station for permission to see the suspected criminal. The occurrence of this murder, which has caused so great a sensation in the district of St. Helen's, will now gradually decrease in its terror, by the termination of proceedings which have brought home to the husband the guilt of murdering his own wife in a most appalling manner.

The place where Elizabeth's body lay was a stable attached to the Eccleston Arms where her inquest was held. Wilton Buckley initially denied involvement in his wife's death, claiming they'd become separated and he'd assumed she'd gone to her mother's. Even the painter's blood-soaked shirtsleeves were passed of as paint – but no one was fooled and Buckley eventually admitted his guilt.

HORRID MURDER AT ST. HELEN'S, AND CONFESSION OF GUILT BY THE HUSBAND.

It is our melancholy duty to record the circumstances of a most atrocious and cold-blooded murder, which was committed on Sunday evening in the neighbourhood of St. Helen's. The victim is a young married female, of very respectable connections, and the wife of a painter named Wilmot Buckley, who has lately been employed by Mr. A. T. Woods, of St. Helen's. The tragedy is aggravated by suspicion which at present attaches to the husband of the murdered woman.

So far as we have been able to collect the circumstances attendant upon this shocking event, it appears that on Sunday afternoon the husband of the deceased went to church, and afterwards, about five o'clock in the evening, took his wife along with him for a walk. The direction they took from the town was up the Liverpool road; and about seven o'clock in the evening they called at a public-house in Eccleston, and on the Liverpool highway, where they each had a glass of rum. Nothing more was seen of them in company, but about eight o'clock in the evening the husband, whose name is Wilmot Buckley, went to the house at which he had been lodging, and inquired for his wife, stating that when at the top of Comb-Shop Brow, nearly half a mile from St. Helen's, he left his wife for a few minutes, and when he returned where he

Manchester Courier December 3rd 1842

The young man said the crime had occurred after he'd mentioned to Elizabeth in passing how when recently visiting Wigan, he had bumped into an old flame. Buckley said his wife was enraged that he'd spoken to the woman, an argument had ensued and in the heat of the moment he had stabbed her. The Cork Examiner wrote:

It was evidently the impulse of a frantic moment, done in the heat of violent and ungovernable passion, and produced by the tantalizing upbraidings of his wife, who was jealous of her husband, and viewed his attentions to other females with distrust.

THE ALBION.

EXECUTION OF WILMOT BUCKLEY AND BETTY ECCLES, FOR MURDER.

Liverpool was, on Saturday last, between the midday hours of eleven and one, a purer and more virtuous community than usual, for there was, throughout the whole morning, but particularly during the hour before noon, an efflux of its scum, its offal, and abomination towards the scaffold erected at Kirkdale Gaol for the execution of Wilmot Buckley and Betty Eccles, condemned to death for murder. It had been known, for some time past, that Saturday, the 6th day of May, at twelve o'clock, was the time fixed for these unfortunate mortals to pay the last fearful penalty of their crimes. Many eager individuals, however, believed not the announcement, but conceived that they were to be cheated out of the anticipated gratification of witnessing the violent death of two fellow-creatures; and some wretches, with more than an ordinary ap-

The Liverpool Albion from Monday May 8th 1843

Despite the trial jury's plea for mercy, the hanging of Wilton Buckley – and the Bolton murderer Betty Eccles – went ahead on May 6th 1843 from a scaffold outside Kirkdale prison. The Liverpool Albion newspaper was scathing of those that went to watch the gruesome deed take place with some of those in attendance having travelled from St Helens. The newspaper wrote:

Liverpool was, on Saturday last, between the midday hours of eleven and one, a purer and more virtuous community than usual, for there was, throughout the whole morning, but particularly during the hour before noon, an efflux of its scum, its offal, and abomination towards the scaffold erected at Kirkdale Gaol for the execution of Wilmot Buckley and

Betty Eccles, condemned to death for murder. It had been known, for some time past, that Saturday, the 6th day of May, at twelve o'clock, was the time fixed for these unfortunate mortals to pay the last fearful penalty of their crimes. Many eager individuals, however, believed not the announcement, but conceived that they were to be cheated out of the anticipated gratification of witnessing the violent death of two fellow-creatures; and some wretches, with more than an ordinary appetite for disgusting exhibitions, have almost constantly bivouacked on the ground.

Several times crowds have assembled opposite that portion of the gaol where executions usually take place, the anxious expectants having been hoaxed or otherwise led into the belief that the criminals were then to suffer. On one occasion, when an unruly mob was present, the people were repeatedly informed that they were mistaken, as no execution would take place that day. They refused to be convinced, and remained perseveringly gazing at the closed aperture whence they looked for the unfortunates to emerge. A gentleman who saw them, losing all patience at their display of depraved curiosity, exclaimed, "You wretches! I wish I had the power of hanging one of you for the gratification of the rest!" This brutal appetite, which seems so strongly to pervade the worst classes, was most strikingly exemplified on Saturday. From eleven o'clock, the roads leading to the gaol were crowded with people, chiefly of the most dissolute orders.

Carts, cars, and coaches bore their loads of individuals, male and female, scoffing, swearing, laughing, shouting, and bandying ribbald jests with those on foot, the chief theme of discourse being the approaching scene of death, intended by the law less as a punishment to the criminals than as a solemn warning and example to the survivors. It is impossible to convey to those who did not witness it an adequate idea of the disgusting effect of such a scene. It seemed as if every brothel, stew, and den of vagabonds in the town had sent forth its inmates; and there they were in, we are sorry to say, thousands, hurrying forward, in high glee, to see two human beings hanged by the neck. It must not be supposed that the entirety of the crowd was made up of the vile classes we have mentioned. There were hundreds of labourers and workmen present, and a few decent-looking young women, whom we were sorry to see present at such a scene and in such company. Many parties of people had come from the country, and we are assured that individuals had journeyed many miles, amongst whom were not a few from Bolton and St. Helens, to be present at the scene.

THE DEATH OF A WATERLOO HERO

In a case heard in St Helens County Court in 1869 a witness claimed to be an old Waterloo hero. However, upon being questioned by the puzzled judge – no doubt thinking he was too young to have fought in the famous battle – the man admitted he was referring to Waterloo near Crosby and not in Belgium! The judge said it was a very good joke but warned him not to repeat it as he could be accused of making a false pretence.

William Bickley was a real Waterloo hero and on January 23rd 1875, the newspaper known as the South London Press published this short piece about his demise at the age of 96:

> On Sunday week there was interred at St. Thomas's Cemetery, St. Helens, a man named William Bickley, who had reached the almost patriarchal age of 96. Bickley had helped to dig the grave of Sir John Moore at the battle of

Corunna, had followed Wellington all through the Peninsula, and fought under him at Waterloo. Many others were cut off at an early age, but Bickley braved shot, shell, and disease for nearly a century. This story and his medals are to be seen on his gravestone.

Bickley had spent the last forty-five or so years of his life living in St Helens and a far more detailed account of his exciting military background was published by the St Helens Newspaper under the headline *"Death of Waterloo Veteran At St. Helens"*:

On Sunday week the grave closed over the remain of William Bickley, well known in St Helens and district as one of the few remaining heroes who fought for their country during the long continuous Peninsular Wars, and also at the memorable conflict on the plains of Waterloo. The deceased for the last nine or ten years, has resided at Sutton Lodge, but his previous history was a most eventful and remarkable one. Whilst a young man he enlisted as a soldier, his object, being to evade some legal process about to be served upon him. As a natural consequence he gave both an assumed name and false age, so that though he is officially recorded as being 92 years of age he was in reality turned 97.

Shortly after he enlisted he was sent with his regiment, the 10th Light Dragoons, out to Spain, and took part there under Sir John Moore, at the battle of Corunna, where he received a severe sabre wound on his left hand. On returning to England his regiment was quartered at Hampton Court, and he and a number of his comrades having taken umbrage at the quality of the bread served out to them, stuck a loaf on one of the spikes of the gates so as to attract the attention of the Duke of York, when he made his official visit. The affair caused considerable notoriety at the time, and in order to avoid the severe punishment likely to follow such an offence, he and five other ringleaders in the demonstration already alluded to, deserted, and entered on board a man of war at Portsmouth. He and one of his companions were found out as deserters, and sent to Brighton, where the regiment was then quartered, and where Bickley also underwent a twelve months' sentence of the "log." At that time this sentence was considered a light one, and Bickley was many times heard to exclaim that had it not been that men were much wanted in the army, his punishment would have been much heavier. As it was he got through it, and was next sent out to the Peninsula to join the forces under the command of the Duke of Wellington.

Here he suffered many vicissitudes, the precise dates of which we are unable to give, but it would appear that he was engaged in at least four severe battles, in the second of which he was taken prisoner by the French, but managed to escape them; and after suffering severe hardships whilst struggling to get to the English lines he accidentally met with Sir William Bentinck. He still continued through the campaign, and was wounded in two subsequent engagements, namely at Corunna, where he had his left hand nearly cut off, and at Vittoria, where he received another severe sabre wound on his left breast. He was also engaged at Waterloo, where he got a most severe wound, a grape shot having exploded just behind his head, taking off a portion of his left cheek and ear, his horse at the same time being killed under him.

He was invalided home, and awarded 3s 6d per week pension, and although the old soldier often complained of the smallness of the amount, he sometimes admitted that had it not been for the "Hampton Court affair" it would have [been] larger. As to this being firmly impressed on his mind may be gathered from the fact that even ten or twelve years since he caused the following epitaph to be written, and which at his request will be placed over his grave:-

> "To the memory of William Bickley, who was out with General Moore, and through the Peninsula, with Wellington also at Waterloo, belonging to the 10th Light Dragoons, and has received 6d per day pension for his services, during fifteen years and nine months. The body and bones of this old warrior lies here, and hopes to meet with a better reward in the next world."

To resume our narrative we may remark that after leaving the army he worked at Cheadle, in Staffordshire, as a copper smelter, and came to St. Helens when the Ravenhead Copper Works were established in 1830, and he continued to work there until about ten years since, when he was pensioned off on account of his age and infirmity. We are happy to state with the combined pension afforded him by the Ravenhead Copper Works Company and the Horse Guards – the former largely predominating – the brave old hero was in moderately good circumstances in his declining age. On the morning of the 15th instant he quietly passed away, in his cottage at Sutton Lodge, and on the following Sunday his remains were interred in St. Thomas's Cemetery, Eccleston. To his last moments he had a martial ambition, his last wish being that he should have a military funeral, but this it appears could not be complied with. We should state that for his services in the Peninsula and at Waterloo, he was awarded two silver medals, the former with two clasps, and these he was very proud of wearing on great occasions, especially when he went to draw his quarterly pension.

The Women Who Accused Their Husbands Of Persistent Cruelty

"Last Friday he thrashed me, smashed a rocking chair to pieces and said he had a good mind to batter my brains out with one of the rockers."

INTRODUCTION

During the late 19th and early 20th centuries it was common for husbands to be charged with persistent cruelty to their wives. The hearing in St Helens Police Court usually involved the husband and wife trading allegations against another – with women often detailing shocking acts of violence. And the public lapped up every prurient detail that the newspaper reports revealed as the hearings poked into hidden corners of a couple's marriage.

One might expect that the outcome for the defendant if found guilty would be a prison sentence, heavy fine or being bound over to be of good behaviour upon payment of sureties. But these were not really criminal charges, despite the hearing being held in the Police Court. The magistrates that heard such cases were in reality considering an application for a separation order.

Not that couples needed permission from the authorities to go their own way. But a separation order came with legally enforceable maintenance payments. And so if the man failed to pay the weekly amounts to his wife, he could expect to be hauled back into court and ultimately might be sent to prison for not complying with a court order.

Such cases do provide insights into what life what like at that time – particularly with regard to the strict demarcation of male and female jobs. When a man married he acquired a cook, housekeeper and mother for his children. For most husbands earning a living was their sole responsibility – virtually every other task was his wife's to perform. For him to be asked to undertake any cooking, shopping, washing or cleaning or look after the kids was anathema to his manhood.

Charles Forman's book *'Industrial Town - Self Portrait of St Helens in the 1920s'* is a collection of oral histories made during the 1970s. The author quotes an unnamed woman born during WW1 who reflected on what husbands were like in between the wars:

> Men were tyrants in the old days. There was an awful lot of wifebeating and the women were the underdogs....The men were horrible. I think the men today are much better – you'd never see a man go shopping, and I never saw a man in a chip shop till after I got married....Mothers could do all the baking and cleaning and cooking, and just have time to go out with a clean pinny on in the evening to sit on chairs in the street and jangle. That was their whole life. They couldn't get ready to go out – there was no social life.

Most men would contest their wife's claim of persistent cruelty – for one thing they did not want to lose their cook, housewife etc. And if they had no choice in the matter, they did not want to have to make payments to their wife but not derive any personal benefit.

Often the husband's mitigation in court for striking his wife involved "offences" that would sound ridiculous in a modern-day court – such as the man's dinner not being on the table when he arrived home from work. Or talking back to him during a row. And a certain amount of violence against the wife was considered acceptable by the authorities.

In one persistent cruelty case in St Helens in May 1903 a woman claimed to have been beaten by her husband on her wedding day and then a few weeks later dragged down the stairs by her hair. Defence solicitor Jeremiah Haslam Fox argued that there were "certain occasions and circumstances in which a man was justified in chastising his wife". Fox also complained that the woman had only detailed three violent acts against her, which, he reckoned, did not qualify as persistent cruelty.

And so the magistrates did not automatically grant such orders. They needed convincing that the split in the marriage was irreparable and would quite often refuse the application as they prioritised the saving of marriages over the safety of women. This chapter is devoted to a number of examples of such cases:

THE RAINHILL QUARRYMAN'S BRUTALITY

On March 18th 1902 in Prescot Police Court, Bridget Coyle of Holt Lane in Rainhill charged her husband John with persistent cruelty – and a dreadful story of abuse was told. Bridget said on the previous Wednesday night her husband had come home and – according to the St Helens Newspaper's account of the proceedings – had then:

A RAINHILL QUARRYMAN'S ALLEGED PERSISTENT CRUELTY

On Tuesday, at Prescot Police Court, before Alderman J. Beecham and Mr. T. Dennett, a Rainhill quarryman named John Coyle, was charged with persistent cruelty to his wife, who stated that on Wednesday night he came in and commenced thrashing her, took her by the hair of the head, and knocked her head against the wall. She had to run out as he said he would finish her. They had been married eleven years, and this was the fourth time she had had to leave him, and every time she had left him he had beaten her black and blue.—Defendant said his wife took up a chair and threw it at him. She then went out and he had not seen her since.

St Helens Newspaper March 21st 1902

> ...commenced thrashing her, took her by the hair of the head, and knocked her head against the wall. She had to run out as he said he would finish her.

The 29-year-old added that she and her husband had been married eleven years and this had been the fourth time she'd been forced to leave him. "Every time I have left him it was because he has beaten me black and blue", Bridget explained to the Bench.

John Coyle was a labourer in a stone quarry and told the court that his wife had thrown a chair at him before walking out. The 31-year-old insisted that Bridget had as good a home as any working man's wife would want and claimed: "She does not want a home; she wants her fling."

Throwing the chair at her husband as she fled from his violence is understandable – but the act was used against Bridget as evidence of her own unreasonable behaviour. The magistrates ruled that there were faults on both sides and said the couple should try to live together peacefully.

And so Bridget's request for a separation order and maintenance payments for herself and her 5-year-old daughter Gertrude was denied and the magistrates effectively sent an abused wife back to live with her brutal husband.

RETURN TO YOUR HUSBAND AND BE A GOOD WIFE

Then on May 8th 1903 the wife of Owen Jones of Parr Stocks Road in St Helens unsuccessfully sought a separation order after accusing her husband of being jealous and "always thrashing me". It sounds like the man gave a good account of himself in court.

He was reported as having emphatically denied his wife's allegations and Mrs Jones had to admit that her husband did hand over to her his weekly wages – as most husbands in St Helens then did, receiving pocket money for drink, tobacco etc. in return.

And so Owen Jones was seen as doing his bit in providing for his family and impressed the Bench by saying he was ready to take his wife back, adding: "I am quite willing to do anything I can – even go teetotal".

The Police Court Missionary (social worker) said he had tried to get the couple back together but the woman had positively refused to return home. And so Mrs Jones was painted as the unreasonable person in the marriage and the Bench dismissed her application for a separation order, telling her to "go back to your husband and be a good wife". Upon hearing those remarks Mrs Jones left the court declaring she would never return to her husband.

But the magistrates could also lecture husbands too. On May 15th 1903 Alice Forrest of Wilson Street in St Helens *(near Boundary Road)* summoned her husband James on a charge of persistent cruelty. The 1901 census shows the couple were then in their mid-30s and had seven children aged between two and fifteen.

In court Mrs Forrest stated that she had been married 17 years but her glassmaker husband did not give her enough cash from his wages and last week he had hit her. However, upon being questioned Alice had to admit that the assault had been the first she had experienced in two years. That placed a question mark over whether the cruelty had passed the persistency threshold.

But Mrs Forrest had an ace up her sleeve. She produced some letters, which suggested that her husband had been having an affair with another woman. The Bench decided to adjourn the case for a month to see if the couple could be reconciled, telling James Forrest to "treat your wife as a wife ought to be treated. If there is any truth in the letters produced you ought to be ashamed of yourself".

PERSISTENT CRUELTY FROM A PIGEON DEALER

On July 7th 1902 Ada Range from Naylor Street in St Helens brought a charge of persistent cruelty against her husband John. Previously Mrs Range had taken out a summons against her spouse in which she'd accused him of desertion.

However, he had claimed that he'd walked out because of his wife's adultery with another man. That was something Ada strongly denied and it was common for men accused of wrongdoing in their marriage to fabricate or exaggerate stories about their wife. Upon appearing again in St Helens Police Court, Mrs Range explained that she had been married for eight years with her husband having been a widower.

The 36-year-old told the Bench that John's treatment of her had been very bad. She said he had struck her several times, put her outside their house and also made a false allegation of her stealing a sovereign. The Bench asked John Range if he was prepared to take his wife back and not make such claims of stealing in future. "She will not get the chance again", was his retort.

Despite the beatings the woman had received, the court was not prepared to grant a separation order and instead adjourned the hearing for five weeks "to enable the parties to come together again", as it was reported. The newspapers only occasionally followed up on such cases. However, in the vast majority of them pragmatism set in and battered wives felt obliged to return to their abuser – mainly for financial reasons.

That is clearly what happened in this case. Although I can find no further report concerning the marital affairs of the Ranges, they were back together again by October 1902. Then Mrs Range gave court evidence against a man for stealing a pigeon.

Although John Range is listed in the 1901 census as a Corporation labourer, he also kept a bird shop at his house near the Wellington Hotel. That would have been another reason why Range would have wanted his wife home despite his court bravado. Not only did she do his cooking, cleaning and seeing to his sons – but she'd have been a valuable asset in looking after his bird shop for free.

THE HUSBAND THAT COMPLAINED HIS WIFE WOULD NOT CLEAN HIS BOOTS

The St Helens magistrates were even less reluctant to grant a separation order if a recently married young couple appeared before them. They needed some persuading that the woman would be in danger of being badly hurt by her husband if she returned to the marital home. At the outset of a separation order application on August 1st 1902 the Bench made it clear that they felt Matthew and Henrietta Davison should be reconciled. That was after hearing that the couple from Manning Street, off Borough Road, in St Helens were in their early 20s and had only wed two years before. But their minds were changed after being told of the catalogue of abuse that had been inflicted on Henrietta by her jealous husband.

Mrs Davison gave the Bench several examples of the many violent acts that she had endured. On one occasion Matthew had "thrashed" her in bed and attempted to strap her down. Another time he had dragged her across the kitchen and thrown Henrietta violently on to the stairs. On a third occasion after half-killing his wife, he had gone out remarking that he hoped when he came back to find her dead. Henrietta added:

> Last Friday he thrashed me, smashed a rocking chair to pieces and said he had a good mind to batter my brains out with one of the rockers.

Most of the abuse was through Davison believing his wife had been flirting with other men. In giving evidence the husband admitted that some of what his wife had alleged was true but he denied that he had ever severely thrashed her and claimed Hettie was often "cheeky" to him.

But his biggest mistake was to complain how once his wife had not cleaned his boots. To that the Chairman said: "Why don't you clean your own boots?" Unimpressed with Davidson's ridiculous excuses for beating his wife, the magistrates granted the separation order and allowed maintenance payments of 6 shillings a week.

SPEAK IF YOU DARE AND I'LL KILL YOU

Like Matthew Davison, James Matthews from Eccleston Street in St Helens blamed his spouse for his wife beating and downgraded the severity of his brutal assaults. Appearing in St Helens Police

Court on July 24th 1903, Matthews said he had only "touched" his wife because of the bad language she had used towards him.

However, Mrs Matthews provided the Bench with a long list of assaults that her husband had committed. Four months earlier he had fractured a bone in her eye, leaving her with a permanent black eye and he'd recently tried to break her leg.

She claimed that he had also taken her by the throat, saying: "Speak if you dare and I'll kill you". Up until recently Mrs Matthews said she had £50 saved in the bank through selling pigs but her husband had gambled it all away on the horses.

Asked by the Magistrates Clerk if over indulgence in alcohol was behind her husband's assaults, Mrs Matthews said no, before adding: "It is just the same, breakfast, dinner and tea time. He has left me black and blue many a time". The Bench granted a separation with an order of 7 shillings a week.

BLAME THE MOTHER-IN-LAW

Upon Elizabeth Houghton explaining that she had summoned her brutal husband to St Helens Police Court on a persistent cruelty charge after only 16 months of marriage, the surprised magistrates' clerk, Bertram Brewis, said to the woman: "Do you mean to say you want to be separated all your life?"

The hearing on November 6th 1903 was told that Arthur Houghton's beatings had begun three months after the couple's wedding. Elizabeth said the final straw had been earlier that week after her husband had knocked her down after coming home early and finding his tea not ready. She also alleged that the 26-year-old had once taken a knife to her.

As well as not resisting their violent husband or taking the odd drink, it was also important for female victims of domestic violence to come across as meek and mild in court. It appears that Mrs Houghton put on too brave a face when giving her testimony.

Henry Riley was the husband's defence counsel and he told the Bench:

> It is not enough in proving persistent cruelty to say that a man in a moment of temper called his wife ugly names or boxed her ears. The cruelty must be deliberate and malicious. With regard to the complainant's manner in the box I think the defendant would have to be a brave man to dare to be cruel to her.

Riley argued that the real problem with the young couple's marriage was that their residence in Grafton Street in St Helens was too near the home of the wife's mother. The pair's problems, he reckoned, would go away if they moved away. Or as Arthur Houghton put it when giving evidence, his wife simply refused to "flit" from her mother.

Brutal husbands often claimed that interfering mother-in-laws were responsible for their marital difficulties – although parents could hardly be blamed for wanting to protect their abused daughter. Upon being pressed by the Bench, Elizabeth said that if her husband world "sign teetotal and stop backing horses" they might possibly be able to get on.

She then addressed her husband, saying: "You said you would make me stand my corners if you could get me away from my mother's". To that the Clerk enquired what stand my corners meant. "It means he will thrash me", came the reply. Upon hearing the husband's denials and counterclaims, the Chairman of the Bench said:

> We are inclined to think there has been faults on both sides. It is a great pity that so young a couple should want to separate, and so we will adjourn the case for a month to see if with the assistance of the Police Court Missionary, you can make up your differences. In the meantime the defendant must get another house.

At that point the Clerk told Mrs Houghton: "If you do not go with him you will get no benefit here". And so the woman was being forced to move away from her mother's neighbourhood. If she did not leave there would be no possibility of a separation order and maintenance payment in the future if things did not work out.

THE INFERNAL BLACKGUARD THAT ATTEMPTED TO GAS HIS WIFE

On May 1st 1916 Frederick Milsop of Park Road in St Helens appeared in court after threatening his wife with a razor while drunk. "It was all a cod", he told the magistrates, "I did it to frighten the missus". And I expect he succeeded too! What his motivation had been to put the fear of God up Mrs Milsop was not reported – unlike that of Robert Critchley three weeks later.

The bricklayer from Victoria Terrace in Rainhill appeared in St Helens Police Court on May 26th 1916 charged with

> **GASSING A WIFE.**
>
> **HUSBAND'S REMARKABLE ADMISSION.**
>
> At the Police Court, on Friday, when the magistrates on the Bench were Col. McTear (in the chair), Sir David Gamble, Bart., Dr. Dowling, and Mr. F. Dromgoole, a case in which some remarkable admissions were made by a husband was heard. A bricksetter named Robert Critchley, of Victoria-terrace, Rainhill, was summoned on a charge of persistent cruelty to his wife, Maud E. Critchley, to which he pleaded not guilty.
>
> Mrs. Critchley said they had been married sixteen months. On Thursday week her husband went to work at five o'clock in the morning, and some time afterwards she felt a stifling feeling and got out of bed and opened the door, never dreaming that the gas was on. She thought she would get into bed again until she felt proper, as she was feeling heavy. She got into bed and lay there wondering where the smell of

St Helens Newspaper June 2nd 1916

persistent cruelty to his wife. In fact, as was pointed out in court, the man was fortunate not to have been charged with murder.

Critchley had left for work at 5am after turning on the gas in the couple's bedroom and deliberately shutting the usually open window and door. Some time later his wife Maud woke up with a suffocating feeling and finding the room full of gas.

The man admitted turning on the gas but said he'd only done it to frighten Maud because he had sometimes arrived home from work to find his tea not ready. The Clerk to the court told him: "If the door had been absolutely airtight she would have died and you would have been hanged."

Mrs Critchley explained to the magistrates that they'd only been married sixteen months and her husband had treated her badly. After the gas incident she'd left home and gone to live with her sister and she was now seeking a separation order. The magistrates granted it and ordered Critchley, who was joining the army in three days' time, to pay his wife 12s 6d a week.

Maud Critchley then asked the court whether she could take a bed from her old home so she could be more comfortable at her sister's house. That I expect was badly overcrowded and she was probably sleeping with at least one other person. However, her estranged husband flatly refused to let her have a thing from their home – even though he was about to go into the army.

That rebuff enraged the Court Clerk Bertram Brewis whose job was to advise the magistrates on matters of law and not to state his personal opinion on defendants.

After explaining that the Bench had no power to deal with furniture, the Clerk told Critchley that if he was not prepared to give his separated wife a bed he must pay Maud £1 a week maintenance. To that Critchley replied: "I cannot pay a sovereign a week." The Clerk then responded with this highly unusual outburst:

> You can pay. Any working-man can pay in St. Helens when he is getting £2 and £3 a week. You are an infernal blackguard. I have a good mind to go and fetch it [the bed] and stand the risk myself.

Critchley stubbornly refused to allow his wife to remove a bed from what had been her marital home and so the magistrates signed an order for him to pay Maud £1 a week.

THE BRUTE THAT ATTACKED HIS PREGNANT WIFE

On July 28th 1919 in St Helens Police Court, Annie Mercer brought a charge of persistent cruelty against her husband John – and a shocking tale of domestic abuse was told. The young couple had wed in November 1915 and gone to live in Parr. However, it only took the man three weeks to give his wife a black eye. There was further violence during the following year but then John Mercer went into the army allowing Annie a reprieve.

ALLEGED PERSISTENT CRUELTY.

On a charge of persistent cruelty brought by his wife, Annie Mercer, of Parr, John Henry Mercer, Back Ville-street, Bolton, appeared before Mr. A. R. Pilkington (in the chair), and Councillor J. Heaton, at St. Helens Police Court on Monday.

Mr. Tickle for the complainant, stated that on the 5th July the defendant came home about 11.30 p.m. His wife was suffering from a large abscess in the neck. He immediately commenced to pick a quarrel with her, and knocked her on to the couch, struck her several times about the head and face, breaking a plant-pot and bursting the abscess, causing complainant considerable pain. Furthermore, she was expecting to be

St Helens Newspaper August 1st 1919

But after being demobilised from the forces the husband resumed his assaults on his wife and had even attacked her while she was pregnant. On that occasion he ordered Annie out of their home, despite her being in considerable pain and requiring a doctor.

Mercer told his young wife that he would find some other woman to look after him – which was how many men then saw their wife's role. The other woman turned out to be his mother, as Mercer debunked to his parental home in Bolton – but not before selling their furniture and keeping all the cash for himself.

In spite of the litany of abuse and graphic nature of Annie's claims, the court resorted to its default position of attempting to save the couple's marriage. And John Mercer was another wife-beater that blamed his spouse's family for his marital troubles and said he'd take Annie back if she lived with him in Bolton. The Court Missionary or social worker, John Holmes, also told the Bench that he felt there had been interference from Mercer's in-laws and thought relocation was the answer.

The Church of England funded such missionaries and it was common for Holmes's court evidence to seem biased in the husband's favour. The Church saw separation orders as a precursor to divorce and disapproved of them being easily granted.

There doesn't appear to have been any censure of the man's conduct by the court. It was seen as the product of quarrels that would likely cease if the couple moved away from interfering in-laws. The magistrates decided to adjourn the case for a month to see if the two parties could resolve their differences.

In the minds of the magistrates they were attempting to save a troubled marriage. But to 21st century eyes the authorities were placing pressure on a vulnerable woman to live with a violent man. The notion that all would be sweetness and light by the family relocating to Bolton appears absurd and certainly Annie clearly did not accept that as a solution. Unusually, the St Helens Newspaper described what had occurred at the adjourned court hearing and on August 29th 1919 wrote:

> Mr. Tickle, [solicitor] for the complainant, said the case had been adjourned from a previous court to see if the parties could come to some agreement, but there had been no reconciliation, and there was not likely to be any in this case. They were married three years ago. There had been one child of the marriage, and another was expected shortly. On Saturday, July 5th, defendant went home about half-past eleven at night nearly drunk, and complainant was suffering from a severe abscess in the neck. He commenced to pick a quarrel with her, and struck her several times on the face and neck, and burst the abscess. She suffered severe pain. After that he opened the door and told her to clear out and not return, as he would get someone else to look after him. As soon as she had gone he sold up the house of furniture, realising about £27, out of which he had not contributed anything towards her keep or that of the child. He

understood defendant had "blued" the money in drink. Mrs. Mercer after the assault was assisted to her mother's, and was so distressed that her mother had to sit up with her all night, and next morning a doctor was called in. Mr. Tickle went on to detail other instances of assault, the first three weeks after marriage.

On another occasion he threw a glass of water over her, knocked her about the bedroom floor, broke nearly all the furniture in the room, threw most of it downstairs, and acted like a madman. He said on that occasion that he would hang for her. Since he turned her out on the 5th July he (Mr. Tickle) understood that defendant had gone to live with his parents at Bolton, and had only sent her one sum of 10s. He had been earning about £3 a week. She was afraid to live with him, and emphatically refused to do so, and she asked for an order of separation and maintenance. They formerly lived at 7, Endowment-row, Parr. Complainant went into the box and bore out the above, and in reply to questions by the defendant she said she would not go to live with him at Bolton if he provided a home for her.

The sister and mother of the complainant were also called, the latter stating that they had lived very unhappily together ever since they were married. Defendant informed the Bench that he had a home for her at Bolton, which was his own home. This was all a family affair. He would never do any good in this town [St Helens], and he was not willing to give her anything as long as she was with her people. If she would come out of the town he had provided a home for her, and he would give her every halfpenny he had got. The Bench made an order for 15s. a week, with costs, and two guineas advocate's fee [for his wife's solicitor]. Defendant: "I don't think I will pay it, gentlemen.

It was not uncommon for such men out of bravado to state in court that they would not make the weekly maintenance payments to their separated spouse. Occasionally their stubbornness would lead to a prison sentence but I expect John Mercer eventually agreed to pay.

The 1921 census shows 26-year-old Annie Mercer living with her widowed mother and four siblings in Waterloo Street in St Helens, along with her daughters Annie (aged 3) and Mary (aged 1).

There were a total of ten persons living at the house and so privacy would have been at a premium – but at least the adult Annie and her children now appear safe.

TOO FRIENDLY WITH GIPSIES

There was nothing funny about persistent cruelty cases. They shone a light on some of the worst traits of many wife-beating husbands. But on February 7th 1902 in St Helens Police Court, it must have been hard not to laugh when Joseph and Ann Bonney traded the most ridiculous allegations against each other.

Sometimes the victims of alleged violence placed huge dressings on their heads to exaggerate the effect of the assault. And Joseph Bonney came into court bearing a massive plaster on his bonce. He claimed to be the victim and accused his wife of not only being the violent party in their marriage but of "jangling" too much and being too friendly with gipsies.

It was also common for husbands to claim they earned very little in order to reduce the amount of maintenance that they might have to pay their wife. But Joseph Bonney made the mistake of dressing up in order to show the magistrates how respectable a person he was, with his sartorial elegance also sending the message that he earned more than he claimed.

This is how the St Helens Newspaper of February 11th 1902 described this mixed up case:

Some curious recriminations were indulged in at Friday's Police Court in a husband and wife case, in which Joseph Bonney, Waterloo-street, was summoned for persistent cruelty. Mrs. Bonney said her husband illtreated her, but defendant promptly asserted that it was the other way about. Mrs. Bonney – I admit I hit him on the head with the poker, but it is not as big a mark as he says. He has plaster on nearly as big as his head. Defendant said his wife gave his child's clothes away to a gipsy to get her fortune told. This gipsy was always coming to the house. Complainant – She is only a poor old woman who sells things, and what I gave away myself I had to work hard for. Defendant – She gives the child mustard and laughs when it cries. The Chairman (Mr. Michell) – What did you do that for? Complainant – He did it himself. The child cried for some, and he put some on its tongue; it was his joke. He thrashes the child worse than thrashing a big man.

Defendant said his wife got aggravated, hit him with the poker, and then flew off to her mother's. She told her mother a lot of lies. His house was always dirty, and there was jangling and bother. The gipsies were always in the house. His wife had threatened many a time to take her life, and when eight years old was sent to a school for trying to do it. He earned 17s 4d. a week on the railway. The Chairman – You don't work on the railway for that. The Clerk – You could not have those clothes on if you only got 17s. 4d. a week. Defendant – They are not my clothes. (Laughter.) Mrs. Bonney – He used to "clem" us to keep himself in finery. Defendant – She is dangerous to live with. The Chairman – You should have found that out before you were married. We make an order for 6s. 6d. a week.

SEPARATION FROM A SAINTS STAR

According to Saints Heritage Society, Tom Durkin was a "tough and mobile, no-nonsense second row forward" who played 85 times for the Knowsley Road club between 1912 and 1920. He was also a savage wife beater.

Durkin of Bruce Street in St Helens was summoned to the Police Court on March 5th 1920 charged with persistent cruelty to his wife Sarah. She told the court that they had married in September 1915 and seven months later her husband had given her an "enormous thrashing" for which she had suffered pain for a considerable time afterwards.

Tom Durkin

On a further occasion when on leave from the army, Sarah said Durkin had slashed her across the face with his braces, blackening both of her eyes. He would also push her out of bed and a week prior to the hearing had punched her in the ribs and struck her twice in the face, cutting her lip and giving her another black eye.

As a result of this beating Sarah had run out of the house to get police protection. Tom Durkin showed his contempt for the proceedings by not showing up. However the magistrates granted a separation order and ordered that he pay his wife £2 per week maintenance.

BLAME THE TROUBLESOME CHILDREN

I've described how brutal husbands would often apportion blame on their battered wives, as well as their in-laws. But Frederick Evans of Market Street in St Helens blamed his own children and his wife's inability to control them for his troubles. On March 2nd 1923 Evans was charged in St Helens Police Court with persistent cruelty to his wife, Sarah. The couple had married in 1916 and had four children. Mrs Evans told the Bench that her husband had abused her and threatened to turn her out of their house. On other occasions Frederick had beaten her face black and blue.

Evans insisted to the court that he had not been cruel to his wife but did admit losing his temper once or twice after his wife had called him abusive names. His children he called "very troublesome" and claimed his wife did not look after them properly.

The police, Evans said, had brought their 9-year-old child home at 2 o'clock in the morning whilst their mother had been away at Prescot, leaving him to look after their kids. Sarah had also taken a woman into their house that had come out of prison and he claimed his wife liked anyone who was "criminal like".

By the 1920s such hearings could last an hour or so and the newspaper reports although detailed were little more than summaries. I would have liked to have known if the magistrates had asked Evans why he felt that as the father of four children he did not feel responsible for instilling discipline into them.

And why when he had been left in charge of the kids, did he consider it his wife's fault that their 9-year-old had stayed out till 2am? Whatever was or was not said in court, the magistrates accepted that the couple's relationship had broken down and issued the separation order with Evans ordered to pay his wife 6 shillings a week maintenance. However, the husband was awarded custody of the children with his claims about his wife's associations having seemingly resonated with the Bench.

"YOU ARE NOT FIT TO LIVE WITH"

The combination of pressure from the authorities, financial need and desire to conform to societal norms could lead to some women repeatedly obtaining separation orders from their husbands – but soon be persuaded to return home to give their violent spouse another chance.

In the 1901 census James Tucker was living in Lyon Street in St Helens, along with his wife Jessie and their three young children. When the 29-year-old glassmaker appeared in the Police Court in August 1902, it had been one of many occasions in which he'd faced a persistent cruelty charge. Mrs Tucker told the court about the last time they had lived together:

> As usual he then promised to be different, but in a fortnight he was smashing the things up and turning the children into the street. He has been dreadful; he often would not work, or he could earn 36s. 4d. a week; and every week end he turned us all out into the street. He had sold up four times.

James Tucker attempted to make out that he was the victim, complaining that three women had held him down while a man had hit him. But Mrs Tucker explained to the Bench that the incident had occurred when her neighbours came into her home to stop her husband from attacking her with tongs. The Clerk to the court expressed his feelings to Tucker, declaring: "You are not fit to live with; you are not safe."

NOT FIT TO LIVE WITH.
A WIFE'S SAD STORY.

James Tucker, glassworker, appeared once more in the Police Court, on Friday, on a charge of persistent cruelty to his wife. It was one of many occasions on which he had been up.

Mrs Tucker told a sad story to the Court. She had been married ten years, and in that time had had several separation orders against her husband. This last time she had been living with him less than four months. As usual he then promised to be different, but in a fortnight he was smashing the things up and turning the children into the street. He had been dreadful; he would not work, or he could earn 36s. 4d. a week; and every week end he turned them all out into the street. He had sold up four times.

Defendant complained that three women held him down while a man hit him on the eye.

Mrs Tucker said that was when the neighbours came in to stop him from killing her with the tongs.

The Clerk (to defendant)—You are not fit to live with; you are not safe.

Defendant offered to pay 12s. 6d. a week, and

St Helens Newspaper August 26th 1902

The man offered to pay 12s 6d maintenance a week to his belittled wife, which was accepted. A slightly higher amount than courts usually ordered but still only a third of his weekly wage.

When St Helens Was Only A Village

"A pretty little village, consisting only of a few streets, mostly cottages, occupied by colliers and workers in the glass trade...the surrounding country was beautifully wooded."

INTRODUCTION

Towards the end of the 19th century there were still people alive that remembered St Helens as a village. The old timers could just about recall when the Greenbank district around Liverpool Road was a green bank along the St Helens / Sankey Canal – instead of being jam packed with low-cost housing occupied by mainly poor Irish folk. And when Westfield Street was a field – or at least open space punctuated by a small coal pit.

Just whether the air in St Helens was quite as pure as they remembered, with roses growing round their doors and fish swimming in sparklingly clear streams was another matter! But the environment would certainly have been much better than the heavily polluted air and water of the late 19th century.

And so this chapter is devoted to such recollections of a time before industry developed on a large scale in St Helens and people poured in to work in the factories and coal mines, leading to the creation of homes, schools, churches – and much pollution.

ST HELENS NOW AND THEN

"St. Helens Now And Then" was the headline to this letter published in the St Helens Newspaper on June 19th 1875 that lamented how rural life had been sacrificed for the sake of industry:

> Sir, – There is not in the whole island of Great Britain a town (in proportion with the number of its inhabitants) that has

sprung up with such lightning like velocity (since ye dayes of Catherine Parr) as the "smoky, sooty, begrimed" and "odorous" town of St. Helens. We have no positive proofs as to the founders of this town, but, safely speaking, the King's Head is about the oldest hostelerie in St. Helens. It is not very many years ago since the old stage coach, well appointed and equipped, ran from the Red Lion Inn to Southport, and Liverpool road was one extent of fields and gardens. It was a very easy matter then for some ancient dame to knit from the top of Church street, down to Market street and back, meanwhile leaving her ball of worsted or wool, as the case may be, at home, without fear of the said wool or worsted being broken by either pedestrians or vehicles. What is now Westfield street once contained a coalpit in full working order, and for miles around there could not have been a brighter or clearer trout fishing steam that now foul and polluted body of water vulgarly called Stinking Brook. Greenbank was then really a green-bank.

But in the face of all this, it can be seen that as the wheel of fortune is gradually revolving and depositing traces of its visit here and there amongst us, that in proportion to the "seed that is sown the crop is scarce." In short, we are far ahead in drunkenness, vice, and immorality. Compare our weekly police court list with any other town of the same size, and there is not one which can reach our average. And it appears that the only remedy is this; we require amongst our clergyman less of the "do as I say," and more of the "do as I do," without sensationalism. It is an old proverb that what the master does "so doeth Jack." Let it be amongst the class termed Masters that the example be shown, and all the Jacks will easily follow, and in the course of time, a full harvest can be gathered in. Yours, &c., **ANON.**

A drawing of the Kings Head Inn which was opened in 1629 and demolished in 1879 to make way for the Church Street post office

Another letter appeared in the following week's edition of the Newspaper criticising Anon's letter as inaccurate, stating that Barrow-in-Furness had grown faster in terms of population during the 19th century than St Helens. But the point of Anon's missive was not disputed.

GLIMPSES OF OLD ST HELENS

In 1891 John J. Dutton published a series of articles in the St Helens Lantern newspaper under the title *"Glimpses Of Old St Helens"*. The reminiscences were based on interviews that the author had conducted with some elderly residents.

Lacey's School in North Road

Dutton had been headmaster of the Cowley British School in North Road that locals called "Lacey's", after the longstanding former head Newton Lacey. Higher Grade School and later Central Modern would be built on the same site. In the 1891 census the

53-year-old Dutton is listed as a schoolmaster living in Cowley Hill Lane.

Mr Dutton reckoned that St Helens townsfolk of a hundred or so years before had not been very receptive to strangers. In fact he claimed that it was common for newcomers to be "welcomed" by having a half-brick thrown at them!

But in those 18th and early 19th century days, St Helens was a very rural and different place. An octogenarian friend had told Mr. Dutton that on more than one occasion in his younger days he had travelled through St Helens by coach and found it to be a:

> …pretty little village, consisting only of a few streets, mostly cottages, occupied by colliers and the workers in the glass trade. The surrounding country, however, was beautifully and thickly wooded.

Dutton described in his articles how the town had no lighting until about 1810 when the streets became lit by oil lamp. Usually, he said, only two such lights were located in each street and often were simply swung from the branches of trees. By the time c.1890 that Mr Dutton wrote his reflections on St Helens' past strangers no longer had bricks heaved at them. Although he still felt that newcomers were resented, writing:

> A stranger coming to reside in St. Helens often finds people distant and shy. It has even been said that the natives of St. Helens treat those whose lot is to be thrown amongst them, with something more than mere shyness. I have been told they resent, in manner at any rate, the intrusion of strangers, and more than one occasion can be recorded of people, educated and in good positions, who have for a time been compelled to take up their abode in our town, feeling that their presence upon the side-paths of our streets seemed to give offence to those they met.

This is my edited version of Dutton's remarkable memories, with thanks to St Helens Archive Service for their assistance:

> To a traveller passing through this neighbourhood in the early days of the present century, the scene would be such as to elicit high encomiums [praise] from its very diversity. Go with me back in your imagination to that time, and let us together take a ramble through the district. Let us leave the Manchester and Liverpool Coach at Bold Heath, and wend our way towards the isolated village [of St Helens], whose name is so familiar to all of us.

GLIMPSES

OF

OLD ST. HELENS,

BEING THE

Reminiscences of Old Inhabitants,

COLLATED BY

JOHN J. DUTTON.

January, 1893.

As we turn our backs upon the busy turnpike, towards the North-West, we enter a shady lane bounded on the right by the ancient park of the Bold family, – with its cluster of fine old oaks, some of which are of vast girth, – covering 40 statute acres of land. Through the thick forest-like park, we get no glimpse of the hall [Bold Hall]. Passing on our way through a rich corn-bearing country, including Sutton and Burtonwood, we skirt the domain of Sherdley, the hall then occupied by Mr. Michael Hughes. Leaving Green End, we pass on and descend into Peasley Vale, a name surely suggestive of holy quiet and rural felicity.

Time has dealt hardly with Peasley Vale, for though the builders' art has not invaded it to any large degree, yet it is shorn of much of its rustic beauty by the overwhelming

203

dragon of modern industry. Here stands a house (now the Fever Hospital) which stood there in the early days of this century, and which was occupied, a few years later than the time I am speaking of, by Mr. Richard Fildes, son of Dr. Fildes, the almost sole representative of the healing art in St. Helens at the close of last century. Still passing on, further down the lane we pass a number of straggling cottages; occupied for the most part by workers in the mines, until we come to the canal.

Now we have reached the village of St. Helens, and stand at a point where we can view two fairly long streets, Parr-street on the right, and Raven-street, with its continuation, Church-street, on the left. Following the latter, we cross the canal by the turn-bridge. Resting a moment here, it needs no stretch of the imagination to fancy the banks of the canal, even then 55 years old, as rustic as any natural waterway. Nor shall I lay myself open to the charge of giving reins to my fancy, if I people its banks with votaries of the piscatorial art. For at a much later period, the men and youth of the overgrown village were wont to take their pleasures in fishing the waters of the canal, and I [am] told with very great success.

Leaving the canal behind us, we ascend Raven-street by a gentle incline, not so steep as at present, leaving several cottages, of the same class as those before named, on our right. We pass the Friends' Meeting House and the Raven Hotel also on our right, and we reach the main street of the village, Church-street. Here we see a mingling of cottages, small shops and the residences of such gentry as the village could boast. Half-way up Church-street there is a small space of unoccupied land, which every Saturday does duty for a market, and according to one informant there stood also the village pump, and the village stocks.

Sketch of Chapel Lane in St Helens made by John Knowles in 1805 prior to the town's leading thoroughfare being renamed Church Street

Let me now take you down a narrow street from the market place, already known as Market-street. This was occupied by business people mostly, though here, as in Church-street, we find a few private houses. Then along Tontine-street to its junction with Bridge-street we come upon the verge of the country, with its green fields and its hedgerows, its farm-yards and orchards. Tontine-street and Bridge-street, like the others, seem to possess a very mixed population, though the former seems to have been the more aristocratic quarter, as in its short length, as many of the gentry lived as in its longer neighbour, Church-street.

Returning by Bridge-street to Church-street we circumambulated that remarkable village, from which has sprung the town of world-wide fame in which it is our lot for the present to be cast. As we stand at the junction of the two streets just named, with our backs to Church-street, we again face the open country. Our view is scarcely interrupted by the few cottages scattered here and there. Following the direction in which we are looking, we notice on the left a primitive building standing in a field, with one gable to the lane. The other gable is topped with a small dilapidated wooden belfry, telling us that it is a house of prayer. The building is not large; it has four windows at the side, and the end nearest to us has one window and two doors; and near this window is a slab on which is cut the year "1710." Around it are gardens and fields, and behind it a bowling green, and within its own borders are two small cottages, wherein reside the veritable guardians of the sacred ashes of the dead, whose resting places are marked by the many memorial stones scattered about.

*The Independent Chapel in Ormskirk Street c.1810.
The Congregational Church was built on the same site.*

This was the Top Chapel – to use the name it was then known by – or the Independent Chapel, the name whereby we should recognise it, of these days. That was the forerunner of the large church close by which we are now sitting. The spot we occupy in this building (Brook-street School) covers a bit of the "God-made country" of that time, yet in the eyes of God and Ruskin surely its presence must be commendable, having for its object the furtherance of His cause, and the mitigation of the evils which always attend the man-made town.

Now let us proceed further along the lane by which we have come; almost opposite to us, two or three small cottages stand at right angles to the road. In one [of] these cottages, dwelt the progenitrix of one of our present worthy County Councillors, whose business it was to deprive men and children of their hirsute growth with scissors and razor. More than one lively story is told of the barber-woman of those days, who only forestalled, by half a century or so, the rage, so common in these days, for the advancement of women, by practically illustrating the phrase scarcely then invented, the equality of sexes.

Windle / Eccleston Workhouse

A little further on we note a small school, and close to this stands that country residence of the poor, the Workhouse [in Ormskirk Street]. This neighbourhood on our right hand with the few scattered cottages behind was then known as Moorflat. These were the only erections until College-lane was reached, then we pass a few cottages on the opposite side with gardens in front, and arrive at Duke street. Here we find almost another village, if one long street of cottages may be so named.

All around and behind these streets are fields of growing corn, pastures and gardens. College-lane, so called from the Charity School behind the Manse, was a veritable lane with its hedgerows and stiles, leading past the lime kilns to

Hares-Finch. Following Duke street we come to another aristocratic neighbourhood, although, as always, there are many humble cottages attending upon their richer neighbours. Many of the houses here are graced with gardens before and behind, and the whole has the appearance of a separate and a secluded village. The rising ground between Duke-street and College-lane is Cowley Hill, and a footpath, starting from the middle of Duke-street, passing the 'Tannery' and passing through the fields which cover the slope of the hill, meets another footpath out of College-lane at the top of the hill. The path thus formed leads past Shooting–Butts-lane and Hard-lane to Moss Bank. At the end of Duke-street we again enter rural scenes; a farm and its adjuncts meet us at the outset. The tall hedges of hawthorn upon high backings of raised earth and at intervals stunted oak trees form continuous lines on each side of the road, only broken by a few thatched cottages.

This rural view of Cowley House and Billinge Beacon was painted by Robert Sherbourne in 1793 and later copied by A. T. Free and is thought to have been taken from near Croppers Hill

[Having] Arrived at Dentons Green, charming scenes await us. On that tree-covered slope which bounds the view on the left, stands Eccleston Hall with its avenue approach. On the rising ground to the right stands Windle Hall, the residence at this time I believe of Miss Gerard, sister of Sir John Gerard, while in front the lordly park of the Derby family fringes the horizon as far as the eye can sweep. At Dentons Green we find several houses of the better sort, the Gerard's Arms, and a few cottages. If we are of an archaeological turn of mind, we shall not omit to step aside for a few minutes, to see that interesting ruin, Windleshaw Abbey.

Windleshaw Chantry / Abbey

We may find it in something like the state the antiquary Mr. Barrett found it in at the close of last century, as recorded in the pages of Baines. We may find it "an old ruinated chapell," with the "upper part" of the steeple "quite surrounded with ivy, whose friendly care seems resolved to preserve the remains of this venerable fabric to the last extremity."

Having said so much with regard to the surroundings of this (to us) interesting village, I will, if I have not already wearied you with my perhaps too roseate view of the district, say a few words of the trades, the people, and some of the social matters that even then occupied their thoughts. Now, although I have taken a very favourable view of the country around St. Helens in those days, and I quite believe the descriptions I have quoted are in the main true, yet the district was not without its black spots.

Of the 4,294 inhabitants who dwelt here in 1811, the great bulk of them were workers in mines or dependent upon those workers. On all sides, wherever you looked, the headstocks of collieries, and air-shafts or ventilating shafts met your view. I believe under the very spot we occupy at this moment, if not directly under our feet, such a shaft as I have named is arched over to form a foundation for the building we are in (Brook Street School). I do not think any description I could give would convey to you the extent and importance of the coal trade in this neighbourhood at the time as this fact, that no less than 10 firms of coal proprietors were enumerated at the census following the date under our consideration.

In 1755 the Sankey Brook Navigation undertook an enterprise, which to the people of those days was no less than the great [Manchester] Ship Canal now in course of construction is to us. It was in all respects a ship canal on a small scale. The original intention of the promoters was to deepen Sankey Brook, but instead of making this the channel of communication, they cut a separate canal from the Mersey, at Sankey, to Ravenhead. "This navigation" says Baines [Edward Baines, gazeteer], "affords a medium of transit to various descriptions of merchandise and tillage including grain, slate, timber, stone, lime and manure, but the principal is coal, which is carried in great abundance to Liverpool, Warrington, Northwich and other places, from the mines in the parish of Prescot; and particularly from those of

St. Helens. Vessels of 60 tons burthen can navigate this water, with 16 feet beam and a draught of 5 feet 1 inch."

Even at this early date two hundred thousand tons of coal were annually conveyed on this navigation [canal]. To produce and send away so large a quantity of coal many workers were required. Men, women and children were employed in this labour. There was no restriction, children of 7 and 8, if not even younger, and women young and old were alike drawn into the dark bowels of the earth to bring to light the "black diamonds," as the toast of the day had it. This is no fancy, but it is very true.

Thus though we find the majority of the people were engaged in making glass, smelting and refining copper and getting coal, yet we have reason to believe other manufactures existed to a limited extent, some of which have died out entirely. There was a cotton mill near to Spray's Bridge, now removed, and the site is covered with cottages; a linen mill; a foundry; a weaving shop and a crown-glass works on a small scale. At a rather later date there [were] several comb-makers, several nail-makers, at least two stay-makers [corset makers], numerous pattern-makers, and, strange to say, one crossbow-maker, named Simkins, had his shop in Tontine-street. This last fact reveals to us the probable use of the Shooting Butts, that gave the name to a lane near the City on the way to Moss Bank. Lastly J. Tasker of Moss Bank was set down as a farmer and a "pinder," the latter a business no longer common, at least in this neighbourhood, namely, the keeper of the pinfold or pound in which strayed cattle were penned.

As to schools and education there was almost a void. Five schools existed, but three of them were dames' schools, and in the words of my informant scarcely deserved the name. H. F. Chorley says in his autobiography "We three boys were put to a not bad day-school in St. Helens, where we were 'brought on,' as the school phrase is, in the classical languages, and in writing and arithmetic, and, I think, were well considered by the masters." From this we have the consolation of knowing that education was not entirely neglected in this embryo city.

I have already spoken of the market, with the stocks at the corner, and the pump not far away. It was considered a very good market if six or eight country people attended to sell goods on market days in summer. I am quoting from information received from an old inhabitant. The market was always over by four o'clock, with the exception of some "mug people," and why mug people above all others should want to stay later than four o'clock after everybody else had gone home, I fail to see, but so it was. My informant bewails the fact that there was no place for the sale of fish – the only treat they could get in that way was by an old man of the name of Wicky Wandy who came from Southport and brought his fish upon two donkeys. Occasionally men would come from Liverpool in the season with herrings for sale, but they could never sell them all, – and do you know why? – because, as the town was without light, the people always took the opportunity of robbing the fish carts.

The parapets of the streets were paved with boulders, and logs of wood were placed across, I presume to give some support to the boulders. Large-headed nails were driven into the ribs to prevent wearing, and particularly to prevent people dancing on them at night, or after working hours, which was a common thing. Before 1810 there were no lights at night except the little that might be obtained from a small candle in some shop window, and under these circumstances we do not wonder that it was a common thing to run against a barrow or other vehicle, or stumble over a load of coal, or walk into something still more unpleasant. I have it in my notes that my informant knows this from experience.

The streets were in perfect darkness, save that now and then a lantern might be seen floating about like a will-o'-the-wisp, to prevent collisions. Notwithstanding all this St. Helens was always considered a prosperous town, although there was not a single lawyer in the place, nor a druggist, nor a stationer, nor post office. What a happy place! The Fleece Inn did duty for the post office, as well as for a station. The coach to Liverpool started here with two horses, two-and sixpence outside, to carry 8 passengers, and five shillings inside, to carry 4 passengers.

Somewhere about 1810 they began to light the streets with oil-lamps, say about two in each street often swinging from the branch of a tree. There were frequent acts of mischief committed; we can very well understand that, and there were no police to detect the perpetrators. If any were detected they had to be taken before Michael Hughes or Colonel Frazer, the only two magistrates in the neighbourhood, and as there was no sitting in St. Helens, all cases had to go to Prescot.

In 1806 a solemn event occurred in this retired village. In August of that year, a severe thunderstorm passed over the town, and a young man named Williams, who had taken shelter in an unfinished house in Bridge-street, and who was uttering profane language at the time, was struck dead by lightning. The awful event seems to have had a profound effect in arresting the serious attention of the people, clerical and lay, to the sad and neglected state of both education and religion. It moved Mr. Sharp the minister of the adjoining Chapel to commence a Sunday School and that Sunday School was the origin of the place we are now in (Brook Street). As this was the first attempt to establish a Sunday School in St. Helens, perhaps it deserves something more than a passing word.

The house where the young fellow Williams was struck dead, was for a number of years occupied by Miss Leadbetter and afterwards [by] Mr. John Kitchen. The Rev. Isaac Sharp "improved the occasion" in a sermon [on] the next Lord's day to a large congregation, and at the close he invited all those who wished to receive religious instruction to be present the following Sunday morning. At the appointed time the chapel was filled with adults and children. A scene of great confusion followed, but after a few weeks, classes were organised, teachers were appointed and order was introduced. The old resident from whom I have learned much of the foregoing information says "the old chapel had forms up the aisle as I well recollect, for I was one of the first scholars there, and repeated the Catechism and Scriptures in the presence of the Congregation in the chapel for four years."

Several cottages stood opposite the Fleece Inn. Betty Mousdell or Mosedale occupied one. It was a thing to be remembered to have seen the mouth of my octogenarian friend water at the thought of, and the gusto with which he related the excellencies of Old Betty's Everton toffey. The pleasant sensations produced by the mere recollection of it were apparent in every feature. So strongly are the impressions of youth sometimes stamped upon the mind.

"In Market-street, five or six yards from Mr. Hodgson's shop, stood the village pump, and all behind it in the space bounded by Market-street, Tontine street and Church-street were a number of gardens."

Naylor-street did not exist in 1821. At the corner of Market-square near to the house occupied by the Speakman family the stocks stood. An old inhabitant who died lately assured me he had seen men put in the stocks. The same garrulous old gentleman, who would have been now 88 years of age, used to tell a story about a cat being in the stocks, but while relating the incident, either the ludicrousness of the situation or the absurdity of the tale so excited his risibility that from his inordinate laughter I could never gather the cause of his merriment.

One custom, which held sway in the early days of this century has been deservedly discarded. It would hardly be believed in these days of temperance and teetotal effort, when we are bringing down lecturers to tell the children there is "poison in the cup," that the Sunday scholars were regaled on warm ale and buns on Christmas day. Happily, this was changed in 1827 to a service on Good Friday, and tea and oranges were substituted for the warm ale. – **John J. Dutton – Published in the St Helens Lantern in 1891**

THATTO HEATH OF LONG AGO

In 1948 the St Helens Reporter published a remarkable article on the development of Thatto Heath during the early 19th century. That included converting its heathen residents – described as "poachers, cock-fighters, bull-baiters, drunkards and pugilists" who indulged in acts of "gross darkness" – into more decent folk.

The uncredited piece was published on October 15th 1948:

A hundred years ago, Thatto Heath was a heath indeed. In fact, it was a barren stretch of undulating common land relieved by patches of rough grass and gorse. In a dip known as "Sot's Hole" – for the men and women of Thatto Heath were hard drinkers – were erected a number of miners' cottages. A few yards away stood a strong post used for bull-baiting, [a] popular pastime in those days; and the locality was further adorned by wooden stocks where inebriates were fastened to "cool off." There was neither church nor school within several miles and as one history writer puts it, "gross darkness held the minds of the people." In 1810, Mr. Jonas Nuttall, of the printing firm of Nuttall, Fisher and Dickson, Liverpool and London, was on the look-out for a country house, and selected a small estate on which he built Nutgrove Hall, so called because of the filbert bushes which grew around it. Jonas Nuttall and his wife Frances, were devoted Methodists and they visited the homes of the people of the Heath and opened the kitchen of their home for religious services.

Soon this became too small to house all who came and the services had to be held on the open heath. The congregation included poachers, cock-fighters, bull-baiters, drunkards and pugilists, some of whom became 22-carat Christians. In time, Mr. Nuttall built a chapel and nearby he erected a school with two cottages, one for the school mistress and the other for the caretaker. In those days Nutgrove Church was in the Liverpool Circuit, which sent preachers who used either a horse or shank's pony. That great literary and preaching giant, Dr. Adam Clarke, was a frequent visitor and he bought Millbrook House; his name is enshrined in Clarke's Crescent. There are many thrilling stories of those days. One man, Hugh Naylor, who kept the "Beehive," gave up the licence on his conversion. His wife was angry with him and one Sunday morning when he arose to attend the seven o'clock prayer meeting, he found that she had hidden his hat, coat and shoes and the key of the door. But, he outwitted her by jumping out of the window and turned up at Chapel without coat or shoes. By the time of Mr. Nuttall's death in 1837, the chapel was too small and his widow, at her own cost, enlarged it to hold twice as many people.

In 1863 there was a revival which moved the whole neighbourhood. Special services were held nightly for thirteen weeks without a break, and the membership of the church was doubled. One of the methods used was one which the Communist Party has since imitated. Each of the members decided to select some particular person and seek to win him for the faith and the Church. John Hill set his heart on a newcomer to the district and prayed in the prayer meeting, "Lord, save that man; I don't know his name, but he's a big chap." The following Saturday John was digging in his garden when he saw the stranger approaching. He rushed upstairs and, dropping on his knees, he prayed, "Yon's chap 'at I want saving, Lord, coming down Elephant Lane." Late that night there was a knock at John Hill's door. It was the stranger with a deep request, "I want you to help me to get saved."

The Champions Of Child Cruelty Cases In Croppers Hill

"You cannot beat a small child like that. You might easily have been here today for manslaughter or murder."

INTRODUCTION

In the early years of the 20th century, St Helens was awash with cases of cruelty. As was seen in a previous chapter, wives could go to court to claim persistent cruelty from their husbands and seek a separation order with maintenance. And during 1902 about fifty St Helens women found the courage to take their case to the magistrates – although that probably only scratched the surface of the widespread brutality that many women then faced.

Neglected and abused children in the town did not have the same legal redress as adults – but from the 1890s they did have their own champion in Croppers Hill. That was the National Society for the Prevention of Cruelty to Children who had a small office there – run initially by **John Thompson** *(1895 - Dec 1902)*, **George Luff** *(1903 - May 1913)*, **Charles Embling Cooper** *(1913 - 1919)* and **Francis Lycett** *(1919 - 1931)*.

These men were responsible for child welfare in St Helens during the Society's early years and always referred to by their title of inspector – e.g. Inspector Thompson. That may, at times, have given some the erroneous impression they were members of the police force. However, they also had another name that many people called them – the "cruelty man".

The organisation had been founded in 1884, initially as the London Society for the Prevention of Cruelty to Children. It took some years for offices to be rolled out throughout the country, as local branches had to be formed to raise the funds needed to pay for the Society's operations in each district.

The NSPCC arrived in Warrington in 1892 and its inspector there also dealt with a few cases of cruelty in St Helens and Prescot. When the Warrington Society's third annual report was issued in May 1895 it said:

> We regret to say the prosecutions have been very numerous, but we were bound to undertake them, as the evildoers would not become amenable to the kindly advice of our officer, or take any heed of the "warning notice" served on them. In the many cases where a drunken woman rules the house nothing has any effect but imprisonment. We have to point out that 86 per cent. of the cases are due to drunkenness.

The NSPCC's office in Croppers Hill in St Helens was also opened in 1895 with Inspector John Thompson in charge. Yorkshire-born, the inspector was then aged about 30 and living in City Gardens in Cowley Hill with his wife Susannah and their two little girls. Thompson had joined the NSPCC six years before coming to St Helens and had worked initially in Birmingham and then in Liverpool.

"YOU LITTLE BASTARD, YOU ARE NOT MINE"

Inspector Thompson's division included Prescot, as well as St Helens, and soon he had his hands full dealing with the many challenges arising from family life in a working-class town. One of his earliest prosecutions took place on July 10th 1897 when Patrick Dillon from Albert Street was charged with ill-treating and neglecting his two children.

These were Margaret – who was only five months old – and two-year-old James. The Society's solicitor, Henry Riley, told the magistrates a shocking story of abuse. Baby Margaret had recently been punched in the face by Dillon and his wife – who was also called Margaret – had needed hospital treatment through the violence that she had endured.

But Dillon's main fury had been against his 2-year-old son, who had been born before his marriage. Three months prior to the court hearing the coal miner had placed the shaft of a pick in the fire and then shoved it against James's leg, shouting:

"You little bastard, you are not mine." The solicitor explained to the court that Dillon seemed to think that he could beat his little child on the smallest provocation and was "constantly thrashing it".

> **Brutality at St. Helens.**
> **A Father Sent to Prison.**
> **A Wife's Alleged Perjury.**
>
> At St. Helens Police Court, to-day, before Alderman Harrison and Mr. Leach, Patrick Dillon, a collier, of Albert-street, was charged in custody with ill treating and neglecting his two children, James (two year) and Margaret (five months), in a manner likely to injure their health. Mr. Riley said the prisoner seemed to think that he could beat his little child two years old on the smalest provocation. The accident that the child was born before the marriage was the apparent incentive to it. He described it to his mother in most opprobrious terms, and was constanty thrashing it. On Friday he and his wife had some controversy about a pawnticket, and he kicked her all about the place. The baby, five months old, he struck with his clenched fist on the forehead. He had thrown a bottle at

Liverpool Evening Express July 10th 1897

The man's wife had made a signed statement to Inspector Thompson of the NSPCC detailing her husband's cruel actions. But when she was called to the witness box she repudiated her written account – and so did her sister Maria with her own statement.

Mrs Dillon had claimed that her husband had struck her with a bottle and then attempted to throw her and the little boy out of a window, with the violence of his push breaking four panes of glass. But she now said:

> On my oath I hove [heaved] a bottle and I trod on it; but being in a temper I said that he had done it. He did not try to throw me out of the window. I broke the windows with my hand. ...He is a good husband when he's sober, and the children are not neglected; they are clean and decent.

However, Inspector Thompson was able to testify of the floor and walls of the Dillons' home being smeared with blood and PC Smith said he had seen the man knock his wife down.

And so the magistrates sentenced Patrick Dillon to two months hard labour and told him he had been guilty of brutal conduct. The man's wife and his sister-in-law were also warned by the Bench that they might be prosecuted for perjury, although that does not appear to have occurred.

So why did Margaret Dillon reject the statement that she had made to the police? Had her husband coerced her? Possibly, but he had been in a police cell since his violence on the previous day – which included the punch in his baby's face.

More likely Mrs Dillon had concluded that it would be better to have an occasionally violent husband that brought a decent income into her home than go without a breadwinner for a few months. But Patrick Dillon went to prison in any case, although the 1901 census shows that the family were still together with a third child having been born.

PUNY AND EMACIATED

But not all married women adopted a "stand by your man" attitude. Some parents fought like cat and dog at inquest hearings or during court cases, with both wanting to apportion blame for the neglect of their children on the other. When the inquest into the death of James Jones was held in 1898, the child's parents were so aggressive to each other that the coroner asked a policeman to stand between them.

The father and mother were Edwin and Sarah Jones of Victoria Street in St Helens. Inspector Thompson of the NSPCC explained to the hearing that after being tipped off about conditions at the couple's house, he had found the three-month-old child lying on a bedstead by a broken window. The inspector described little James as "puny and emaciated". He said the mother had told him that her husband only gave her a few shillings a week out of his wages – but Sarah denied suggestions that she went out begging with the child.

On the same day that Inspector Thompson visited the house, PC James Sellars said he'd seen three of the Jones' children *(aged nine and under)* sitting on their doorstep from 12:10pm to 1:30pm. They were crying and waiting for their mother to come and give them dinner – but she never came and they returned to school without food.

The constable added that on two further occasions the children had been locked out of their home, with their neighbours having to take them in and feed them. PC Sellars also described a time when baby James was left alone in the house for over two hours and had to lie on a bed with virtually no clothes on.

> **A ST. HELENS STARVATION CASE.**
>
> **THE ADJOURNED INQUEST.**
>
> **STRONG REMARKS BY THE CORONER.**
>
> Mr. Brighouse, county coroner, this morning held the adjourned inquiry into the death of James Jones, aged three months, son of Edwin and Sarah Jane Jones, of 64, Victoria-street, St Helens, who died at the Whiston Workhouse on February 19. The father and mother, who are in the hands of the St. Helens police on a charge of neglecting deceased and four other children, were present in custody. Mr. H. L. Riley, St. Helens, appeared for the National Society for the Prevention of Cruelty to Children.—The Coroner, addressing the father and mother, said they would hear all the evidence and be able to ask any question they might wish.—The Father: I want to say a few words first about her (his wife)—how she has been neglecting the child.—The Wife: I did not neglect the child.—The Coroner: We are going to hear the evidence of other people, and you must wait a bit. You will be able to make a statement on oath if you desire.—As the parents were making hostile demonstrations, the coroner directed a police officer to stand between them.—Inspector Thompson, of the National Society, gave evidence, and said his attention was called to
>
> *Liverpool Echo February 28th 1898*

Dr Challoner told the hearing that ten days before James had died he had seen the baby and he "looked very ill indeed". The weather was very cold and he'd told the mother that on no account was she to take her child out of the house.

But Mrs Jones took no notice and she took James outside just the same. Sometime later Dr Challoner signed a certificate that stated that the child's poor condition was through his mother's neglect and if he were not removed to a hospital immediately he would die. He also certified that the house was not fit to live in.

Dr Hall, the medical officer at the Whiston Workhouse infirmary, told the Coroner that when baby James had been admitted to the institution he was very weak and emaciated. Two days later he died from congestion of the brain induced by cold and neglect.

The Coroner asked for the Jones's remaining four children to be brought into the room and when he saw them he said he could imagine the youngsters sat on a doorstep in the cold crying for their dinners. He then declared:

> The finest thing in the world would be to starve Jones and his wife for a couple of days, and then they would have some appreciation of what it was like.

The Coroner was then reported to have administered a severe rebuke to the father for not proving proper food and clothing but said he thought Mrs Jones had been coerced, adding:

> How a father could sit unmoved and hear a tale of woe and suffering such as they had heard that morning, passes my comprehension. I feel strongly that the justices would not be doing their duty unless they sent the father somewhere where he would have time for reflection.

The mother and father subsequently appeared in St Helens Police Court to face charges of neglecting their five children. At the first hearing Inspector Thompson claimed that Jones had twice previously deserted his family and while at Wigan had tried to give two of his children away.

At a second hearing the charge against Sarah Jones was dropped in the light of the Coroner's comments at the inquest. But her husband Edwin was committed to Liverpool Assizes, where he appeared on May 5th 1898.

However, the case for the prosecution was rather thin as it relied exclusively on a charge of Jones only giving a small proportion of his wages to his wife. The Liverpool Weekly Courier explained how that arguably amounted to cruelty and neglect:

> Of the little she had received [from her husband] she was compelled to provide him with good and sufficient food, no matter what became of the children and herself. The consequence was that the children were not properly fed or clad, and were so neglected as to cause them injury and suffering. Inspector Thompson, of the National Society for the Prevention of Cruelty to Children, spoke to the destitute and comfortless condition of the prisoner's house, and to the ragged and half-starved appearance of the children.

But Edwin Jones's wife Sarah had now changed her tune. The prospect of her husband going to prison no doubt induced her to tell the court that her husband's wages were 17 shillings 6d per week and of that he gave her all but 3s 6d – the opposite of what she had previously claimed. The judge was Justice John Bigham who was developing a reputation as being hostile to the NSPCC and he directed the jury to acquit Jones. Bigham later, incidentally, became Baron Mersey of Toxteth and is caricatured here in Vanity Fair magazine.

ILL-CLAD, FILTHY AND VERMINOUS CONDITION

For a number of years there was suspicion and even downright hostility to the activities of Inspector Thompson and the NSPCC. Some called the Society persecutors of the poor and intrusive meddlers in people's private affairs. Even some judges (like Bigham) and magistrates were opposed to their prosecutions, as they seemingly did not realise that most of the Society's work took place behind the scenes.

And so monthly reports were issued to explain their activities. For example, in November 1902 the St Helens and district branch of the NSPCC declared that they had 16 new cases on its books that affected the welfare of 59 children. Thirteen of those cases were dealt with by warning and advice and only three resulted in prosecution. The inspector had also made 89 supervision visits to old cases.

Although such transparency helped to satisfy the courts, the public took much longer to fully appreciate the activities of the "cruelty man". This is exemplified by the reaction to a court case that took place on October 3rd 1902 in which an unmarried couple were charged with neglecting and ill-treating four children.

Annie Sellers and Patrick Kelly lived in Victoria Street – which used to be in Gerards Bridge, near Cowley Street. The Society's solicitor, Henry Riley, told the court that the four children had been found in an "ill-clad, filthy and verminous condition" and on several occasions had been subjected to violence. He then said:

> The eldest girl, Amelia, told her grandmother of the carrying on that she had seen in the house and was then thrashed and put out of the house. The man threw a poker at her and threatened to kill her. Kelly did not work but spent his time drinking with the woman.

Amelia then bravely took the stand in court and gave evidence as to how Patrick Kelly had threatened to put her on the fire and roast her. The 12-year-old said he had asked her mother: "What would you say if I killed her?" and she'd replied, "I would not care, as she would deserve it."

PC Heaton gave evidence of having heard Annie Sellers and Patrick Kelly making the threats and seeing the girl later being put out into the street. "Her lip was bruised and her face was as pale as a corpse", remarked the constable. Another of the children contradicted the evidence of her sister Amelia. However, in cross-examination the girl admitted having been told by her mother what to say.

Despite the strong evidence and Mrs Sellers accusing PC Heaton of being a liar, the magistrates were quite generous with the couple. Patrick Kelly was discharged from the court, as being unmarried and not the children's father his legal liability for their welfare was debatable.

But Mrs Sellers was found guilty, although the Bench said they did not wish to separate the woman from her children. The Chairman explained that they wanted to give the mother an opportunity of correcting a "very bad state of affairs".

After Annie Sellers gave a promise that Kelly would no longer live in the house, they merely bound her over to come up for judgment when called upon. In other words if the woman returned to court for any reason, the case would be taken into account.

THE CRUELTY MAN'S INFORMER

Then after the couple were liberated from the court, the revenge was planned! Margaret Gilheeney was a neighbour of Annie Sellers and her boyfriend Patrick Kelly and had given evidence against the pair at the hearing.

However, the St Helens Newspaper only felt her testimony merited a few lines in their report. But her involvement in the case – despite seemingly not being of great importance to its outcome – was sufficient to infuriate some members of the local community.

MOB RULE AT GERARDS BRIDGE.

THREATENING A WITNESS.

At Friday's Police Court a number of defendants were brought up on warrant, charged with threatening and assaulting Mrs. Margaret Gilheeney, a woman who, the previous week, gave evidence in a neglect of children case. The offenders' names were Ann Jane Baines, 56, Victoria-street, Annie Baines, 85, Victoria-street, Margaret Greenhalgh, 90, Victoria-street, Winifred Shields, 20, Stanley-street, Mary O'Keeffe, 73, Victoria-street, Emily Jones, Victoria-street, Daniel Baines, 73, Union-street, David Baines, 85, Victoria-street, and William Baines, Union-street. Of these only the prisoner Annie Baines was charged with assault as well as threats. Mr. H.

St Helens Newspaper October 14th 1902

On October 10th six women and three men from Gerards Bridge appeared in St Helens Police Court after a campaign of harassment against Mrs Gilheeney who, according to prosecuting solicitor Henry Riley, had been living in a "state of terror" since giving evidence against Annie Sellers. He continued:

> They had made her a prisoner in her own house, had made bonfires outside the door and had shouted "Thompson's informer" and "police spy" at her.

Mrs Gilheeney added that she had also been called the "cruelty man's informer". The mob had, she said, threatened to blind her and burst her mouth. They had also burned mattresses in front of her house while giving cheers for Paddy Kelly and Annie Sellers. The St Helens Newspaper wrote:

> Mrs. Gilheeney in evidence stated that they serenaded her with cans and concertinas, and threw stones at her house. She was afraid for her life.

One of the defendants was discharged but the other eight were found guilty and bound over to keep the peace.

DISGUSTINGLY FILTHY

Also during 1902 the magistrates treated a young woman called Ellen Cooper very lightly in spite of a shocking catalogue of abuse committed against her own baby. The evidence showed that the 22-year-old from Walkers Lane would violently strike her child when it cried and when she was in a temper.

Henry Riley was again prosecuting for the NSPCC and told the Bench that the woman had:

> ...smacked it violently until it was black in the face and apparently could not get its breath. She had been

remonstrated with over and over again by the other mothers in the neighbourhood.

On one occasion Mrs Cooper had struck her baby several times because the child had lost part of its bottle. That led to the child's nose bleeding and a swollen ear. The woman and her husband rented a room from a Mrs Stanley who told the court her tenant "used the child cruelly" and when vexed took it out on her baby.

"She is very stupid and will not be told anything", added Mrs Stanley. She added that the child had gone black in the face and nearly choked through her mother's ill-treatment. Another witness told the court that Mrs Cooper had almost choked her child by putting her hand on its mouth to stop the baby from crying.

Inspector Thompson of the NSPCC described the disgusting condition of the room in which Mrs Cooper lived and said the bed was only fit to be burnt. Dr O'Keefe also told the court that the room they rented was "disgustingly filthy" and said the 8-month-old child was emaciated, weighing only 8 pounds when it should be at least 14 or 15 pounds.

Mrs Cooper insisted that she had never wanted to hurt her baby but her husband was a miner. He often worked nights and she did not want the child disturbing him while sleeping during the day. The Clerk to the court said:

> You cannot beat a small child like that. You might easily have been here today for manslaughter or murder.

In delivered their verdict the magistrates said they had considered taking the child from its mother and giving it to the mother-in-law. However, they had decided to bind Mrs Cooper over to come up for judgement when called upon.

The Chairman said the magistrates were loath to send a young woman like her to prison but she must try to behave herself and look after the child.

There was a balance to be struck between whether ignorant, abusive mothers like Ellen Cooper needed educating how to bring up their child as opposed to punishment. And Inspector Thompson would, no doubt, have made regular visits to inspect the child and talk to the woman's landlady.

But by today's standards a huge risk was being taken with the welfare of the baby – who doesn't appear to have ever been named, just referred to as "it", as was usually the case.

TEEMING WITH VERMIN

The vast majority of cases dealt with by the NSPCC in St Helens concerned neglect of children – rather than violence towards them. That could include not obtaining medical assistance when their kids were sick.

In 1916 Dr Joseph Cates, the St Helens Medical Officer of Health, complained that parents of ill children did not call in the doctor until they were "practically dead". He was referring to outbreaks of diphtheria and scarlet fever in the town but more minor complaints could also have fatal consequences if unattended.

In October 1902 Inspector Thompson of the NSPCC investigated the children of John and Ann Murphy of Bold Street in Greenbank. That was after the father had walked into the police station to say his daughter Mary had died. When Sgt. Small entered the Murphy's house he said he'd found the 6-year-old deceased girl's head "almost one complete sore" and "literally swarming with vermin".

When Dr. O'Keeffe arrived to sign Mary's death certificate, Mrs Murphy failed to tell him that she had another sick child in the house. That was four-year-old Catherine who had been suffering from a sore head for five weeks. When the little girl was eventually examined, she was described as "teeming with vermin".

Inspector Thompson had Catherine removed to the infirmary at Whiston Workhouse but she died nearly three weeks later. The cause of death for both Catherine and her sister Mary had been blood poisoning. Before the introduction of antibiotics, deaths from sepsis – as blood poisoning is more commonly known today – were quite common.

Child neglect was often blamed on uncaring parents who spent their money on drink and left their kids badly clad. Their home was also usually in a shocking state. However, after investigating John Murphy the police described the 35-year-old as a "hard-working, sober, steady workman" – and they'd also heard nothing bad about his wife Ann.

The home of the Murphys was also described as having been "tolerably well furnished" with a very clean kitchen and the parents themselves had been badly affected by the loss of their children. But Inspector Thompson decided that their negligence warranted a prosecution and so brought charges of manslaughter against both husband and wife.

By the time the case reached the Liverpool Assizes on December 6th 1902, the charge had been downgraded to "wilful neglect of children in a manner likely to cause unnecessary suffering and injury to health".

The prosecution claimed that Ann Murphy had not called in a doctor because she did not want the neighbours to know her children had lice. But the 32-year-old also insisted that she had not thought their condition that serious, having never heard of a death occurring through a sore head.

The parents' defence counsel submitted to the jury that it was nothing but sheer ignorance on the part of the woman and not wilful neglect, as she had had no wish to injure the health of her two girls. He then said:

> This case is not one of a class usually brought forward, where there is hard treatment and starvation, or neglect of the ordinary decencies of life, which even in poor families

could be maintained, but a case where husband and wife were apparently living a respectable life and attending to the house. The children suffered from a terrible visitation to the head, and it would be for the jury to say whether it was so palpable that the woman should be taught by some punishment that she should not have acted in such a manner. It was said she should have called in a doctor, but the jury must take into consideration the position of the prisoner's lack of education and knowledge.

In the case of John Murphy the defence argument was that he was completely blameless, as sending for a doctor was "a department in the house over which the wife naturally had control". As a result the jury found both of the defendants not guilty of wilfully neglecting their children.

Next to the St Helens Newspaper's report on the case was their account of the proceedings at the annual meeting of the NSPCC's local branch. That had recently been held in the Town Hall and distrust of the organisation was still being discussed.

This is what the paper reported that the Mayor of St Helens, Councillor Frederick Dixon-Nuttall, had said:

> He did not doubt that a very great deal of good was done, but as an outsider he saw many dangers in having a society like that. Speaking of the general work they could not close their ears to the adverse things that had been said about the society. Many of those things had been answered fully, and he felt that the good that had been done far over-balanced any injury that had resulted from the work of the society. Still, some of the judges and magistrates were very much against them, and the only way he could see in which they could gain back the friendship and good opinion of everyone was by careful administration.

THE ALLEGED CHILD NEGLECT.

TRIAL AT THE ASSIZES.

At the Liverpool Assizes, on Saturday afternoon, before Mr. Justice Jelf, John Murphy (35), labourer, and Ann Murphy (32), his wife, were charged with having wilfully neglected their children, Mary Murphy, six years, Catherine Murphy, four years, and Annie Murphy, ten months, in a manner likely to cause them unnecessary suffering and injury to health. A charge of feloniously slaying the child Mary was withdrawn.

Mr. Mellor and Mr. Rigby Swift (instructed by Mr. H. L. Riley) were for the prosecution, and prisoners were defended by Mr. Madden, instructed by Mr. E. W. Swift.

Mr. Mellor, in opening the case for the prosecution, said the prisoners were husband and wife and had for some time lived at St. Helens. The male prisoner worked at Crosby as a brickmaker and earned about 25s. a week, returning home at week-ends. The couple appeared to have been steady and respectable, and to have kept their house respectably clean. The charge against them was of neglecting their children by not calling in medical assistance when it was necessary. The matter was reported to the authorities, owing to the death of the child Mary being reported to the police on the 16th of October. It was found upon inquiry that the children suffered from blood poisoning, caused by neglect. Their heads were covered with scabs and sores, and the female

THE CHILDREN'S SOCIETY.

THE MAYOR'S ADVICE.

The annual meeting of the St. Helens Branch of the National Society for the Prevention of Cruelty to Children was held at the Town Hall on Thursday afternoon last week. The Mayor (Councillor F. R. Dixon-Nuttall) presided, and there were also present the Mayoress (Mrs. Dixon-Nuttall). Sir David Gamble, Bart. C.B., Alderman and Mrs. J. C. Gamble, Miss and Miss G. Gamble, Mrs. Martin Hammill, Mr. W. Gamble, Mrs. Reid, Mrs. Hayward (Haydock), Mrs. Cook, Rev. B. S. Clarke, Mr. C. Sharples, J.P., Mr. and Mrs. C. C. White, Dr. Harris, Mrs. Riley, Mrs. F. W. Marsh, Mrs. Richardson (Rainford), Miss Turnbull, Mr A. J. Speeden (hon treasurer), Mr. J. Hammill (hon secretary), and others.

The Mayor said he had the greatest pleasure in taking the chair at the annual meeting. He looked upon the society with the deepest respect. It was a society able to do an immense amount of good, to save an immense amount of suffering amongst the children, but at the same time it was a very powerful engine. It was a powerful machine and like all powerful machines required very careful handling to produce the most good. He did not doubt that a very great deal of good was done, but as an outsider he saw many dangers in having a society like that. Speaking of the general work they could not close their ears to the adverse things that had been said

St Helens Newspaper December 12th 1902

However, the Newspaper was very much on the side of the NSPCC. A week earlier in criticising a lenient sentence passed by the aforementioned Judge Bigham, they had written:

> Every person who knows anything about the Society is perfectly satisfied that no more beneficent institution exists. That it should be necessary is a painful reflection on our boasted Christianity and twentieth century civilisation. That the pages of its annual report should contain a list of barbarities practised by ignorant or cruel parents on innocent children little worse than those committed in the Pagan empires of old, or by the savage and semi-civilised

233

nations of to-day, is only too sadly convincing argument for the Society's claim to the support of the enlightened.

The brutalities which children in hundreds suffer daily in every large town in England, and not less perhaps in St. Helens than in other places, must bring hot indignation to the heart and the blush of shame to the cheek of every right thinking man and woman, and the uninformed criticism of Mr. Justice Bigham is not likely to lessen interest in the Children's Society, but rather to stimulate it. St. Helens people perhaps stand in some need of awakening to the claims of the Society upon their influence and liberality. The operations of the Society in St. Helens, the work of its discriminating and energetic inspector, have undoubtedly been of untold service to the community.

Only in the last resort are police court proceedings taken against cruel or neglectful parents and guardians. But the almost weekly prosecutions of extreme and hardened cases show the appalling need of the Society's active labors [sic] in the town. The children who in hundreds are being brought up amid the most sordid and brutal surroundings, will, if they are not saved in time, grow up degraded and brutalised themselves, to prey on Society and fill the workhouses and jails at the expense of the ratepayers; and this is the very lowest ground on which the Society bases its claim to the financial support of the people of St. Helens and the country generally. We understand that so far the subscriptions from St. Helens have not done more than pay half the cost of the inspector stationed in the town, the other half being paid from the central funds of the Society. We do not hesitate to say that it is little short of a disgrace to a town which has so many wealthy churches and individual citizens, and a town which has such a pressing need of the Society's work in its midst.

A SHOCKING STATE OF FILTH AND DILAPIDATION

The same edition of the Newspaper described a prosecution of an extreme case of child cruelty. Although these tended to have many common characteristics, each usually had unusual aspects. And that of Patrick Kenny and his wife concerned a legacy of £90 from their family in Ireland that they had received a year before.

For most working-class folk that amount would have been the equivalent of a year's wages and the couple from Back Merton Bank Road could have invested the cash to improve their family circumstances. But they didn't. Instead they went on bender after bender with no apparent thought for their kids or the shocking condition of their home.

Dr. Patrick O'Keeffe told the court that the children were in an extremely filthy condition, infested with vermin and insufficiently clad. The house was practically without furniture and he said the only bed consisted of an "abominably dirty sack of fluff". And the only bedding was a thin canvas cloth and he considered the house completely unfit for habitation.

Inspector Thompson of the NSPCC stated that he had visited the property on November 19th and found it to be in a "shocking state of filth and dilapidation". Most of the windows were broken and so was the kitchen sink that dripped water on to the floor. The inspector said the only furniture in the house consisted of two broken chairs, a table and a bag of straw that a young woman named Egan and her two children occupied.

PC Whalley told the court that he had cautioned Patrick Kenny time after time and had seen the two defendants drunk for three weeks at a time. Before their inheritance had been received, the husband was described as having been hard-working and he blamed being out of work since June for his troubles.

Kenny told the court that he would be prepared to sign the pledge if the Bench would let him off easy. But that was not likely to happen and he was sent to prison for three months with hard labour and his wife received six months. It was common for such offenders not to appreciate the gravity of their crimes and Mrs Kenny was reported as having created quite a scene as she was being taken down to the cells.

A WRETCHED HOME WITH A PILE OF FEATHERS AS THE ONLY BED

Another bad case was heard in St Helens Police Court on December 19th 1902. That was when John and Mary Seerey of Vernon Street in Pocket Nook were charged with neglecting their five children. Unusually, the NSPCC inspector had been keeping the family under observation for more than two years but despite Inspector Thompson's warnings and advice, things had gone from bad to worse.

A court order had been obtained enabling the children aged between 3 and 15 to be removed to the workhouse. There the three youngest were found to be seriously underweight. Detective Inspector Strong gave evidence of having seen one of the children begging in the street on a bitterly cold day. He described their home as "wretched" and "destitute of furniture", with their only bed being a pile of feathers thrown on the floor and covered by a sack.

Inspector Thompson of the NSPCC stated that he'd had the family under observation since 1899 and the children had always been in a very bad state with little food in the house. At one time he said he had found the girl black and blue all over after being beaten by her father for stealing some of his money.

Dr William Haslam, the resident medical officer at Whiston Workhouse, described the children upon admission as being in a filthy condition and emaciated through prolonged under feeding. And PC Heaton described the defendants as "drunken and dirty people".

John Seerey was another defendant that blamed being out of work for both the condition of his house and the state of his children. But PC Heaton said the man often chose not to work and when he was in employment, he spent his wages on beer. Both John and Mary Seerey were committed to jail for four months with hard labour.

THE ABONIMABLY DIRTY HOME THAT MADE A POLICEMAN VOMIT

Some parents were sent to prison on multiple occasions for neglecting their kids. When Mary Maloney of Fern Street in Gerards Bridge appeared in St Helens Police Court on March 6th 1903 charged with neglecting her five children, it was revealed that she had served two previous prison terms for the same offence. In 1898 she had been committed for two months and a further six months was served three years later.

The 1901 census describes Mary as aged forty with nine children between four and nineteen. Although listed as married, no husband is shown living at her abode. At Mary's latest court appearance it was revealed that Peter McQuillan was the father of her five youngest children – but he'd failed to appear in court. George Luff was now the NSPCC's Inspector for St Helens and District and he had issued the two summonses against Maloney and McQuillan.

The Society's solicitor, Henry Riley, told the court that when Dr Fred Knowles had visited the house he'd certified that the children were in a "state of chronic dirt, vermin bitten and covered with festering sores." The doctor also considered that the kids were insufficiently clad, with their house that was located near North Road being overcrowded and exceedingly filthy.

PC Heaton then remarked:

The state of things is entirely due to drunkenness. There is a general battle in this house every week. McQuillan was recently in a serious condition for several weeks as a result of a poker wound. They fought with lamps, pokers, or anything else that was handy. McQuillan, Mrs. Maloney, and the five children slept in one room, ten feet square. There were two sets of old mattresses, but no bed clothing.

Mary Maloney told the court that McQuillan earned 28 shillings a week working at Pilkingtons but he only gave her 10 shillings. She admitted being ashamed of the condition of the house but insisted it was not her place to clean it, as it was not hers. The Bench sent the woman to prison for six months and issued a warrant for the arrest of Peter McQuillan.

What Mrs Maloney had meant about it not being her place to clean the house was that John and Mary Connolly were the actual tenants and they had sub-let a couple of their rooms to her and McQuillan. And the Connollys' living and sleeping quarters were in an even worse state than theirs!

In a separate case held on the same day, the Connollys were charged with neglecting their four children. Dr Knowles described their home as "abominably dirty" and NSPCC solicitor Henry Riley said their sleeping rooms would be an "offence to animals".

Inspector Luff stated that he had visited the house with PC Heaton. The beds were "quite black, stinking and verminous" and the place was so filthy that it had made the policeman vomit. But this was not a case of abject poverty. John Connolly, and one of his sons that was working, earned a combined 30s 9d per week and the sub-let rooms brought in an extra three shillings.

Women were seen as responsible for the home and so tended to get the blame when things went wrong. And so Mary Connolly – who insisted to the court that she had never been a cruel mother –

was imprisoned for three months and her husband bound over to come up for judgement when called upon.

THE MINER THAT RAPED HIS DAUGHTER

Sexual abuse of children certainly occurred during these times in St Helens, although it is hard to judge its scale. It's likely that only a few of many such assaults were reported to the police and there was often vague newspaper reporting of those that came to court.

Phrases like "criminal assault upon a child" effectively became code for sexual assault and rape, with few other details provided. Rarely did such cases figure in the St Helens branch of the NSPCC's annual report – but that of Peter Doward was an exception.

The 40-year-old miner from Havelock Street in Croppers Hill raped his 14-year-old daughter Harriett on two occasions. The first was in June 1903 when his pregnant wife Margaret was out shopping. Upon her return home, Harriet told her mother what had happened and, according to the girl, her father confessed to the crime but promised it would never happen again.

But it did on September 7th and Doward threatened his daughter with serious harm if she told her mother. Eventually Harriett did tell her mum and that led to Margaret Doward informing a midwife and a nurse, which led to the NSPCC being brought in.

Inspector Luff interviewed Harriett and had her medically examined – but corroboration could not be obtained from the mother as Margaret and her baby both died soon after the birth. However, Inspector Luff still thought he had a strong enough case against the father, despite his strenuous denials.

On November 20th 1903 Peter Doward appeared in St Helens Police Court and after the evidence was presented he was committed for trial at the next Liverpool Assizes. The St Helens Newspaper in reporting the hearing said the case had created a "great sensation" in the town and that hundreds of people had waited outside the town's police station during the afternoon to catch a glimpse of Doward being taken to Walton Prison on remand.

At Liverpool Assizes in December, the 40-year-old miner faced this charge: "At St. Helens in the month of June, 1903, feloniously against her will did ravish and carnally know Harriet Doward." The father was found guilty and sentenced to ten years penal servitude – meaning hard labour.

A TERRIBLE CHARGE.

PRISONER COMMITTED TO THE ASSIZES.

A great sensation was caused in the town last week end by the arrest on a terrible charge of a collier named Peter Doward, of 45, Havelock-street. He was brought before the Court on Friday charged with a serious offence against his fourteen year old daughter. The Bench on Friday adjourned the case to Monday, when the circumstances were inquired into by Messrs. W. Tyrer (Chairman) and W Gamble.

The prosecution of Doward was undertaken by the National Society for the Prevention of Cruelty to Children, for whom Mr. H. L. Riley appeared. Prisoner, a respectably dressed man apparently not more than forty years of age, was undefended. The girl, Harriett Doward, who looked older than the age given, fourteen and a half years, was also well dressed, and in mourning for her mother who died this month.

Mr. H. L. Riley for the prosecution stated that according to the certificate of registration

St Helens Newspaper November 24th 1903

The 1911 census shows the then 21-year-old Harriet working in London as a domestic servant and in 1921 living in Rainhill working for Albert Fletcher at his home in Lawton Road in Rainhill. He was a pawnbroker with premises in Junction Lane in Sutton.

THE WORST TOWN FOR CHILD CRUELTY CASES

As previously stated each branch of the NSPCC was supported by a local committee that raised money to pay for the Society's work in that town. Any income greater than expenditure went to the NSPCC's headquarters to pay for their administration costs and to dole out to places like St Helens that were in deficit.

At a public meeting held in St Helens Town Hall on May 19th 1913, it was revealed that a total of £1,000 had been received from the central fund managed by the NSPCC's HQ in order to keep the local branch afloat.

> **CRUELTY TO CHILDREN.**
> **IS ST. HELENS A BLACK SPOT?**
>
> A public meeting, to draw attention to the great need for more adequate support of the St. Helens branch of the National Society for the Prevention of Cruelty to Children, was held on Monday afternoon at St. Helens Town Hall. Mr. E. H Cozens-Hardy presided, and said the local branch of the society had drawn upon head-quarters to the extent of £1,000 from the amounts contributed to the central fund by branches in other parts of the country. They needed an additional inspector, but so far they had not subscribed nearly sufficient for one.
>
> The Hon. A. Holland-Hibbert, of the society's Central Executive Committee, said he had just read a report by the inspector of inspectors, who reported on some slum children just outside Liverpool as the worst he had ever seen, and on the top of that they had just received a report from the St. Helens Chief Constable, who said that "in spite of the close attention given by their local inspector, there appeared little improvement, and that St. Helens was most certainly the worst town with which he had been connected during his police career of twenty years. There is about sufficient work here for four inspectors." During last year their one

The St Helens Examiner May 24th 1913

A report had also been received from the St Helens Chief Constable that said that in spite of the good work of the local NSPCC inspector, there appeared little improvement in the number of child cruelty cases and explained how St Helens was:

> ...most certainly the worst town with which I have been connected during my police career of twenty years. There is about sufficient work here for four inspectors.

The meeting was told that in 1912 their single inspector in St Helens had dealt with 323 new cruelty cases concerning the welfare of 1,076 children, as well as having to check on cases that had arisen during the previous year.

Another inspector was said to be vital to cope with all that work but presently they did not have the funds to pay for another man. It was decided that a determined effort would be made to obtain more donations and at the NSPCC's annual meeting in 1914, it was revealed that their efforts had paid off with income received in St Helens boosted by £146.

It was also disclosed that during 1913 the number of new child cruelty cases investigated by their inspector had been 305, a slight drop from the previous year. Members of the public had reported 129 of them and only 4% of cases had resulted in prosecution, as parents had responded well to warnings and advice.

CHILDREN'S EYES WERE CLOSED BY ULCERS

What was believed at the time to have been the worst ever case of child cruelty in St Helens occurred on October 17th 1914. Then Ellen Critchley of Raglan Street was sentenced to a total of 12 months hard labour and her husband James to six months. NSPCC Inspector Charles Cooper told St Helens Police Court that the couple's five children had been removed to Whiston Workhouse in a shocking condition.

The two eldest girls aged five and nine had a mass of sores all over their heads and their eyes were closed through ulcers. A doctor said it would take months for their eyes to heal and the children would likely be left with serious defects. Inspector Cooper also described the condition of the house:

> The upstairs rooms were filthy. There were scarcely any bedclothes or furniture, and there were only one cup and three plates for the whole family.

A LIVING SKELETON

During the war the dependents of soldiers and sailors received a separation allowance from the government. In 1917 it worked out at 12 shillings 6d per week for the wife, with a further 5 shillings for her first child and 2/6 for each additional child. For some women with large families, they received more money than before their husband went to war. Sarah Abbott from Bickerstaffe Street in St Helens was said to be one of those who was better off. With six children at home she was receiving £1 10 shillings a week, which was not far off the average weekly wage.

> **BABY THAT WAS A LIVING SKELETON.**
>
> Sarah Ann Abbott, 10, Bickerstaffe-street, St. Helens, was sent to prison for three months with hard labour on Saturday for neglecting her children. Accused, it was stated, has six young children, and her husband had been ten weeks in the Army. Inspector Roe said she was now getting a good deal more money than when her husband was at home, but the children were in a dirty and neglected state. The baby of twenty-two months weighed 11lb. instead of 28lb.
>
> Mr. Garner, who prosecuted for the N.S.P.C.C., said the child was a living skeleton, and was apparently being starved to death. It had no organic disease.
>
> The magistrate said the woman ought to be ashamed of herself.

Liverpool Daily Post - June 25th 1917

On June 23rd 1917 the NSPCC charged Sarah with neglecting her six children, one of whom was described as a "living skeleton". The woman's children were in a dirty, neglected state and her youngest child of 22 months weighed just 11 pounds. The norm for a child of that age was 28 pounds.

Inspector Cooper of the NSPCC told the Bench that the youngster was apparently being starved to death. After hearing this evidence the magistrates told Sarah that she ought to be ashamed of herself and they sent her to prison for three months with hard labour.

TOO MEAN TO DO ANYONE A KINDNESS

On July 6th 1918 a street collection was held in St Helens in aid of the local branch of the NSPCC, which raised the considerable sum of £220. This amount included monies raised from collections held within the Theatre Royal and the town's cinemas.

On September 6th of that year Harriet Lee of Argyle Street *(near North Road)* appeared in St Helens Police Court charged with leaving two of her children alone in the house for nine days.

Inspector Cooper of the NSPCC told the Bench that the practice of leaving youngsters alone while their parents were away was very prevalent in St Helens.

He said he'd brought the case in order to impress on parents that they must arrange for someone to take care of their children if they had to leave home. Inspector Cooper also told the court that once he'd learnt of the children's situation, he'd placed them in the workhouse until Mrs Lee returned home on the following day.

The inspector said she had told him that she hadn't asked her neighbours to look after her children as "they were too mean to do anyone a kindness". Harriet Lee told the Bench that her husband was on active service in France and she had been to Edinburgh to see her sister who was ill. She added that her 13-year-old daughter Hilda was capable of looking after herself and her 6-year-old brother Ernest. The magistrates bound Mrs Lee over for 12 months in the sum of £5.

HAD TO PAWN HER SHAWL FOR FOOD

On April 16th 1919 John Smith appeared in St Helens Police Court accused of child neglect through refusing to work and support his family. The 35-year-old from Parliament Street in Thatto Heath had been discharged from the army at the end of December 1918 after undertaking nine months' military service.

Since then Smith – a mine labourer by trade – had simply refused to do any work. Initially the family lived on his army demobilisation pay but by early March they had to be kept by small allowances that the NSPCC provided.

Inspector Cooper told the Bench that he'd received numerous excuses from Smith for not working – included having a bad back. The man had had an offer of work at a St Helens coal mine but never turned up and at one point Smith's wife had to pawn her shawl for food. The inspector told the Bench that he had "talked to the defendant like a father, and begged of him to go to work". However, it was to no avail – Smith simply would not budge.

Two days before the court hearing, the inspector had found nothing in the house apart from a quarter pound of dry bread that someone had given the family. Mary Smith gave evidence that her husband had told her that he had finished work for good and did not intend doing any more. But John Smith put the blame on Mary, telling the Bench:

> I have not worked because she brought Mr. Cooper [of the NSPCC] to me. She brought Mr. Cooper to me before she had any need to do.

To that the Chairman, Cllr William Collier, said: "She had a right to complain if you did not provide her and the children with food." The Chairman added that it was a:

> ...disgraceful thing for a man to leave his wife and children dependent on charity or doles. If you are going to take that stand there is nothing for it but to make you work. You will have to go to gaol for three months at hard labour.

However, this wasn't Smith's first prison sentence as he had been given three months in December 1917 for "neglecting to provide the necessaries of life for his children". Evidence was then given that the man had not worked for six weeks and his neighbours had been forced to feed his kids.

ADDICTED TO METHS

Alcohol abuse was behind many cases of neglect. But when Thomas Moore appeared in St Helens Police Court on August 23rd 1919 charged with neglecting his three children, an addiction to methylated spirit was blamed for his refusal to work. When the NSPCC's Inspector Cooper had visited his home in Silkstone Street he found it very poorly furnished with the bedding "very scanty" and not a particle of food in the house. Moore had sold many of the items – including his children's slippers – to buy meths and in order to survive his family had become reliant on food donations.

Inspector Cooper told the hearing that the man's wife had told him that her husband had been sacked from his job for drinking and was "wandering about day after day" looking for meths. In his defence Thomas Moore told the Bench that he had been "proper bad" with his nerves and could not get work.

The case did not appear to be connected to the unrecognised mental health crisis that swept the country in the post-war years and affected huge numbers of former soldiers. The St Helens Reporter's lengthy account made no mention of Moore having served in the army.

But he bore all the hallmarks of someone with a serious addiction that needed help. Mrs Moore described having found three bottles of meths in her husband's jacket the other day and despite his many promises to reform had been unable to do so.

The man had spent several short periods in Whiston Workhouse but, of course, they were not geared up to helping people with addictions. Neither were the prison authorities but the magistrates felt a three-month-long custodial sentence was the solution to Moore's addiction and neglect of his family.

1,658 CASES OF CRUELTY IN SIX YEARS

It was the policy of the NSPCC for their inspectors to be transferred elsewhere after around six to eight years of residence. In October 1919 when Charles Cooper announced his impending departure to Norwich, he provided a detailed account of his 6¼ years in St Helens. Since Inspector Cooper had arrived in the town from Bath in August 1913, he had investigated the circumstances of almost 5,000 children.

These had been involved in 1,658 cases of cruelty of which 1,542 were for neglect, 59 for ill-treatment and assault, 2 for abandonment, 12 for failing to register nurse children, 29 for being in immoral surroundings, 12 for exposure for begging and 2 miscellaneous. Of these cases involving 4,957 children, 1,404 parents received warnings and only 60 were prosecuted.

Out of the 1,658 cases that Insp. Cooper had investigated, the general public had reported 480 of them, the police 487 and schools 226. More than 350 of the kids had required hospital treatment.

Insp. Cooper had also made 6,112 visits to parents that had been warned during his predecessors' time. The St Helens Newspaper described the inspector as an:

> …indefatigable worker among the children, many of whom have to thank the great interest he has taken in them for their present improved conditions.

Inspector Cooper's successor in the Croppers Hill office in St Helens was Francis Lycett and one of the worst cases that he investigated was brought to court on November 28th 1921 which the Liverpool Echo described in detail:

> At St. Helens, to-day, Mary Devlin and Thomas Twist, of 32, Havelock-street [off Eccleston Street] were sent to prison for twenty-eight days for child neglect. The evidence showed that the neglect and filth was of a very revolting description. Mr. Garner, prosecuting for the National Society [NSPCC], said the woman was a single woman, aged twenty-four. The man was married, and had been living apart from his wife. The woman had three illegitimate children by him, and he understood that he had three other illegitimate children by another woman, and he was paying 3s a week for the maintenance of one. The man was a gasworker and earned

£3 6d a week. Mrs. Mary Houghton, Twist's married daughter, who lived in the same house, said that the woman, although she received £2 15s a week, would not keep the place clean or use the money to advantage.

Whenever the little child cried she poured water down its throat. Dr. Donnelan gave evidence as to the state of the bed and bedroom. Inspector Lycett [of the NSPCC] spoke as to the stench in the bedroom, where the man and woman and children used one bed only. The woman was a dirty, filthy, useless person and was too lazy to keep herself clean. The man had allowed her good money, but she went about the house in such a state as not to be decent or presentable.

Twist said his wife left him eighteen years ago. He wished to be married and thought that that would cure a good deal of the trouble. He had tried to find his wife but could not hear anything of her, and so he had put the banns up to be married on December 14 to this woman, and he hoped the bench would allow him to make a fresh start. The bench decided that instead of this the couple must go to gaol for a month each.

Inspector Lycett was often outspoken in St Helens Police Court about the abusers that he brought to justice. In June 1922 the magistrates were told that a miner called James Davies had regularly left his wife without cash to buy food for their children – while he was having an affair with a widow.

The inspector described Davies as a "callous, worthless, inhuman fellow" who had "maintained an attitude of defiance and indifference" throughout his investigation. Davies was sent to prison for two months with hard labour.

Then in January 1923 Inspector Lycett described Sabina Deacle from Elephant Lane in Thatto Heath as the "most fiendishly brutal, violently uncontrollably tempered woman possible, and I have never seen anyone to equal her." She was the archetypal wicked stepmother who looked after her own children well but severely abused her stepdaughter.

Thirteen-year-old Margaret had been repeatedly beaten and kicked over a long period. The girl told the court that her stepmother had hit her on the head several times with a poker. She had also been cut behind the ear with a knife and the bruises that were on her legs had been caused by the woman kicking her.

Mrs Deacle was sent to prison for three months with hard labour and her husband – who was considered fearful of his own wife and under her thumb – received a month's hard labour for not stopping the abuse.

> **'MOST FIENDISHLY BRUTAL'**
>
> **AMAZING STORY OF A STEP-MOTHER'S CRUELTY.**
>
> **CHILD'S CUTS AND BRUISES.**
>
> **WOMAN AND HER HUSBAND SENT TO GAOL.**
>
> A charge of cruelty to a child, on which a stepmother was sent to prison for three months with hard labour, was heard at St. Helens to-day.
>
> The defendants were James Deacle, collier, of 82, Elephant-lane, and Sabina, his wife.
>
> Dr. Donnellan said that the girl, Margaret (13), one of Deacle's children by his first wife, had two cuts on the head, and was bruised all over the arms, shoulders, and legs.
>
> **MANY SCARS ON BODY.**
>
> The body had many scars, showing that she had been very badly ill-treated.
>
> Mrs. M'Cann, wife of a colliery fireman,
>
> *Liverpool Echo January 27th 1923*

In 1931 Inspector Lycett retired from the NSPCC after over forty years service with the organisation. His successor in the Croppers Hill office in St Helens was Inspector Bayliss who transferred from Deal. Although he would be kept busy for some years, a combination of better education and the welfare state reduced the need for the cruelty man and such cases became the exception rather than the rule.

Francis Lycett, incidentally, remained in St Helens and in 1972 his son Allan became Mayor of St Helens.

Unusual Things Said In Court

"The Chairman: Do you produce Anne Boleyn as a witness? Complainant: I don't know her, your worship; she does not live near me. I hear she is a queen somewhere."

This final chapter is largely an extension of the first as it consists of examples of curious sayings that defendants made in court – or which the police or prosecutors stated had been said at the time of the prisoner's arrest.

HE TOOK THE LIGHT OUT O' MY EYES, GLORY BE TO GOD!

The man and woman at the centre of a court case held on June 23rd 1873 appeared to be competing as to who could make the most outrageous statements to the Bench. Thomas King was charged in St Helens Petty Sessions with assaulting Ellen Bowe from Parr. She told the court that King had "rolled" into the shop where she worked and asked to see her "man".

Mrs Bowe replied that her husband was at work but that she always stood in for him. That offer of being her spouse's proxy probably did not extend to violent assaults. But, nonetheless, King gladly accepted the opportunity and bashed Mrs Bowe. She told the court that he: "…took the light out o' my eyes, glory be to God."

Then she claimed that her assailant had yanked out some of her hair, which she produced from her pocket for the court to see. However, the defendant denied making the assault, and, as the St Helens Newspaper reported:

> …protested his gentleness of spirit, and averted that it would be just as reasonable of her to say that he had pulled her

house down, and swallowed the backdoor. The bench fined him 10 shillings and costs.

I'D BE A RASCAL IF MY HEAD WAS CHOPPED OFF!

William Pilkington was the Chairman of the Bench on August 11th 1873 when Michael Brennan was fined 5s and costs for assaulting James Coyle. The defendant did not deny making the blow – but pleaded that he'd thumped Coyle to save himself from decapitation. That was by the spade that his opponent was holding in his hand. And Brennan said after making the punch he'd had to run into the yard of Pilkingtons Glassworks in order to protect himself. Michael Brennan told the Bench:

> Of course, I struck him, sir. But I'd be a great rascal to let him chop my head off. I had to run into your Worship's yard to escape from him and his wife.

BRINGING THE GESTAPO AND MARTIAL LAW INTO ST HELENS

St Helens Police must have received countless threats over the years while making arrests. But I don't think the one that a 57-year-old Haydock chap made to them in July 1972 would have worried the bobbies that much! In St Helens Magistrates Court Inspector David Johnstone described how the man from Juddfield Street in Haydock had been found drunk and disorderly in Cotham Street.

And when a policeman told him he was taking him to the police station he replied: "If you take me away I'll bring the Gestapo into St. Helens." In court the defendant sighed and said "It's no use" before being fined £10 for his 14th offence of drunkenness in just two years.

There must have been something in the water – or beer – in Juddfield Street. Eighteen years before James Lyden had announced his intention to bring martial law to St Helens. "I will overthrow the Queen", he promised the police. The man had been standing in the middle of Victoria Square in St Helens at ten minutes past midnight when he threatened to instigate a revolution.

Asked in court on July 26th 1954 if he had anything to say in defence of the charge of being drunk and disorderly, the 30-year-old glassworker from Juddfield Street told the Bench "I think we will let it go." Very wise! Lyden was fined £2.

OVER THE CHIEF CONSTABLE'S DEAD BODY

Thomas Durkin from Johnson Street in Parr was fined 20 shillings in the Police Court on September 23rd 1922 after being convicted of drunkenness. He was another individual emboldened by drink at night who made big threats against the police – which in the cold light of day in court must have sounded rather silly. A policeman said he had seen the miner leaving the Soldiers Club in Parr Street in a very drunken state and so had spoken to him. His friends attempted to take Durkin home but he shouted:

> You are not going to take me home. I am not afraid of the police. The first man who tries to lock me up, his dead body will be beside me, even if he is the Chief Constable.

ALL SWIFTS ARE NOWT!

When Thomas Swift appeared in the St Helens Petty Sessions on June 30th 1873 accused of defaming the character of Ellen Thompson, Thomas Swift represented him in court. The defendant was not defending himself – but had hired his namesake solicitor to represent him. That created a rather comical moment in court as Ellen Thompson did not think very much of Swifts.

She accused Thomas Swift (the defendant) of having called her very insulting and degrading names in Baxters Lane in Sutton and said that since the incident her husband had been on bad terms with her. When Thomas Swift (the solicitor) put it to Mrs Thompson that she had accused Thomas Swift (the defendant) of being a thief and stealing from the railway company, she denied having said it.

She also claimed not to have told Thomas Swift (the defendant) that "all Swifts are nowt". However, she did concede to Mr Swift (the solicitor) that there was not much good in any of them! To that Thomas Swift (the solicitor) said: "I hope I am not included in that", to which Mrs Thompson assured him with a smile that he was not.

But she did not smile for long though, as Thomas Swift (the defendant AND the solicitor) had a star witness in a Mrs Helm. The woman from Baxters Lane had heard the row between the two parties – indeed she had fully opened a window in her home so she and her five children could enjoy the fun! Mrs Helm told the court that she'd heard Ellen Thompson call the defendant Swift very offensive names and had even challenged him to a fight, and so the Bench dismissed the charge.

THE DOGS ARE BARKING THE GOSSIP!

The phrase the "dogs are barking it" was used four times in the St Helens Reporter's account of a 1930 court hearing. That was not, seemingly, a reference to canines going "woof woof" – but the defendant's odd metaphor for rumour mongers in Thatto Heath. And just what the tales actually were, the report did not specify – but seemed to suggest that Annie Mooney of Springfield Road had been having an affair.

Her neighbour Eliza Jones, appeared in St Helens Police Court on February 14th 1930 charged with using offensive and

SLANDEROUS TONGUES

THATTO HEATH WOMAN DEFAMED

TRADUCER BROUGHT TO COURT

A charge of using offensive and defamatory language was preferred against Eliza Jones of Springfield-road, at the Borough Police Court, on Friday

The complainant, Annie Mooney, who was represented by Mr J. Davies, referred to certain slanderous statements alleged to have been made by Mrs. Jones and her daughter about a fortnight ago. When taxed with uttering the slander, Mrs. Jones replied that, "the dogs were barking it."

St Helens Reporter February 21st 1930.

defamatory language to Mrs Mooney. But Mrs Jones had not been one of the "dogs" spreading the gossip – but had entered the woman's home to find out the truth of the claims. Her refusal to name any of the disseminating dogs – what might be called rumour mongrels (!) – had led to the summons being issued. This is how the Reporter described the dialogue in court between Annie Mooney and her solicitor:

> **Mr. Davies:** Did Mrs. Jones call at your house?
> **Mrs. Mooney:** Yes. She came in and said, "What is all this jangle about?" And I replied, "What is all this scandal about?"
> **Mr. Davies:** What did Mrs. Jones say to you?
> **Mrs. Mooney:** She said the dogs were barking it round about.
> **Mr. Davies:** You asked her for further information, and who were the persons concerned? What was her reply?
> **Mrs. Mooney:** She said she did not know. I told her I was going to put my foot down on the scandal, and I told my husband the following day.

Upon learning of the gossip from his wife, Francis Mooney went with her to see Eliza Jones. This what he said in court:

> I asked Mrs. Jones if there was any truth in the statement that had been made, and she replied that it was the talk of Thatto Heath, and the dogs were barking it. I told Mrs. Jones she was making a very serious statement, and I asked her for the names of the persons referred to. If she could not tell me both, I asked her to give me one, and she replied, "No. It would not do. I have only heard it."

When Mrs Jones gave evidence, she insisted that she knew nothing "wrong" about the complainant, but had simply repeated gossip. "You had no right to repeat it," retorted the solicitor. "Well, you can't shut people's mouths and ears," replied Mrs Jones, who was bound over for 12 months.

I WANT TO BE LOOKED AFTER!

When John Conway was charged with vagrancy in St Helens Police Court on March 12th 1923, he asked the magistrates to deport him back to his homeland in Ireland where he said he'd be looked after. "I wish I had never seen this country and would be glad to get out of it", he added.

> **"GLAD TO GET OUT OF THE COUNTRY."**
>
> **IRISH VAGRANT'S LAMENT IN POLICE COURT.**
>
> When John Conway was charged at St. Helens, to-day, with vagrancy, he said he wished they would deport him to his own country, Ireland, as he would get looked after there. He wished he had never seen this country, and would be glad to get out of it.
>
> Liverpool Echo March 12th 1923

No doubt the people of Britain would also have been glad if he'd kept away. Conway had 52 convictions in various parts of the country – although mainly around Southport, where the local police called him a "station loafer". That was a reference to the local railway station that in most towns – including St Helens – was often a magnet for undesirables to hang around.

The St Helens magistrates sent Conway to prison for a month and after completing his sentence, advised him to return to Wigan where he claimed to belong and settle down. This was his reply:

> They are sick and tired of assisting me, and I can get no money at Wigan. I ought to be taken to the workhouse, and kept there altogether.

Conway appears to have taken no notice of the advice as six months later he was back in court in Southport where he was charged with being drunk and disorderly.

The 40-year-old was reported as making his 56th court appearance, which suggests it had been his third arrest since coming out of prison. Conway was fined 20 shillings or 14 days in prison but chose the latter option telling the Bench: "I am better off in gaol. It is a good home for me".

INNOCENT AS AN UNBORN CHILD

In St Helens Police Court on December 22nd 1902 William McIntyre from Merton Bank Road vehemently protested his innocence. He had been charged with stealing a box of groceries valued at 13 shillings 4½d from the front parlour of his neighbour, William Priestley.

In court he declared he was "as innocent as a child unborn" but when arrested by PC Whalley had admitted stealing the items while drunk. The slight chance of McIntyre's innocence claim being accepted by the magistrates evaporated as soon as they heard he had two-dozen previous convictions and he was sent to prison for two months.

I'M NOT DRUNK – IT'S THE ROTTEN BEER!

The state of the ale during and immediately after both world wars certainly had its critics. The strength of the beer was reduced and shortages of ingredients led to its taste altering. I'm not sure that it made drinkers vomit – but Moses Glover certainly thought so. In September 1946 the driver from Milton Street in Sutton Manor appeared in court to face a charge of committing a nuisance. A police officer gave evidence that when the 20-year-old was spoken to about the offence he had replied: "It's the rotten beer; I was being sick". Moses was found guilty and fined 10 shillings.

IS ANNE BOLEYN IN COURT?

People did say the most peculiar things to their antagonist when the red mist rose. When Mary Noonan summoned Bridget McGarry to St Helens Petty Sessions in July 1873 for assault, she told the court that the woman had called her "shocking names" and said she was "one of Anne Boleyn's breed".

Mrs Noonan claimed Mrs McGarry had said she would "come in for the same reward as that unfortunate woman received". Well, those were the words used in the St Helens Newspaper's report, which were probably not precisely what was said in court. But the paper did quote this comic dialogue between the Chairman of the Bench and Mary Noonan.

> **The Chairman:** Do you produce Anne Boleyn as a witness?
> **Complainant:** I don't know her, your worship; she does not live near me. I hear she is a queen somewhere.
> **Mr Spencely** [court clerk]**:** She said you were Anne Boleyn.
> **Complainant:** No, that I am of her breed, and just such another.
> **The Chairman:** We shall fine her 5s. and costs.

MOUTHY MARY GRIMSHAW

On July 26th 1873 the St Helens Newspaper described how Mary Grimshaw had appeared in St Helens Petty Sessions accused of causing a disturbance near her home in Red Cat Buildings in Crank. Let us just say the 36-year-old Irishwoman was not a quiet, reserved person! This what they wrote about her conduct in court:

> A policeman had to be stationed beside this woman for the purpose of keeping her tongue within some sort of bounds, but he might as well have been in London for all the success he had. She was bound over.

I'M PART OWNER OF THIS PUBLIC PARK

The argument that as a member of the public you automatically had part ownership of public parks and so could do whatever you wished in them was never likely to impress a court.

Or that being illiterate and so unable to read notices that stated the park's rules and regulations absolved you from responsibility when committing vandalism. But Michael Malley tried on the first excuse in St Helens Police Court on June 19th 1903.

The park keeper at Victoria Park gave evidence that Malley had damaged a seat by chalking over it and scratching it. When he'd spoken to him about his vandalism, Malley had claimed to be a "part proprietor" of the public park.

Albert Preece of Tontine Street was also charged with damaging the seat and he employed the second illiteracy excuse, adding: "I only used a little bit of chalk on the seat; it was the smallest offence a man could be guilty of." The two defendants were each fined 1s. and 5s. 6d. costs.

Benches in Victoria Park were not to be chalked on

THE SHORT-SIGHTED BEGGAR

In January 1930 PC Jones told St Helens Police Court that while off duty in plain clothes, William Owen had approached him in Duke Street at 10:50pm and asked him for money. He said he told the man he was a police officer and warned him against begging. The constable then saw Owen cross the road and continue asking people for cash before disappearing inside a fish shop.

When he came out of the premises the beggar crossed the road and without initially realising who he was cadging cash from, said to PC Jones: "Will you give me 7d towards this…" Owen then looked up, realised his mistake and said: "Oh, you are the constable, are you? Lock me up then." And he did, leading to William Owen making his 65th court appearance and a month's stay in Walton Prison. After hearing his sentence the man politely said to the Bench: "May I have it without hard labour, sir?" "Yes, all right", came the reply.

TWO WOMEN OF EVIL NOTORIETY

Honesty was not always the best policy in court. When in June 1873 Maria Callaghan was charged with stealing a patchwork quilt from Maria Smith of Garden Street in Greenbank, the St Helens Newspaper described the defendant as a "woman of evil notoriety".

Mrs Smith had allowed Mrs Callaghan to lodge with her for some time, which puzzled the Bench and so they enquired why she had allowed such a woman to rent a room from her. Maria Smith could have said: "Well, I have a generous spirit", or "I was hoping she would reform", etc.

Instead she blurted out: "She's just as bad as me, herself, sir", which condemned herself as a drunkard, thief and, perhaps, prostitute. Then Mrs Smith started arguing with Mrs Callaghan, leading to the magistrates dismissing the charge.

THE QUAINT AMERICAN JUGGLER

On July 10th 1903 under the headline *"A Quaint Figure At The Police Court"*, the St Helens Newspaper published this short piece:

> George Mullins, an elderly man, who said he came from New York, and had the appearance and manner of a well-known Dickens character, was charged with causing an obstruction in Church-street by performing as a juggler. The officer said the man had a large crowd round him. In front of the Fleece Hotel he was performing with five hats at a time. Mullins addressed the court and said he was "only four

months over at this side," and was making his way to Liverpool to return by cattle boat. He would clear out of the town. The Chairman (Mr. Oppenheim): Well, let's see how quick you can do it. Mullins thanked the court, but took some little time to gather up his hats and bundles, and then walked down the court a most comical figure. He paused at the door and bowed, and smiled at the bench saying, "Thank you," and disappeared amid the laughter of everyone in court.

SHE HAS TOO MUCH GUFF

There is nothing beats an entire change from St Helens

This picture postcard lampooned the overcrowding of homes in St Helens during and after WW1, suggesting the situation was no better in guesthouses in resorts like Blackpool. Overcrowded houses often led to friction between their inhabitants. In May 1923 Andrew Keeffe from Albion Street was fined 20 shillings in St Helens Police Court for assaulting Mary Leavesley. The woman was his landlady and she told the Bench how Keeffe had been eating a meal when her little girl called Doris began walking round the dining table.

That had annoyed the 29-year-old lodger who said if the 3-year-old did not go away, he would "have her away". When Mrs Leavesley objected to little Doris being threatened in that way, she said Keeffe struck her several times on the head with a canister. The defendant's version of events was that the child had stolen his egg off his plate when his back was turned, adding:

> Mrs Leavesley then flew up and I told her if she did not shut up I would shut her up – and I did. Her husband then piled in to me and other members of the family held me down. Her own husband will tell you that she has too much guff.

TAKING THINGS EASY MAKING MOONSHINE

When Michael O'Brien appeared in St Helens Police Court on May 17th 1923 there was considerable amusement at his silly statements. At one point the Chairman of the Bench said: "Do you know what the truth is?" The seaman had only been discharged from the court a few days before after being charged with "lodging out", i.e. sleeping rough.

But after leaving the court at St Helens Town Hall, O'Brien had stolen a bicycle from outside the Lamb Hotel. Upon being stopped by a police inspector while wheeling his machine on the road to Liverpool, O'Brien

"DON'T MIND SO LONG AS THEY FEED ME."

AMUSING PASSAGES IN A POLICE COURT.

Michael Joseph O'Brien, seaman, caused much amusement at St. Helens to-day when charged with stealing a bicycle, valued at £3. Prisoner was arrested and brought before the court last Saturday, when he was discharged. He left the building, and was later seen by a police-inspector going in the direction of Liverpool, wheeling a bicycle. When questioned, he said the machine was his own, and that he bought it in Boston, U.S.A.

The officer noticed that the bicycle was of large size, and he asked prisoner to get on and ride it. Prisoner got on the machine, but could not reach the pedals properly.

He was arrested, and later it was learned that he had stolen the bicycle from outside the Lamb Hotel, in Corporation-street.

Liverpool Echo May 17th 1923

insisted he had bought the bike in Boston, USA, but proved completely incapable of riding it. Back in court to face a charge of stealing the bicycle, O'Brien first stated that he had been born in Ireland but then said it had been Philadelphia. He later added that his father and mother were Welsh – but he was Irish! And then O'Brien said:

> I have done nothing since 1921 but walk about the country making moonshine and taking things easy. I am married and had some children but I have not seen my wife for 16 years. I am a solicitor and can speak seven different languages and can talk on any platform as well as Lloyd George.

O'Brien said he planned to go to Southampton and sail to New Zealand to claim some property there and then he would settle down. To that the Chairman of the Bench said:

> Perhaps someone has done with the property like you did with the bicycle – pinched it? You will have to go to prison for fourteen days.

O'Brien replied: "I don't mind so long as they feed me."

A TEST FOR FITS

Drunks arrested on the streets of St Helens would sometimes claim in court that they had not been inebriated but had instead been suffering epileptic fits. When Jane Clingen appeared in St Helens Police Court on February 7th 1902 charged with drunkenness she claimed to have had ten fits in the street.

Sgt. Stewart told the court that the woman had pretended to have another fit in the corridor of the police cells but he said he'd employed a simple means of proving her attack was a fake: "I put a pinch of snuff to her nose and she jumped up and started swearing at me." The Clerk to the court then said: "Is that a test?", to which the policeman replied: "Yes, and a good one." Mrs Clingen was fined 5 shillings.

DRIVING THE DEVIL AWAY!

There were several unusual, if not comical, aspects to the case heard in St Helens Police Court in December 1920 in which James Ashton was accused of persistent cruelty to his wife Rose. For a start she was 39 and her husband was 85.

The couple lived in Ormskirk Street in St Helens and the man was accused of committing various types of spousal abuse during their six years of marriage. These ranged from refusing to give Rose housekeeping money to attempting to strangle her. However, Mr Ashton blamed his wife for being unreasonable and said it was not safe for him to live with her.

There was laughter in court when the elderly man described the night his wife sprinkled water over him in bed. He said he asked her what she was doing and Rose replied: "Driving the Devil away". On the following night she did the same trick but this time James said he was prepared. He had his own jug of water ready at his bedside and threw its contents over her! The wife wanted £2 per week from her husband but the Bench were not impressed with such a difference in their ages and dismissed the case.

ONLY A CAGED BIRD

When Alice Potter of Cowley Street in St Helens was sentenced to six months in prison in July 1902 the 35-year-old thanked the Bench and invited them to a game of ping-pong, as table tennis was then called. And as she was removed from the dock, Mrs Potter burst into 'She's only a bird in a gilded cage'.

That was then a hugely popular song and although Alice Potter may have considered it appropriate to her situation, others might have felt the line that went: "'Tis sad when you think of her wasted life", to be more relevant. The woman had been imprisoned for ill-treating her children who were described as being in a very filthy state and covered with vermin. Mrs Potter was a confirmed drunkard and had told the court that she had been to jail four times and could do three months on her head.

TALKING TO ME LIKE I WAS A LITTLE DOG

When Thomas Callaghan of East Street was fined ten shillings by St Helens magistrates in 1930, he was making his 56th appearance before the Bench. Callaghan had been charged with placing himself in a position to receive alms and with using obscene language to a policeman. The man had made the mistake of singing for cash outside the home of PC Griffin.

SANG FOR MONEY

And Got a Copper

Thomas Callaghan, East-street, stood before the Magistrates for the fifty sixth time at the Borough Police Court, on Monday, where he was charged with placing himself in a position to receive alms, and with using obscene language.

P.C. Griffin was in his home at Hillside-avenue, on Saturday afternoon, when he heard the prisoner singing outside. He went after Callaghan, whom he overtook at the top of Gamble-avenue. He told

St Helens Reporter Nov 11th 1930

The constable subsequently came out of his house and collared Callaghan in Gamble Avenue and told the court that as he escorted him to the police station, he had used obscene language. Some of the swear words were written down on a piece of paper and handed to the Bench. However, the defendant had a complaint of his own, saying:

> I couldn't walk any faster, and the officer was just in front of me saying, "Come on, Tommy. Come on, Tommy," as if he were talking to a little dog.

"TELL THE F****** CHIEF CONSTABLE TO....."

On July 7th 1905 in St Helens Police Court, Thomas McCormick was charged with being drunk and disorderly. A constable told the Bench that the man's antics had put the district of Greenbank "in an uproar". Then the Chief Constable of St Helens told the court a surprising story of how he had previously gone out of his way to give assistance to McCormick.

Arthur Ellerington said that when the man had come out of prison in May, he had sent for him and "tried to point out to him the folly of his ways". McCormick had promised him that if he could get work he would turn over a new leaf.

So the Chief Constable provided him with breakfast and supper and found a job for him at Lea Green Colliery – despite the mine not needing any more workers.

INCORRIGIBLE.
UNEMPLOYED WHO DON'T WANT WORK.

At the St Helens Police Court, on Monday, before Mr W I Thomson and other magistrates. Thomas McCormick was charged with being drunk and disorderly on Saturday night, a constable stating that prisoner had Greenbank in an uproar.

The Chief-Constable said that when McCormick came out of gaol in May he sent for him and tried to point out to him the folly of his ways. McCormick then said that if he could get work he would turn over a new leaf. He (the Chief-Constable) thereupon provided him with his breakfast and supper, and found work for him at Lea Green Colliery. Mr

St Helens Reporter July 7th 1905

Another man was similarly taken on. But they only worked for three weeks and then they "threw down their tools, and said they would rather lounge about than work." They also told someone to tell "the _____ Chief-Constable that they did not want work." Thomas McCormick was sent to prison for 28 days.

Acknowledgements / Credits

St Helens Archive Service

Eccleston Library, St Helens

British Newspapers Archive

Newspapers.com

FindmyPast

Charles Forman, Industrial Town – Self Portrait of St Helens in the 1920s (Cameron & Tayleur, 1978)

Equal Justice Initiative – (2017) 'Families Torn Apart by Slavery Desperately Sought Reunion After Emancipation' – Accessed June 17 2023 through https://eji.org/news/families-torn-apart-by-slavery-sought-reunion/

Saints Heritage Society, Tom Durkin – Accessed June 23 2023 through http://www.saints.org.uk/saints/player.php?num=15242

Most images are from the author's own personal archive or reproduced from newspapers on microfilm at Eccleston Library.

Thanks to Diane Charnock and Gyles Charnock for their proof reading and support.

Newspaper Sources: Belfast Newsletter, Cork Examiner, Liverpool Albion, Liverpool Daily Post, Liverpool Evening Express, Liverpool Weekly Courier, Manchester Courier, Manchester Daily Examiner, Nantwich Guardian, Police Gazette, Prescot Reporter, South London Press, St Helens Examiner, St Helens Lantern, St Helens Newspaper, St Helens Reporter, Stroud Journal, Surrey Mirror, The Era, Western Gazette, Wigan Observer, Yorkshire Gazette.